TABLE OF CONTENTS

SUMMER 2024
VOLUME 4 / NUMBER 4

Liberties is a publication of the Liberties Journal Foundation, a nonpartisan 501(c)(3) organization based in Washington, D.C. devoted to educating the general public about the history, current trends, and possibilities of culture and politics. The Foundation seeks to inform today's cultural and political leaders, deepen the understanding of citizens, and inspire the next generation to participate in the democratic process and public service.

Engage
To learn more please go to libertiesjournal.com

Subscribe
To subscribe or with any questions about your subscription, please go to libertiesjournal.com

ISBN 979-8-9854302-5-7
ISSN 2692-3904

EDITORIAL OFFICES
1101 30th Street NW, Suite 310
Washington, DC 20007

DIGITAL
@READLIBERTIES
LIBERTIESJOURNAL.COM

Liberties

PAUL BERMAN

A Stupid Cartoon and the University Ideology

Among the thousand currents of the university turmoil during these last several months, the tiny ripple that most securely caught my eye was a distinctly minor scandal at Harvard back in February, which caused not a single broken window or student riot or mass invasion by agents of the state. This was a scandal over a cartoon. The minor scandal had the virtue, however, of casting a retrospective light on an earlier scandal at Harvard, the original scandal, which was pretty much the founding moment of what eventually became the enormous tide of university protests and controversies.

The original scandal was a statement signed by more

than thirty Harvard student groups in the first days after the October 7, 2023 massacre blaming Israel ("entirely responsible") instead of Hamas (unmentioned) for the atrocities — after which came the clumsy dithering of Harvard's president, Claudine Gay, to speak up in a sufficiently articulate fashion about the massacre and the student statement, which led to her notorious failure in testimony to Congress to find anything condemnatory to say about students calling for genocide of the Jews ("depends on context"), which led to everything else. And this was not just in America. In Paris, Sciences Po, aka the Institut d'études de politiques de Paris, which is more or less the Harvard of France, generated its own scandal, beginning in March. The Sciences Po students held a pro-Palestine meeting. A Jewish student got up the courage to enter the amphitheater. And the Jewish student was greeted in a manner that was sufficiently obnoxious to attract the attention of Emmanuel Macron himself, who thought it his duty to underline the "unspeakable and perfectly intolerable" behavior — which led, by late April, to a student occupation of a stairwell, the intervention of riot police, indignation over the menace to academic freedom, and generally the turmoil that any number of universities and arts organizations have come to know. In this fashion, the enormous and sometimes scandalous wave of protests against Israel and Zionism that got started at Harvard has turned out to be, well, maybe not universal. Problems and protests like these seem not to have occurred in the Latin American universities, which is curious. Nor in various other regions. But the wave has been very large.

The cartoon scandal — the mini-event at Harvard in February — was brought on by two student organizations, the Harvard Undergraduate Palestine Solidarity Committee and the African and African American Resistance Organization, with the unfortunate support of still another organization called Harvard Faculty and Staff for Justice in Palestine. The two student groups set out to show and acclaim the historical origins of African-American solidarity with the Palestinian cause. This reaches back to 1967 and the rebellious young activists of the civil rights movement. The Harvard student groups wanted to explain that, in adopting the Palestinian cause, the young rebels of those long-ago times took a major step in advancing the larger struggle for black liberation. The students composed an infographic making those points, and the graphic within the infographic was a charcoal-line cartoon by an artist named Herman "Kofi" Bailey, which the students lifted from the young rebels' newsletter from 1967.

The cartoon showed blacks and Arabs being jointly oppressed by their enemy, the Jews. A black man and an Arab man (who might have been Muhammad Ali, the boxer, and Gamal Abdel Nasser, the president of Egypt) gazed helplessly upward from the cartoon with nooses draped around their necks. At the top of the cartoon a white hand, bearing on its back a Star of David tattoo encasing a dollar sign, held the two nooses loosely in its fingers, ready to give the fatal yank. But salvation was in sight. This was a scrawny arm brandishing a machete, with the arm and machete labeled "Third World Liberation Movement," ready to slice the ropes and liberate the doomed. The cartoon was, in short, a melodrama of victimhood (blacks, Arabs), victimizer (Jews), and savior (Third World Liberation). The Harvard student groups saw sufficient value in the cartoon to post it on their Instagram site. Someone at the Harvard Faculty and Staff for Justice in Palestine was sufficiently impressed to repost it, signaling approval (even if, in reality, the faculty-and-staff group had no idea what was being reposted). And the mini-scandal was at hand.

On this occasion, Harvard's new interim president — Claudine Gay was gone by then — demonstrated that he had learned from Gay's mistakes and was quick to condemn. And the dean of Harvard College, Rakesh Khurana, did the interim president one better. Dean Khurana called the Instagram post "unmistakably anti-Semitic and racist," which was a sharp phrase, given that, at Harvard, the two student groups surely regarded themselves as racism's boldest enemies. And the phrase was doubly sharp, given that Harvard Faculty and Staff for Justice in Palestine had made a point, in their founding statement, of disputing the claim that "critique of the Israeli state is anti-Semitic." Their own critique of the Israeli state turned out, however, to be anti-Semitic. Said the dean: "It's become clear that some members of our community are intent on testing the limits of how low discourse can go — and it now appears that we are hitting rock bottom."

Everyone apologized. Harvard is civilized. And yet, no one likes to be insulted. And the people under accusation by their dean may have felt that, even if they had failed to examine their cartoon closely enough, the general opinion among students at Harvard, and among a good many faculty as well, was on their side. Harvard Faculty and Staff for Justice in Palestine accordingly lamented their participation in the affair with a fine panache of the passive tense: "It has come to our attention that a post featuring antiquated cartoons which used offensive anti-Semitic tropes was linked to our account."

The student apologies ventured still further into the zones of passive aggression. The student groups expunged the disgraced cartoon from their Instagram post. But they replaced the cartoon with a photo of the leader of the young rebels whose newsletter, back in 1967, had originally published it. This was Stokely Carmichael, in later years known as Kwame

Ture, a charismatic man whose most famous slogan was the stirring "Black Power," but whose second most famous slogan (famous, at least, within the corner of the public that was singled out for death) was the off-hand snarl, "The only good Zionist is a dead Zionist."

The aspect that catches my eye now was how ghostly the scandalous element turned out to be, as if haunted by the truly original scandal, not the one at Harvard immediately after October 7, but the original's original, which was in 1967. The rebellious young people in 1967 were members of the Student Non-Violent Coordinating Committee, or SNCC, pronounced "snick." In the period leading up to 1967, SNCC was — if I may put it this way — the most glorious student organization that has ever existed. Martin Luther King, Jr. and a solid bloc of experienced stalwarts were the commanders of the civil rights movement in its adult division, and the young people in SNCC, who were black and white alike, were the human-wave foot-soldiers, marching across the South to undergo arrests and beatings and ultimately achieve victory. Young John Lewis in Atlanta was SNCC's chairman. In South Carolina, young James Clyburn was among the SNCC stalwarts. In New York, SNCC's high school division mobilized the youth of the youth.

By 1965, though, Stokely Carmichael and his fellow-thinkers were beginning to take over the organization. They succeeded in expelling the whites, which tended to mean the Jews. By 1967, young Lewis had left the organization. Carmichael inherited the chairmanship. The Six Day War broke out in the Middle East. In the Arab countries, the shock at seeing so many Arab armies defeated so quickly and ignominiously by Israel set off a political earthquake, which meant radicalization, a major event across the region. The Palestinian terrorist campaigns got underway. And the war set off an additional earthquake in the American civil rights movement. The new team at SNCC rebelled against the civil rights old guard and its many alliances, above all the alliance with the American Jews. And the SNCC newsletter ran an article making the case against Zionism.

It was a ferocious case. Zionism in SNCC's portrayal was ugliness itself. Zionism was racist even against darker-skinned Jews. It was exploitative of black Africa, hostile to African liberation, and Nazi-like against the Palestinians in Gaza. Zionism was a creature of British and American imperialism. Zionism's purpose was to help white America exploit Arab oil. Zionism was a product, finally, of a Rothschild "conspiracy with the British" — the Rothschilds, who, in capital letters, "CONTROL MUCH OF AFRICA'S MINERAL WEALTH." The noose cartoon faithfully illustrated the article. And the spirit of that article and its cartoon became a trend, visible in SNCC and in the brand new Black Panther Party, too, which went on to publish its own cartoons on similar themes.

Those were big developments, which perhaps *could* be presented, as the Harvard students and their faculty supporters did a few months ago in their infographic, as contributions to a "heightened awareness" within the black struggle for liberation. But it also could be argued that, all in all, the young people's anti-Zionist rebellion in SNCC in 1967, together with the rise of the Black Panthers, pretty much blew up the national political coalition that King and Rustin and the old-school civil rights leaders had so brilliantly put together. The blow-up took place at a crucial moment, too, just when, under Rustin's inspiration, King was taking early steps to bring about a basic transformation of the civil rights movement.

The historic movement was a campaign for legal rights. By 1967, though, the major specific demands of the historic movement had made their way into law, voted by Congress and signed by Lyndon Johnson. But Rustin had come up with a new idea, which was to convert the movement for legal equality into a campaign for economic equality. The idea was to expand the civil rights coalition into an immense multi-racial campaign for social democratic reform, under the command of the old civil rights leadership, which meant King himself and his circle. This was a proposal to move United States social policy significantly to the left, in the European style, with the collusion of the Johnson administration. Only, the entire universe conspired against Rustin and King and this very ambitious project.

It wasn't just the young radicals in SNCC, together with their comrades in the Black Panther Party and everyone who admired SNCC and the Panthers, which was a lot of people. The social-democratic trade unions — the historically Jewish garment unions, that is, plus the Auto Workers — maintained their own youth auxiliary, which was the mostly white Students for a Democratic Society, or SDS, who took pride in being SNCC's loyal allies. And the young white hotheads of SDS and their own friends among the hippies and "freaks" were already doing their own bit to blow up the old coalition, though not generally in the name of anti-Zionism or hating the Jews. In truth, not everybody did hate Zionism and the Jews. But everyone hated the older generation — everyone in the left-wing and activist youth movements, that is, except for a few. It was rough on the fifty-year-olds. Rustin's vast social democratic project depended, in any case, on King and his charisma, and the assassination in Memphis, which was in April 1968, brought the project pretty much to an end. And Richard Nixon was elected president. And Stokely Carmichael departed for a new life in Africa.

SNCC's turn toward anti-Zionism has always seemed a little puzzling, and that is because of Carmichael himself. Carmichael was born in the West Indies, but he came of age in the Bronx, New York, where Jews were not an exotic species. At the Bronx High School of Science, which he attended, the scions of the Jewish Bronx crowded the corridors, and none of those students were Rothschilds, and various of them came from backgrounds not lacking in enthusiasm for King and the civil rights movement. Todd Gitlin was one year behind Carmichael at Bronx Science — Gitlin, who went on to Harvard, where he became a national leader of Students for a Democratic Society. Harvard expressed an interest in Carmichael, too, and offered him a scholarship. Carmichael preferred to go to Howard University in Washington, the most distinguished of the black colleges.

And yet, at Howard one of his more significant friends appears to have been Tom Kahn, who was yet another socialist from a Jewish family, in this instance from Brooklyn. It was young Kahn who brought Carmichael into the circle around Rustin — Kahn, who went from Max Shachtman's famously clever socialist faction to strategizing for Rustin, and from there to strategizing for the AFL-CIO. How, then, could someone like Carmichael, with any number of friends and comrades from the world of Jewish support for the black cause, have made his way to "rock bottom," in the Harvard dean's phrase, amid the ancient superstitions and the belief that African-America's oppressor was international Jewry? The descent into that sort of thing can make people wonder if some terrible incident didn't drive him to a crude response — a knavish landlord, a nasty math teacher, a catty high school clique, or who knows?

But those are silly speculations. Carmichael was a serious man, and his evolution was a matter of serious reflection — a matter of intellectual sophistication, in some degree, and not a lack of it. The classic civil-rights idea, in Rustin's version, was itself a mighty sophistication. It was an internationalism, with inspirations drawn from India's anticolonial rebellion and the non-violent philosophy of Mahatma Gandhi, mixed with support for the anticolonial campaigns of black Africa, which Rustin deftly mixed with still more inspirations drawn from multiple currents of American Protestantism and the African-American tradition, and still more inspirations from the social-democratic wing of the labor movement and their Shachtmanite advisors, together with the particular corner of American liberal reformism that tended to be Jewish. That was a fabulous concoction. But those were ideas from the 1940s and 1950s.

Young Carmichael was a man of the 1960s. He drew his own inspiration from Frantz Fanon, the philosopher of decolonization, who was a psychiatrist from Martinique — and Fanon's ideas seem to me key in this development. Fanon was angrier than Rustin, and bitter — which accounted for his appeal to a younger generation. And he was an ambitious thinker. His ideas unfolded in phases. Initially his project was to sharpen and affirm a black consciousness adapted to the mid-twentieth century — a trans-national black consciousness, suited to his own French Caribbean, to the blacks of France, to various regions of West Africa, and even to the blacks of the United States. He became active in the Algerian struggle against France, and he extended his purpose to speak on behalf of revolutionary Arabs as well, though I am not sure that his insights into Arab consciousness amounted to much. He broadened his purpose still again to animate and illuminate what he considered to be a worldwide program of anti-colonial revolution and post-colonial development — which mostly that meant the black and Arab worlds, with side glances at other corners of the globe, sufficient to suggest the universality of his ambition.

Ultimately his goal was to help the whole of humanity achieve a full and undeceived self-awareness. This is the self-awareness that is made possible, at last, by a human recognition from others. He wanted to promote a self-awareness of this sort among blacks internationally, and among broader populations of color, and then universally. He was, in sum, an unapologetic Hegelian, and, given his background in Martinique, this gave him an undeniable power, analytically and emotionally. Hegel was, after all, the philosopher who stipulated that slavery and the struggle against it are the starting point of all of history — which might sound like a philosophical metaphor to people in other parts of the world, but was actually the case in the Caribbean.

C. L. R. James, the Trinidadian intellectual, was Fanon's predecessor in thinking along those lines. James wrote a history of the Haitian slave revolution, *The Black Jacobins*, in 1938, which was also a contemplation of the African decolonization movement, and, in doing this, he, too, gazed on events through a lens of Caribbean Hegelianism. Only, James's Hegelianism was Marxist. He converted Hegel's abstract categories — the Master, the Slave — into concrete realities of class struggle, where the traits and interests of one class might intermingle with traits and interests of the other class. James's anger at slavery was volcanic, but his Marxism allowed him, even so, to identify ways in which the Haitian slaves, who had every reason to hate the French, were able to borrow ideas and ideals from France. And the slaves were able to benefit, if only fitfully, from the solidarity of France's revolutionaries, and were able even to offer a solidarity of their own to France's revolution, quite as if the struggle, which was deadly, contained within it a negotiation. And the negotiation pointed to a possible better future — which made for an angry book that was also a subtle book.

Fanon's Hegelianism, though, was not a Marxism — not in his early book *Black Skins, White Masks,* and not in his more famous *The Wretched of the Earth*, in 1961 (even if the title is a line from the revolutionary anthem The Internationale). Fanon recognized the reality of economic conflicts and struggles. But his vision of the world emphasized, instead, conflicts that were psychological, or perhaps cultural. He recognized the existence of social and economic classes, but his vision of the world emphasized the clash of entire nations against one another, instead of social classes. These were the colonized nations against the colonizing nations, and their struggle was the global struggle of the Third World against the European empires (and the second Europe that is the United States). Sometimes he spoke of entire races, and not just of nations. In a number of rhapsodic passages here and there, he spoke of a higher synthesis emerging from the worldwide conflicts. But mostly he pictured a struggle that was going to lead to a victory for the colonized and a defeat for the colonizers, or the opposite, without any intermingling of traits that might contain within it a hidden negotiation, and without much prospect for a higher synthesis, except in the vaguest of ways.

Fanon was not, on these points, a proper Hegelian, which he punctiliously acknowledged. His vision of the struggle was blunter than Hegel's, and blunter than James's, and the bluntness led to a strictly violent concept of the struggle. He considered that violence was unavoidable for the oppressed. And he considered that, in some respects, violence was positively good. In his view, power relations defined identity, such that the oppressed were defined by their oppression, and not by any cultural or religious wealth that might be their own. (That is why, in *The Wretched of the Earth*, the various colonized nations are indistinguishable, one from another, since all of them are victims of the same colonialist oppression.) And since the oppressed are defined by their oppression, the only way for them to assert a new and better identity and resolve their psychological problems is through an exercise of force, which means violence. Gandhi and the Gandhians and their American civil-rights emulators considered that non-violence was a tactic which was also a principle. In their eyes, non-violence conferred meaning. But Fanon looked on violence as a tactic which was also a principle. It was violence that conferred meaning. Violence was therapy for the colonized. Violence allowed oppressed people to become fully human, or "men."

In his recent biography of Fanon, *The Rebel's Clinic*, Adam Shatz offers a satisfyingly intelligent and thorough account of the man, and argues that Fanon has been subject to a lot of unfair criticism on the violence question. "The violence of the colonized," in Fanon's interpretation, as Shatz explains it, "was a *counter*-violence." The imperialists were to blame, not the enemies of imperialism. This explanation may not survive a reading of *The Wretched of the Earth*. Something is alarming in Fanon's odes to the violence of the oppressed: "At the individual level, violence is a cleansing force. It rids the colonized of their inferiority complex, of their passive and despairing attitude. It emboldens them, and restores their confidence," and so forth. Violence makes Fanon sit upright in his chair. He is electrified. He was, in this respect (and in other respects), a true disciple of Sartre, who spent a lot of time sitting upright in his own chair, excited at the prospect of open conflict. Or Fanon ended up looking like Georges Sorel, the syndicalist — Sorel, the author of a once-famous book called *Reflections on Violence*, whose revolutionary doctrine rested on the direct-action anarchists of the 1890s, and found encouragement in the violence of the frightening lumpenproletariat, and hinted at the fascists of the years to come.

You could be excused for wondering if the nationalism-violence-and-lumpen combination in Fanon's imagination likewise didn't flirt with extreme-right possibilities — though Fanon was plainly more a man of moods than someone with an extremist vocation. And, in scattered passages of *The Wretched of the Earth*, his better judgment allowed him, as his biographer correctly observes, to grant that violence was not, in fact, an ideal, and could even be a big mistake, tactically speaking. And Fanon was eloquent, finally, on the meaning of freedom. But this meant only that, on a series of fundamental questions — violence, the nation — Fanon was ambiguous.

His emotional force, though, his power of condemnation, which was a power that comes from being frank — *this* was not ambiguous. The anger in him and even the ambiguities seemed to speak for vast percentages of the human race — the vast percentages that were in the course of throwing off the European empires and trying to construct a new world system. The man himself was appealing, with his enthusiasm for ideas and his effort to get at the real psychology of people, and this made it easy to overlook his infelicities of one sort or another. If he contradicted himself, which he did almost systematically, this, too, was not without appeal. He was a man in a hurry because world events were in a hurry, and there was no time to straighten out every little contradiction. Besides, he was immensely self-confident, and self-confidence made him glamorous.

His glamour was rendered official, too, by an endorsement from Sartre himself — Sartre who, in the 1960s, floated on a sea of worldwide prestige. Sartre endorsed him by writing a wild preface to *The Wretched of the Earth*, more violent even than Fanon himself: "Murderous rampage is the collective unconscious of the colonized...." And on every continent, the hippest-of-the-hip in the 1960s, who were the young, understood intuitively that Fanon's ideas and even his excesses were the spirit of what was, in fact, a revolutionary age. Wasn't that Stokely Carmichael's experience? I am sure that it was. I imagine Carmichael turning Fanon's pages and saying to himself, "Yes, that is me he is talking about. And the world he describes is the world that actually exists."

I imagine this because, in a fashion that could hardly be more different, that was my own experience. My copy of *The Wretched of the Earth* — the copy on my table right now — is a $1.25 paperback, which I purchased in 1969. The faded yellow magic marker lines running through its pages remind me how earnestly I studied it. I did that at Columbia College in the spring semester of 1969, under the guidance of my professor, Edward Said, who himself was still in a stage of voraciously absorbing influences from Fanon and the French philosophers. I took from my reading that Fanon's *Wretched of the Earth* offered a schema, which was neither liberal nor Communist, for analyzing every conceivable thing. The violent passages — there were many — alarmed me not at all. "For the colonized, life can only materialize from the rotting cadaver of the colonist," wrote Fanon, and the rotting cadaver seemed to me, from my standpoint at the age of nineteen, creepy with energy, which made it marvelous. I, too, believed that Fanon spoke for vast portions of the previously silent or silenced human race.

Only, I found myself wondering about the many populations that might not fit into a simple tabulation of the colonized and the colonizers. Not everybody does fit into those two categories, after all, or into any two categories. The Jews, for instance — where did *they* fit? I wasn't much concerned with Jewish issues, but, still, as I bent to the task of drawing yellow lines, I did wonder. And I wondered again as I faithfully attended a campus teach-in, at the urging of my professor, in order to learn about the secularist and progressive ideals of the Popular Front for the Liberation of Palestine, who were represented to me as the true exponents of Fanon's philosophy, but whose secularist and progressive ideals left me uneasy — as if a little voice whispered in my ear that, fifty-four years later, the Popular Front for the Liberation of Palestine was going to participate, as it did, in the October 7 massacre. So I responded with excitement to Fanon, and also grew reserved.

Now, Fanon himself, it must be said, did give some thought to Jewish questions. He ruminated over the psychological situation of the Jews, perhaps more than he ever did over the psychological situation of the Arabs — though mostly he did this in reference to his study of psychological circumstances among the blacks, which was his chief concern. His thoughts were sympathetic. In *Black Skins, White Masks*, he made clear that nothing in his sympathy for the Jews and their plight was begrudging: "Anti-Semitism hits me head-on: I am enraged, I am bled white by an appalling battle, I am deprived of the possibility of being a man, I cannot dissociate myself from the future that is proposed for my brother." He understood that hatred of Jews and hatred of blacks tallied up, in the last analysis, to the same sum. "It was my philosophy professor, a native of the Antilles, who recalled the fact to me: 'Whenever you hear anyone abuse the Jews, pay attention, because he is talking about you.'" Or, in other words: "an anti-Semite is invariably anti-Negro."

He drew up comparative observations on the oppressive prejudices that descend variously upon Jews and blacks, and on Jewish and black psychological reactions. He was tolerant and charitable. He proposed a diagnosis of a Jewish psychiatric patient who, in "a fine example of a reactional phenomenon," angrily and pathetically sided with the anti-Semites. "In order to react against anti-Semitism," Fanon explained, "the Jew turns himself into an anti-Semite" (with the acuity of this diagnosis revealed by the fitness of his present tense).

But *Black Skin, White Masks* is not so widely read. In *The Wretched of the Earth*, he occupied himself with other matters. But even there he paused to note, if only in passing, that Germany was paying reparations to Israel, which he seemed to approve. And his approval left no doubt that his approval extended to Israel as well, even if he did not spell out his approval explicitly. Does this seem surprising? I suppose that, in the atmosphere of our own moment, Fanon's evident sympathy for the Zionist project might, in fact, seem surprising.

But it should be remembered that, in 1961, when *The Wretched of the Earth* came out, an approving view of Israel was entirely normal and natural among intellectuals of the traditional left. Israel was, after all, a refugee state, and everyone on the traditional left did understand this. Israel was filled with people who, in Fanon's phrase, "were forced to leave" other countries, and who, in their new country, which was also their ancestral homeland, were trying to avoid getting massacred — which made the Israelis objects of sympathy as a matter of left-wing instinct. The concept that a nation of refugees ought to be regarded as an imperialist imposition, soon to be erased ("the world's last settler-colonial state," as Adam Shatz confidently puts it in his Fanon biography), had not yet taken hold. Fanon made clear that he expected Israel to endure: he speculated about a new collective unconscious emerging among the Jews, after a hundred years of Israeli existence. And then, at the age of thirty-six, he succumbed to leukemia, and there was no opportunity to work up further thoughts on Jewish or Zionist themes.

Fanon's very early death was a tragedy in a dozen ways, but one of those ways, I think, touches precisely on those themes. A man with his acuities and philosophical breadth, and his recognition of Jewish suffering and its complexities, might have been able to explain Israel to the Arabs in a fashion that no one else has been able to do — or so I like to imagine. He could have made clear that Jews fleeing to Israel from places like Algeria were not the equivalent of people from France deciding to become settler-colonists in Algeria. He could at least have pointed out a few realities along those lines to the American professors who pride themselves as experts on oppression. Perhaps he could have explained a few things to the Jews, too, in his role as kindly psychiatrist.

Then again, in connection to Zionism, his early death might have been a tragedy also for the blacks of Africa and maybe in other parts of the world. He wanted to affirm a lucid black consciousness, wanted to define a distinctly black perspective, which meant that he wanted to cast off the white insistence on imposing white definitions on everything touching on blacks. His finest pages explored those themes. And, in connection to controversies over Zionism, there was an obvious point to make — obvious, I would think, to someone like him, who, in drawing up his analysis, paid careful attention to an additional sophistication that was Sartre's. This was a sophistication in regard to dishonesty. Sartre fixated on what he called "bad faith," which was a great theme of Sartre's, maybe his greatest theme of all — a grand theme, at least, in *Being and Nothingness*, which Fanon made a point of invoking. "Bad faith" meant the particular mendacity of someone who knows the truth, but does not like the truth, and therefore prefers to lie about it, and lies about having lied. And it is the mendacity of someone who may even convince himself that his lies are truths, and his lies about lying are likewise truths — even while knowing that lies are lies. Bad faith, in short, is a twisted consciousness.

The black perspective, then, in regard to Zionism — what was it? What *should* it have been? In recent decades, the black liberation struggle has acquired a worldwide prestige that Fanon could only have fantasized about. The black struggle has become the modern ideal of a righteous struggle for a better world. And in the context of this development, the anti-Zionist movement, beginning in a small way in the 1960s, and continuing in a large way in the years after 2000, has taken to arguing that, in the modern age, Zionism ought to be seen not as one more liberation struggle, but as the enemy of liberation struggles. Zionism ought to be seen as a participant in the white supremacist and colonialist movements that oppressed blacks in the past. Zionism ought to be seen not as an enemy of Nazism and its systematic exterminations, but as a counterpart to Nazism. And anti-Zionism, by contrast, ought be seen as the heir and brother of the black struggle. Or better still, anti-Zionism ought to be seen as indistinguishable from the black struggle, given that Zionism is white supremacism itself. The success of this argument has been, of course, extraordinary in different parts of the world, which is why on various continents the anti-Zionist cause has acquired the supreme moral prestige of our moment, not just in the universities.

But someone with an orientation like Fanon's can only notice that, amid the worldwide din on behalf of the anti-Zionist cause, the actual black liberation struggle — the struggle by actual black people, that is — has once again, exactly as in the past, been drowned out by non-black voices. And everyone knows this to be true, and pretends not to know, in a classic display of Sartrean bad faith. The largest ethnic horror of the last several months has taken place, after all, within the Arab world, but not in the poor stricken corner of it that is Gaza. The ethnic horror has been the sustained assault on the Masalit people of Sudan, who are black, conducted by the predominantly Arab forces in Sudan's renewed civil war, with disastrous consequences for the blacks, measured in deaths (*Le Monde* has put the figure at something like 75,000 in the last several months), and rapes, and a refugee crisis consisting of eight million people, and a dire food shortage for some eighteen million people. I say that everyone knows this because these events do get reported, not just in obscure human rights publications.

But the anti-Zionists have succeeded in commandeering the language of black liberation, and they have used the language to drown out the actual blacks who are suffering. To drown out the cries of victims in other parts of the world has been a main function of the anti-Zionist movement for many years now. This point was elegantly made as long ago as 2001 by Bernard-Henri Lévy in an essay called *Les Damnés de la guerre*, or *The Wretched of the War*, which invoked Fanon in its title. (Lévy's *Les Damnés de la guerre* rhymes with Fanon's *Les Damnés de la terre* — though Lévy's rhyme disappeared in the English translation, and along with it the invocation of Fanon.) But who will make that point about anti-Zionism today? Anti-Zionism as an instance of what used to be called "false consciousness"? And who will point out that, by contrast, a function of Zionism itself — when Zionism is healthy — is to raise a cry on behalf of the tiny nations, instead of the enormous nations: the little populations that, like the Zionist nation itself, are surrounded by enormous hostile states and populations?

So the voices of the Masalit people go unheard by everyone around the world (even though everyone does, in fact, hear), except the specialists in human rights and a handful of reporters. At Columbia University just now, as I am writing, the student uprising is led by the group called Columbia University Apartheid Divest, with reference to the white supremacist social system of not-so-long ago in South Africa — quite as if the uprising at Columbia amounted to an uprising in favor of oppressed blacks resisting racism in Africa.

But the Columbia uprising merely claims to have done so, with its invocation of apartheid — oh, perhaps with a perfunctory nod to Sudan now and then, in passing. A main student leader of Columbia University Apartheid Divest has become famous, instead, for saying, "Be grateful that I'm not just going out and murdering Zionists" — which is not, after all, a bizarre thing to say, since it merely reprises Stokely Carmichael. And it reprises the Hamas charter. But since everyone by now has read the charter, everyone ought to know, as well, even if they do not know, that in Article Thirty-Four and elsewhere the charter calls for slavery, too. Perhaps that deserves a comment, too? But no one is going to ruminate over Islamist fundamentalism and the history of Arab marauders attacking African blacks.

Mightn't *those* be Fanon's observations, if he were alive? — the observations that reflect a black bitterness, alert to the layers of falsity that bear the stamp of bad faith? But I do not pretend to know. I am not Fanon. And I am not an oppressed Sudanese. But I am definitely sorry that he is gone.

Fanon's died in 1961, the same year as the publication of *The Wretched of the Earth*. His outpouring of acute moral observations and psychoanalytic complications and simple and too-simple angers and political analyses reached its end. And, under those circumstances, his readers were bound to succumb to the allure of his sharp division of world affairs into a conflict between the good nations and the bad nations. And his readers were bound to succumb to that idea without regard to what anyone's ideas and intentions might be, on the assumption, which was his, that identity is conferred by power relations, and not by what people actually think and believe.

The Algerian Revolution figured within the larger Arabist movement, which, in its struggle against the French and British empires, could only be seen, from Fanon's simple standpoint, as the last word in progressivism. But the Arabists also nursed an absolute hostility to Zionism, which suggested that absolute hostility to Zionism must be, by definition, likewise a progressive sentiment. Everyone who thought along the lines of good nations versus bad nations was likely to reach that conclusion. And everyone was likely to set aside as irrelevant the ideas and intentions of the Arabist movement in regard to Zionism and the Jews.

But what if ideas and intentions do, in fact, matter? What if Fanon's habit of excluding ideas and goals from his analyses was bound to produce a systematic blind spot? The grand French philosophers could never make up their minds on this question — on whether ideas matter. Or should every struggle around the world be judged simply on the basis of who appears to be down and who, up? Sartre was a model of confusion on these matters. His sympathy for the downtrodden led him to line up on the Algerian side against the French, and likewise to line up on the Palestinian side against the Zionists. He did so with a lot of vehemence, too, such that, having applauded random violence against the French in Algeria, he went on to applaud Palestinian violence against random Israelis, too — Israeli athletes, for example. He thought hostility was justified, and he did not worry about how the hostility was expressed, so long as it was, in fact, expressed, and the more ferociously, the better. He, too, thought that violence has meaning. This made him an exciting thinker, of course. He took ruthlessness to be the sign of honesty, and he was the philosopher of honesty.

Then again, it ought to be obvious that Sartre went a little crazy in these ways. Fanon in *Black Skin, White Masks* speculated about a syndrome that he called, drawing on the psychoanalytic literature, a "Manichaeanism delirium." This meant a delirium based on the Manichaean idea that everything in the cosmos reflects a battle between Good and Evil, in eternal conflict. In Sartre's case, surely it was a Manichaeanism delirium that led to his repeated impulse to applaud murderous violence against people whose guilt, if they were guilty, was merely a matter of extrapolation or second-order imputation.

And yet, Sartre did live through the Nazi era and the German occupation, and though his knowledge of Jewish life was minimal, he drew the requisite conclusions. He had no trouble recognizing that anti-Semitism's victims were one more downtrodden population. And, though he would never have put it in these words, Zionism was the downtrodden's obvious resort. So he roused himself from his delirium sufficiently, at least, to sympathize with Israel, after all. In 1967, when the Six Day War broke out and Israel's survival appeared to be at risk, he put his prestige on Israel's side. It was a choice. He was reluctant to make the choice. He wobbled. He had to be pushed. Still, he did it — which might seem impossible, given his preference for the Palestinians and his deliriums. But vacillation is conscience, sometimes. And conscience, too, is honesty. And Sartre did not mind looking foolish, so long as he was authentic, or, at least, *looked* authentic.

Fanon's widow was furious when she heard that Sartre had chosen to stand with Israel. But when I look back on Fanon's *Black Skin, White Masks* and its impassioned pages about solidarity with the Jews and hostility to anti-Semitism, I find it easy to imagine that Fanon himself, if he had lived, would have thought hard about Sartre and his choice. I can even imagine that, gathering his courage, Fanon might have joined Sartre in his waverings, perhaps in recognition that he, too, had succumbed for long periods at a time to a Manichaeanism delirium, all too visibly in whole portions of *The Wretched of the Earth*. And he ought to pull himself together. Fanon's biographer, Shatz, gives this possibility a thought and declares it "unlikely." But I wonder if Shatz, for all his admiration of Fanon, hasn't underserved him in certain ways, mostly by underplaying how seriously he took his engagement with Jewish themes and how closely his instincts meshed with Sartre's.

Sartre's waverings, in any case, set a pattern. Michel Foucault followed that pattern a few years later. Foucault watched the Iranian masses overthrow the tyrannical Shah. That was in 1978 and 1979. Foucault watched the Islamist mullahs come to power. And he was ecstatic. He considered that Iran's revolution was an outbreak of freedom, which led him to spend some time in Iran, relishing the joys. But the time he spent there led him to discover that Iran's outbreak of freedom was actually a festival of ideology, and the ideology was anti-Semitic. Iran's revolution against tyranny was an outbreak of tyrannous bigotry. Which Foucault found repulsive. And the ideas and intentions that people cultivate do matter, and what may appear at first glance to be progressive may turn out to be, at second glance, not so progressive. Such were, in any event, the repeated shaky conclusions of the wobbling French philosophers — not all of them, but perhaps the greatest of them, whose wobblings might be the very thing that rescued them from the temptation of philosophy, which is rigidity. A consistent philosopher is, after all, a madman.

And in America? Stokely Carmichael, the sophisticated young champion of Black Power, took his own view of these matters. His instinct was to accept the national-identity vision of worldwide struggle, and not to engage in any wavering of his own. So he accepted Arab nationalism's absolute hostility to Zionism, and he preferred not to fret over any contradictory aspects or complexities that might have crept into the hostility. This required, of course, a willful blindness on his part. The accusation against Zionism — the real-life accusation, and not just the philosophical ideal of an accusation — was a layered affair, and contradictory aspects and complexities did creep into some of those layers, and they did so from the start.

Is it inappropriate for me to note what those layers were? On the surface, the anti-Zionist accusation was a local accusation about land, which was easy to understand. At a deeper layer, it was a more grandly scaled accusation about imperialist colonization, which could seem accurate, if you viewed it from one angle, or maliciously distorted, if you viewed it from another angle. There was a still deeper layer to the anti-Zionist accusation, the bottom-most substratum, which was theological. This is what you can see in the Hamas charter. It was an accusation against the Jews drawn from ancient Islamic texts, as interpreted by the grandees of the Muslim Brotherhood and the modern Islamist movement, who made clear that Judaism was a plot against the Prophet Muhammad and the whole of Islam. A cosmic crime.

The accusation drew on a German influence from the later 1930s and the early 1940s. This, too, you can see in the Hamas charter, with its scrupulous invocation of the mother-document of modern European insanity about the Jews, *The Protocols of the Elders of Zion*, respectfully cited as if *The Protocols* were one more revered and ancient Islamic text, which they are not. *The Protocols* are a compendium of nineteenth-century European fantasies about Jewish conspiracies, which were published as a hoax in Russia in 1903 and went on to enjoy a spectacular success on the extreme right.

Adolf Hitler invoked *The Protocols* in his own charter, which was *Mein Kampf*. The German government during the Hitler era distributed *The Protocols* in Arabic and other languages in the Middle East, where they enjoyed still more success because they appeared to confirm and modernize the many imprecations against the Jews in the ancient Islamic texts. The accusation against Zionism, then, managed to compile in layers the reasonable and the absurd, the progressive and the appalling, the Middle Eastern and the European, the ancient and the modern, all squeezed together into a sandwich of resentments, loyalties, exaltations, ideas, theologies, and superstitions.

But attention to complication was foreign to Carmichael's image of himself. He read the wavering French philosophers (his reading of French philosophers figured in his own glamour), but he chose to be a radical instead of a philosopher, and he signaled his radicalism by choosing Fanon as his favorite philosopher. A radical is defined by his refusal to waver. Carmichael preferred, instead, to provoke. The TV interviewer David Frost famously asked him who among white men he most admired. And Carmichael boldly displayed his fidelity to the anti-Zionist cause by answering in the fashion that, from time to time, the leaders of the Muslim Brotherhood have always liked to do, which is slyly and provocatively, with the explanation that, although he felt no admiration, the greatest of white men was Hitler, "a genius." Hitler — even if "what he did was wrong, was evil, etc."

That was in 1970. The interview shocked a great many people who admired Stokely Carmichael. This he must have enjoyed. All those kids he used to know at Bronx Science? Bayard Rustin? He stuck it to them! But no one should have been surprised. The cartoon in the SNCC newsletter in 1967, the one that reappeared at Harvard back in February of 2024, had already made obvious what sort of intellectual evolution was at work.

The cartoon was a small thing, artistically speaking. Ideologically speaking, though, it was capacious. It was the anti-Zionism of the Middle East in its grotesque sandwich version, minus the tasty fundamental ingredient of Islamic theology, which was not suitable for Western palates. This meant a joining together of the global revolutionary left and the extreme right, anti-imperialists and fascists alike — a cartoon whose iconography drew on the Cuban left-wing poster-art style of the 1960s (visible in the machete that is about to sever the nooses), and drew as well on Nazi graphic art of the 1930s and 1940s. Or perhaps the cartoon drew on the iconography of the anti-Semitic campaign during the Dreyfus affair in France in the 1890s, with its images of a hidden and sinister Jewish power, lurking fiendishly over a helpless world.

This fateful and miserable cartoon, then — how did this minor revenant make its way into the Harvard University turmoil, five months after the October 7 massacre? Harvard has established a further commission on anti-Semitism, now that a first commission has fallen apart, and the members of the new commission, unless it, too, has fallen apart, are bound to pause over that cartoon and its ghostly reappearance. But I suspect that inquiries into university anti-Semitism are never going to get to the heart of this particular controversy, nor any of the related controversies across the academic world.

There is a problem even in the subject of the inquiry, which by now everyone has come to notice. The definition of anti-Semitism, after all — how is that going to be nailed down? If someone says that anti-Semitism nowadays consists of holding Israel to standards that apply to no other country, somebody else is bound to reply, "Well, I do think that Israel is the worst country on earth. And a white settler-colonialist state has no right to exist just because it happens to be Jewish. And how dare you drag in the Nazis! These are slanders demagogically deployed to prevent large numbers of us from expounding the well-supported human-rights conclusions of our scholarly research, which are endorsed by seventeen Jewish professors!," and so forth — which will sink the inquiry into a muddle from which only bubbles will rise to the surface.

If I were a university president with the autocratic power to make professors do what I want, I would mobilize the more level-headed ones under my command to undertake a broader investigation. This would be an inquiry into a climate of opinion that hovers over the university humanities departments and maybe a few other places, and over the art world and the literary world, and seeps at times into the mainstream press. The climate of opinion is conventionally described as a leftism. But I think it is more usefully described as a politicized legacy of the avant-garde, which is why the arts and the humanities departments tend to be its principal center, instead of the social sciences and the economics department, where leftwing opinions normally ought to flourish, if they are going to flourish at all. This is the avant-garde that has oscillated for more than a century from extreme left to extreme right, and from the marvelous to the horrendous, and back again, always in pursuit of a single notion, roughly speaking.

The single notion is the idea that deep truths lurk invisibly beneath the falsities of modern life, and, if only the truths were revealed, a new era would dawn. The new era might be described in different ways. It might be a new literary religion, according to the splendidly creative anarchist poets and their friends in France in the 1890s, who largely founded this strand of the modern avant-garde; or a return to the barbarian glories of authentic experience, according to the right-wing German philosophers in the 1920s and 1930s; or a social emancipation, a ccording to the French post-modernists, whose genius consisted of drawing together the artistic flashes and playfulness of the left-wing poets and the profundities of the right-wing philosophers. And the deep truths might likewise be described in different ways. They might be a binary truth of language, based on a contrast of signs and differentiations. Or a binary truth of music, based on a contrast of sounds and silence. They tend to be, in any case, almost mathematical in their symmetries. They are elegant truths, pleasing to the religious imagination, or the Platonist imagination, or the poetic imagination — truths suited, in short, to the arts and to the vagaries of metaphysics.

The version of this sort of thing that has lately condensed into a climate of opinion in the humanities departments and the world of the arts is less abstract, therefore less pleasing. But the simplicity has remained appealing. It is a social analysis, in which the deep truth is considered to be Fanon's conflict between the colonized and the colonizer, or the oppressed and the oppressor. Everyone has noticed the more-than-political success of this analysis. You see it in the art reviews, where the critics are likely to detect in the biography of artists under review an aesthetic of oppressed-versus-oppressor, whose dialectic accounts for whatever it is the artists may have done. Or you see it in the museum labels of older works, where the artists of the past are routinely deplored for having contributed to dreadful oppressions of times gone by, instead of doing what artists are supposed to do, which is to advance the progressive cause. Or you see it in the art itself, which turns out to be a visual commentary on an imputed verbal text, which, by implication, recounts a story of oppression and resistance.

This sort of thing may strike some people as very exciting for political reasons, or for moral reasons. It may seem uplifting, the way that bourgeois arts in the nineteenth century were supposed to be uplifting. The excitements may be philosophical-and-aesthetic. There is a satisfaction in supposing that art can be reduced to a dialectic of two elements. To see complexities and simplicities dissolve into one another is always stimulating. And if other people see a species of higher idiocy in the relentless art-world insistence on radical reductionism and moral sermonizing — well, better yet! Provocation is beauty, and beauty, provocation.

But the primary victim right now of this sort of thinking has turned out, somehow or another, to be the Jews. I suppose the somehow-or-another has been inevitable, given the allure of the either/or habit of mind. Stokely Carmichael was a man of our own moment, in this respect. It ought to have been obvious, in connection to Israel and Palestine, that reductionist simplicities of the colonized/colonizer sort were never going to apply in any ordinary or realistic way. It is not just a matter of mistaking refugees for colonialists. Everybody does know, after all, or sort of knows, that a good half of the accused white colonialist settlers, perhaps a slight majority of them, fled to Israel from the Arab countries and the largely Muslim zones of Central Asia, not to mention a couple of Jewish demographic percentage points that fled to Israel from East Africa.

If the planet is to be divided into — still another Manichaean phrase — "the West and the Rest," it ought to be obvious that Israel falls into the West and the Rest at the same time, ethnographically speaking, which ought not to be possible, Manichaeanly speaking. The war right now in Gaza may even hint at Israel's bifurcated nature. Israel's army and its commanders turn out to be extremely capable, disciplined, and conscientious in the style of a modern Western army. But the army and at least some of its commanders also appear to have worried about mass suffering only begrudgingly, and some of the better-known leaders of Israel's disastrous government make a display of worrying about mass suffering not at all. Or they stand openly in favor of mass suffering, quite as if Israel, which appears on the map to be merely one more Middle Eastern country, may be, in fact, one more Middle Eastern country, militarily speaking. And just as Saudi Arabia's anti-Islamist intervention in Yemen produced a humanitarian disaster, so has Israel's anti-Islamist intervention in Gaza, even if not on the Saudi scale, in all-too-faithful conformity to the regional style.

But everything about the prevailing climate of opinion in corners of the academy and in the world of the arts makes it difficult to look the various complexities and nuances in the face. So there are a great many people who gaze at Israel and prefer to see South Africa and its past. They do not see one more bloodbath in a history of even larger Middle Eastern bloodbaths. They prefer to see what the Islamists have always claimed to see, which is the crime against God, or the maximum crime of crimes, namely, an outright extermination of an entire people, such that "genocide," the word, has become a catch-phrase. They see the Jews as Nazis, which has been a theme of the Islamist hysteria against Zionism for many decades. They decline to see anything at all about Hamas's nature, doctrines, and practices, even if they do see those things. They see that resistance to what they imagine to be white settler-colonialism is righteous, and self-defense is monstrous. And the October 7 massacre seems to them — such is the logic, it is inescapable — a good thing, not just *on balance*. The October 7 massacre is a good thing *absolutely*. A good thing in the name of humanitarianism. And in the name of enlightenment, no less. It is a good thing, morally speaking, or psychologically speaking. An occasion for joy. Which some people express openly, even while denying that they want to kill the Jews; and other people merely infer, while denying they are inferring anything of the sort; and other people claim to oppose, but infer anyway.

The celebration of bad faith reaches its acme in the dreadful chants, "From the river to the sea" and "Globalize the intifada," which mean, of course, the reduction of fifty per cent of the world's Jewish population to statelessness (in the first instance) and a worldwide terrorist campaign against Jews (in the second instance) — but which, we are told, mean, instead, "human rights for Palestinians" and "spirited worldwide protest." Except that everyone knows that, on the contrary, those slogans are ventures into transgression, which is why young people like to chant them. And no one wants to acknowledge what the transgression is. And no one wants to acknowledge how shocking it is that, in the United States and in France and perhaps in other places, a mass movement of students, led by the student elite, has arisen in favor of those unacknowledged transgressions.

What should the universities do? I would mobilize my imaginary committee to confront the broader climate of opinion as a whole. This would mean recognizing that the wave of virulent campus anti-Zionism, hidden and overt, together with the wave of virulent hatred in the art and literary worlds, amounts to something more than a failure of civility. It is an intellectual crisis. And the source of the crisis is not the students, and not a handful of radical organizations, either, even if the radical organizations are awful. Nor is the source merely the handful of professors who look and sound crazy. The source is a series of doctrines and assumptions that have degenerated from something authentically interesting into something grotesque, quietly presided over by professors who look and sound not just reasonable but attractively up-to-date. It is a development similar to the intellectual degeneration many decades ago of the brilliant and fiery Stokely Carmichael, except on an enormous university scale.

I would mobilize my committee to inquire into the origin and evolution of the doctrines and assumptions, and the manner of their degeneration. My model for this would be Marx and Engels, who formed a two-person committee of their own to do something similar in their own day by composing a book called *The German Ideology*. This was a study of the German philosophers in their era and the climate of opinion they generated, with "ideology" understood in the Marxist sense, which is pejorative. I would mobilize my committee to produce something along similar lines, to be called *The University Ideology*. It would be a study of the delusions of the humanities departments and related fields in our own era, with "ideology" likewise meant pejoratively. An intellectual revolution would be my committee's goal — a self-revolution in the universities, in the hope that the art and literary worlds might respond with similar self-revolutions. This would be wonderfully stimulating.

But it may be that self-revolutions are not every university's first instinct. It may be that, in the university administrations, a good many people, having observed the coarsening of discussion and debate over the last few months, will prefer a different course of action. They will prefer to mount a scapegoat persecution, intent on singling out the more obstreperous students. They will blame the "outside agitators," who plainly do exist. Or they will focus their attention on the more outrageous and embarrassing professors, who are not too numerous, in the hope that, if only the obstreperous, the outsiders, the outrageous, and the embarrassing were suspended, expelled, arrested, chastised, fired, or demoted, the universities could breathe in peace for a moment. And then, at last, the universities could move on to the main step. This will be a call for renewed civility, for academic freedom, for tolerance, and for reasoned debate. It will be, in short, a search for the perfect speech code.

Am I right about this? If I am, the university response to the crisis of the last many months will end up as an institutional effort to avoid looking into what is fundamentally the problem, which is not an outbreak of incivility, but is, instead, a bad-faith bad turn, ultra-left and ultra-right at the same time, in the evolution of ideas, not just in the universities but in the art and literary worlds, not just in America, but also in Europe.

SERGEI LEBEDEV

The Heroic Illusion of Alexei Navalny

Alexei Navalny was killed in the far north above the Arctic Circle, in the small town of Kharp, where the Ural Mountains are intersected by a railroad leading to the city of Labytnangi on the Ob River. This place of death, this scene of the crime, is not random. It puts a period to the argument with fate that Alexei Navalny led as a man and politician — even, one could say, to his argument with Russia and its history. The man who came up with The Beautiful Russia of the Future as image and slogan died in the horrible Russia of the past.

Approximately fifty kilometers southeast of Kharp, beyond the Ob, is the city of Salekhard. The sadly famous Road

501, the Dead Road, leads east from there. It is one of the last projects born of Stalin's megalomania, a railroad branch to the Enisei River that would traverse uninhabited places unsuitable for construction across the permafrost and the swamps of western Siberia. All that remains of that pharaonic project are a few hundred kilometers of embankments, dilapidated camp barracks, and steam engines rusting in the tundra. And corpses. Corpses in nameless ravines and pits, without a cross or a marker, unknown, buried without funerals, the dead whose killers and torturers remain unpunished.

This is the region of the Gulag, the wasteland of the murdered and the murderers. In these places, geography helps the work of the jailers, and the climate serves as a means of torture. Here, in this ideal geographic nothingness, a space beyond history, beyond evidence, the Soviet state cast out people doomed to annihilation. This is the place where Russia's historical sin is preserved in material, sometimes even imperishable, form — permafrost, after all. Here lie Russia's guilt and responsibility.

Alexei Navalny's political credo, which changed over the years and is not easily summarized, did have one constant premise, one characteristic feature. He denied — or rather refused to consider — the power of the totalitarian past. He would not recognize the genealogy and the continuity of state violence, and most importantly, its long-term social consequences.

Yes, he would come to the Solovetsky Stone — a monument to the victims of communist crimes in Lubyanka Square in Moscow, consisting of a large boulder brought a great distance from the very first Soviet penal camp — every year on October 30, the day commemorating the victims of political oppression, and lay a bouquet at the monument:

the proper gesture. But his image of the "real" Russia was always that of a tabula rasa, an ideal community over which the past had no power — the strange notion of a society that experiences the oppression of an authoritarian regime but somehow automatically aspires to democracy and is in a certain sense innocent, historically undetermined, without, so to speak, a medical record. His "beautiful Russia of the future" was already here, it already existed in the present, in his own generation, it only needed to be unblocked, unveiled, unpacked, affirmed in reality.

Yet it is unlikely that he could explain how it came to be, how it was born. He announced it with the disproportionate confidence of a fakir with a grateful audience that also wished to believe that you can turn over a new leaf without acknowledging historical guilt or admitting historical responsibility, without recognizing the stubborn presence of the past, without punishing the criminals and thereby severing the umbilical cord of violence.

Navalny told a fairy tale about a miracle. In classical myth, crimes and sins give birth to monsters, chthonic creatures, the embodiment of fate. He offered a postmodern reverse myth, the story that monsters are capable — simply by the force of history's progressive course, or because you want to believe it — of giving birth to beautiful, ideal children. In other words, this was a rather spectacular case of a denial of trauma. It was premised on a population without memory and without unhealed scars. But history cannot be fooled. Monsters, if not completely killed, give birth only to monsters.

I may seem cold and too critical. After all, the earth is still fresh on the grave and the period of mourning is not yet over. But already I see the stirrings of an uncritical heroization and canonization that will confer upon Navalny's views, and his temperament, a sacred status, and this, I believe, will inevitably lead to a repetition of his mistakes. His mistakes were fatal — not only to his person but to the trajectory of Russia's opposition movement. He personified some of the most profound errors that a dissident leader can make: he was a moral leader whose moral authority was in fact based on a kind of amorality, a catastrophic substitution of hierarchies of values and an extremely optimistic populism.

Amorality? Isn't that too harsh? For many people in Russia and abroad, after all, Alexei Navalny was the very symbol of moral behavior. He did not betray himself; he did not break in prison or under torture; he died for what he believed to be a just cause. An extraordinary man. No one can deny Navalny's personal bravery. His courage and the habits of a free man distinguished him and attracted others to him.

But there were things that even he did not dare do. He did not dare do them, I believe, for a simple reason: he was a born politician. He had a better understanding than most for the mood of the liberal youth. He loudly and cleverly criticized the Putin regime and fought against it — but where was his criticism directed? For a very long time Navalny's target was corruption. His greatest exposés were in that area. He addressed himself to the material concerns of citizens whose money and votes had been stolen. He played on legal outrage, and on common sense.

The problem is that, from the very beginning, corruption was not the most terrifying aspect of the Putin regime. Vladimir Putin came to power as a war president. The second

Chechen war raised and solidified his ratings, turning him into a national leader. That base and ruthless war turned the Russian Army into a punitive tool, because it not only fought with Chechen troops but it also "pacified" the population. It was a war with tens of thousands of victims; a criminal war from start to finish. It certainly was a crime that on the scales of justice — and in common sense — significantly outweighed any number of stolen billions and any amount of cheating at the polls. It is strange to judge a murderer for the theft of office supplies, or to accuse a serial killer of forging lottery tickets. The right to life is the highest value. Vladimir Putin — like Boris Yeltsin before him — took away that right from tens of thousands of Chechens.

Before 2014, before the annexation of Crimea and the war in Ukraine, this was Putin's greatest crime. Without acknowledging the guilt and punishing the perpetrators in the two wars against Chechnya, which set Russia back on its old imperial and colonial path, and unleashed the spiral of state violence, and turned Chechnya into a "black hole," a zone of lawlessness from where the lawless practices spread throughout Russia — without confronting all this, no bright and real "Russia of the future" would be possible. Without an answer to the cardinal question of the right to secede, without a recognition of the centuries of repressive policies toward ethnic minorities, the Russia of the future will always be the Russia of the past.

Alexei Navalny was silent about the main crimes of the Putin regime and of Vladimir Putin personally. If you think about it, it seems inexplicable. Or, perhaps, explicable but not justifiable — but the explanation destroys the very concept of the beautiful Russia of the future that needs only to be released from Putin's regime to emerge. Navalny was silent either because he did not consider the Chechen war significant or because he understood all too well that even the liberal part of Russian society did not care about dead Chechens, about crimes far away in the Caucasus committed in the name of Russia. The discouraging truth is that Russian society had grown accustomed to war, it no longer reacted to pricks of conscience, and it became alert only when it came to matters of personal interest — for example, the reforms of social benefits, or the crushing of hopes connected to the allegedly more liberal rule of Dmitri Medvedev (during whose administration Russia attacked Georgia in 2008), or the news that Putin would go for a third term.

Then came 2014 and the invasion of Ukraine by Russian troops. The number of military and civilian dead was in the thousands, but Russia's main opposition figure stubbornly continued to expose the economic crimes of Putin and his henchmen. As if no blood had been shed and international law was not being cynically and odiously violated. Whereas it could be said, in explanation of Navalny's earlier behavior, that Russia's war against Chechnya took place before he became a famous opposition politician, no such extenuation can be made of his diffidence toward the war against Ukraine, which occurred when he was already the informal leader of the opposition and a brand name.

That extraordinary status, one would have thought, demanded only one strategy: to speak out against the war clearly and consistently, and to create a broad antiwar coalition. As we know, Navalny cannot be accused of cowardice. It was not fear of repression by the government that kept him from taking this path. But I am certain that in this regard he felt fear — a fear of a different kind, the fear of every populist politician. He was afraid of losing support.

Again, this is just my supposition, but I think Navalny sensed that a radical antiwar position would not increase the number of his supporters but would in fact decrease it. In 2014–2022, almost all of Russia accepted Putin's formula of pretend war, a limited conflict in which Russia was not even involved. Of course, everyone understood that Russia was deeply involved; I doubt that anyone was fooled by the clumsy camouflage, all those "volunteers" and "national republics." The pro-war radicals demanded that the cards be shown without shame and organized in support of war. What did the antiwar people do? It would require a work of literature, a novel in the spirit of Musil's *The Man Without Qualities,* to capture their delinquency — the mix of semi-apathy, semi-activity, intentions without intentions and protest without protest, that the liberal part of society used to delineate its Fronde, refusing to confront the issue for an either-or answer, continuing to cooperate with state institutions, seeking positive aspects in the capital's urbanistic changes — in other words, to live an ordinary life.

Navalny, wittingly or not, played into the hands of that mass pretending to be a mobilized protest by lowering the drama and the ethical intensity of the situation, with his dominating anti-corruption agenda.

In August 2020, after an obvious falsification of the results of the presidential election, the people of Belarus went out onto the streets. It was truly a mass protest, not like the Russian ones. For a few days it seemed that the situation was balancing on a hair: President Lukashenko could flee to Moscow like President Yanukovich did in the Ukrainian revolution in 2014, to add to Moscow's collection of retired dictators — or Putin could invoke the status of Belarus as a Union state and dispatch the troops to complete the annexation of Belarus.

It was during those days that Alexei Navalny was poisoned by Novichok, the poison of choice of the Russian security agencies, which has been used in several attacks. There is much speculation on whether the intention was to kill him. My own view is that the more important fact is that Novichok was used, because it is the calling card of Russian state violence. It was a clear signal to all Russian oppositionists, and the poisoned Navalny transmitted the signal.

It is very possible that Navalny had no intention of following the radical example of the Belarussians. But from the point of view of the Kremlin, he was the only person capable of stirring up a serious wave of protest in Russia, and that was why he was left in a coma, so that any Russian echo of the Belarussian turbulence would die before it was born. But it left something like a legend of the peaceful protest that almost won — as opposed to the brutally violent repression of the Ukrainian protest, with the burning tires of Maidan.

Nothing contributed to the demobilization of the pro-democratic community in Russia more than the temporary loss of its leader and the persistence of the narrative, presented as perfectly obvious, of peace, as if the liberal opposition had only to wait for the right moment (which would definitely come) for everyone to go out onto the streets. Then came the brilliant investigation by Bellingcat, which proved beyond a reasonable doubt that Russian special services had attempted to assassinate Navalny, and Navalny's extraordinary phone call to one of his unsuccessful killers, when Navalny, playing a state official, literally forced him to confess.

So the proof of the regime's culpability was there. But again Navalny preferred bravado, laughter, the merry mocking of the stupidity of the agents. This, instead of a serious conversation about the system, about the institution of political murder that had reappeared under Yeltsin, about the dozens of people who were poisoned, shot, beaten to death: Politkovskaya, Shchikochikhin, Yushenkov, Starovoitova, Kholodov, Litvinenko, the Skripals, Nemtsov, Estemirova, and many, many others. (Vladimir Kara-Murza, for example, survived two poisonings and is now in a Russian prison.)

When he recovered and was literally back from the other world like a mystical hero, Navalny could and should have presented Putin with the bill: to speak out about first principles and on the behalf of everyone whose life Putin had taken. But Navalny did not submit the bill in full. Even though he had had one foot in the grave, he preferred to play (it was not an act, it was his nature) the apostle of the beautiful Russia of the future that does not demand unsettling revelations about the past.

Some might say that this insouciance was the highest level of heroism, the highest bravery — literally to be resurrected and behave as if death had no business in your body and to troll the hapless executioners. I agree that there is courage there, and nerve. But sometimes it is more useful to be scared, to comprehend and proclaim the historical continuity of murders and murderers, to speak in the name of all who had been killed secretly, who were led in the 1930s to execution pits by the same Cheka agents with the same headquarters on Lubyanka. But that was not for him — too old-fashioned, perhaps. I can't find a better word.

It would have put him among the ranks of denouncers and prophets such as Valeria Novodvorskaya, whom the liberal public liked to put down with the humiliating tag *demschizo*

— democratic schizophrenics who were rabidly against the regime. Navalny did not want to be a *demschizo*. He did not want to be a harsh and bitter prophet. He wanted to be the less distressing harbinger of hope.

In the declassified archive of the Lithuanian KGB, I have seen documents concerning an attempted political assassination. In 1980, local officers wrote a letter to Moscow, to General Filipp Bobkov, head of the infamous Fifth (ideological) Directorate. It was about "special measures" that were planned for a Catholic priest. Of course the letter did not contain the word "assassination." The Lithuanian KGB asked Moscow to approve the mission and to send two "technical specialists." Later these "specialists," disguised as traffic police officers, stopped the priest's car on a night road under the pretext of checking documents.

The priest was not surprised. He was used to highway patrols stopping him more frequently and combing through his papers. It was more of the usual harassment. But this time, while one Moscow visitor opened the hood and checked the engine number with the priest, another sprayed some kind of substance on the driver's seat. A few hours later, the priest was brought to the hospital with a diagnosis of "radiation burns." He survived. But a few years later he died in a very strange road accident.

Nothing was said about it in his operational development file. And General Filipp Bobkov, who should have been in prison, after 1991 became a member of media mogul Vladimir Gusinsky's Mediamost Group, which owned, among other things, the independent television channel NTV. Bobkov was head of security. Amazingly, the many decent people, the bold journalists who worked for Gusinsky, never asked any questions. How could their security be guaranteed by a monster? But Bobkov could scare off the pettier monsters who multiplied in the freewheeling early 1990s.

The KGB's murderous reputation and its connection to the political liquidations in the Soviet era were well known, even if not always proven. But no one quit, or even complained. Everyone chose the required cohabitation with evil. As did the citizens who later accepted the generals who fought against Chechnya as politicians and governors, such as Andrei Lugovoi, the assassin of Alexander Litvinenko, a member of parliament. It was a kind of covert social agreement that even the democratic community accepted: not forgetting the past completely, but also not exaggerating, not going to extremes, not shouting "killer" at killers. Or not shouting it loudly.

This house of cards fell apart halfway on February 24, 2022, when the Russian army openly invaded Ukraine. Hundreds, even thousands, of smartphone cameras filmed how the Russians fought and showed it to the world in its full barbarity. Russians are often rebuked for protesting too weakly against the invasion. They defend themselves by pointing to the number of anti-war protestors who were arrested. I admit that I can understand people who would not risk protesting against the regime with the radical methods of Maidan. Not everyone can be a hero. The problem, rather, is that we did not notice, we were not aware of, how we ended up at that point of impotence.

In truth, we got there in part because of all the lulling speeches about how Russia was actually different, how we were an undeniable force, how there were so many of us — all the naïve speeches that we are the power here and Putin fears us.

One of the most frequent reactions of liberal Russians to the atrocities of Russian troops in the early weeks and months of the invasion was shock. Could Russian soldiers really behave this way? Some tried to shift the blame to the units from the Russian Federation's national republics: it was the fault of those savages. But those who remembered the actions of Russian troops in Chechnya were not surprised at all. It was the familiar pattern of violence: mass reprisals against civilians, the wanton destruction of civil infrastructure, executions on the spot.

Our civic memory seems to have had its long-term function disabled. Every political generation now starts from scratch, zeroing out the account of responsibility and denying (or being utterly shocked by) the continuity of violence in both the state and the society. Alexei Navalny was a brilliant tactician, but when it came to larger questions of morality and strategy he was a perfect avatar of this terrible tendency.

Russia's open war against Ukraine revealed yet another fatal flaw in the Russian opposition: a systemic inability for decolonizing thinking, an unwillingness to admit that Russia itself consists of subjugated and partially "digested" nations that have undergone, in the words of the Ukrainian dissident Ivan Dzyuba, a process of forced denationalization. Without the voices of these nations, without their equal representation in the opposition, no conversation about the future of Russia has the right to take place, or will lead to a just result.

Navalnyism always bypassed or ignored the issue of national rights. When Navalny, who began his political career among Russian nationalists and made chauvinistic comments in the early period of his activism, emerged as a recognized leader, he turned out to be a kind of supra-national democrat. He did not divide his supporters by nationality, or recognize their specific national demands; instead he addressed them as conventional people of goodwill who are conscious (or modern) enough to also rise above national feelings and unite for the sake of the beautiful Russia of the future.

This point of view is dominant in the bearers of Great Russian Culture. It is a mixture of a sense of superiority, neglect, chauvinism, colonial-educational fervor — and a subconscious fear of finding out one day that these Others do not really want to be part of Russia at all.

And here the approach of the irreconcilable opponents, Putin and Navalny, surprisingly converged. In Putin's case, this perspective is clear. But it is sad to admit that his most talented and certainly his most relentless opponent turned out to be a hostage of the same imperial paradigm. Navalny had a chance to change history — but for this he had to first accept it himself, to hear voices in other languages presenting a historical account. And Navalny was too Russian for that.

It is noteworthy that there is something here that Navalny had in common with Soviet Russian dissidents of the past. They (there were some exceptions who proved the rule) often treated with a cold lack of understanding the ideas and the agendas of dissidents of the national republics who spoke about the colonial role of Russia, about language rights, about the right to self-determination. To Russian dissidents, it probably all seemed too archaic, a dead-end; and without noticing it they regarded these aspirations for emancipation through the optics of high Russian culture, into which are embedded a hierarchy of cultures and the idea of the national as backward and obsolete. The texts of the dissidents of the republics of the USSR contain bitter philippics addressed to conditional "Muscovites" who talk about human rights, but the "human" in their human rights does not seem to have a nationality.

Soviet Russian dissidents, whose personal qualities were certainly extraordinary, failed to become a tangible and independent political force. Navalny, by contrast, became such a force. But the dissident project contained at least half of the needed reckoning with the past: the memory of the victims of Soviet terror. Navalny's project, directed into the future, did not offer even that half. Therein lay his power: people wanted to forget, to seal a compact of silence, as in Spain. And therein lay his weakness: because it was in that field of silence, in that agreement to forget about spilled blood, that Vladimir Putin's multiple tyrannical ambitions flourished and eventually destroyed Alexei Navalny himself.

Rationally speaking, Vladimir Putin had no need to fear Alexei Navalny. Navalny would not have been serious competition for Putin even in honest elections. He would have gotten a maximum of ten to fifteen percent of the votes of the liberal electorate — a lot, to be sure, but not enough even for a second round. Stories that Navalny would have beaten Putin are the electoral fantasies of his supporters, a fairy tale with a happy ending, with no convincing sociological or political basis.

So Putin's worries about Navalny, his fears of Navalny, were completely irrational. To understand them we need to take an excursion into the dictator's head — a voyage that a writer, rather than a scholar, is perhaps best qualified to take.

Putin was and is an officer of the secret police, counter-intelligence, a trained paranoid whose picture of the world is irreversibly deformed by ideological indoctrination and professional "education." I have read enough internal KGB documents to say this confidently.

The key word, the key concept, of this worldview is "object." The idea is to depersonalize people, to cleanse them of subjectivity, of selfhood. Object of surveillance. Object of influence. Object of operative interest. Object of development. Yours or someone else's. In the world of objects, no one acts on his own. There are always hidden reasons, there are always puppet masters. But Navalny's personality, his charisma, his preternaturally unflappable spirit, was a challenging anomaly for Putin, who was certain that all people were objects; and this exception to the rule, this man who somehow could not be made into an object, created an almost superstitious feeling in him. It is known that Putin never called Navalny by his name until after he died in the camps.

To better understand the genesis of Putin's attitude toward Navalny, we must go back to Dresden in late 1989, where Putin was serving at the time. The local Stasi office and its corresponding KGB office were on the outskirts of the city, in an idyllic area of two-story villas near the Elbe. Right there, about two hundred meters away, stood a typical urban five-story building, which housed families of Soviet officers. A walk along those streets today reveals that it is all one tidy whole, a cozy corner where apartment and work are close together. The neighborhood is so sentimental, so *gemutlich*, so safe.

But in late 1989 the coziness ended suddenly, when demonstrators surrounded the Stasizentrale building and blocked the KGB officers inside their neighboring villa. Descriptions of those turbulent days share an important feature: the protestors acted wisely and in an organized way, while both the Stasi and the KGB were in disarray.

And biographies (and hagiographies) of Putin mention the moment when he allegedly came to the gates and calmed down the crowd that was ready to storm the KGB villa, behaving like the tamer of wild elements, a man with a cool head. Journalists recorded the event: Moscow was silent, Moscow gave no orders, and Putin acted independently, at his own peril.

That was the moment, I think, of his deepest and most destructive fear. Those East Germans, the obedient sheep, the objects that he and those like him were used to bossing around — they rose up, they acted with a firm and free collective will, they invaded a space that he was used to considering private and inviolable. Besides the threat to him and his family, he must have felt a deep-rooted fear, which is always absolute in a state security officer, of people who turned in a flash into subjects of their own fate and history. It was no accident that on his first visit to Germany as president, just a bit more than a decade after the event, he travelled to Dresden. They had thrown him out of there, but he came back — and as master of the situation. Putin would carry that fear — call it the Dresden fear — throughout his life: the fear of "color revolutions," of Ukrainian Maidans, of any street protests where he can imagine the sudden doubling of a crowd's energy and the invented foreign power behind it, the eternal conspiracy of Western influence.

There is another event in Putin's life that is important in this context. In 1996, he was deputy mayor of St. Petersburg, a man little known at the federal level and unknown to the general public. Yet only three years later, in 1999, he was prime minister and Yeltsin's heir. That promotion cannot be described in terms of a consecutive career. There were no such careers. It is Fata Morgana, a postmodern composition in which one of many (and a career counterintelligence agent to boot) accustomed to conspiracies and to manipulations behind the scenes is suddenly elevated and made heir to the throne.

He would spend the rest of his life arguing that it was not an accidental choice, that he in fact was a leader, a historical figure, a messiah; part of the historical pattern, not just Yeltsin's whim. Hence his obsession with history, his search for the ideological genealogy of his power. He is like a commoner determined to create an aristocratic background for himself. Trained to be no one, anonymous, a gray man in a gray coat, he is possessed by a megalomania stemming from a deep fear of imposture. His perception is schizophrenically distorted: he is simultaneously sure of his right to rule the kingdom and waiting in dread to be finally exposed, in the fatal end of the play in which he was once assigned a role.

The two fears converged in the figure of Alexei Navalny. In contrast to Putin, Navalny created himself. In contrast to Putin, Navalny was a genius of the masses, a born leader of the protest minority. Putin's passion for history is profoundly pathological because it is only in the external world, the world of acts of power, acts of aggression, that he can confirm over and over that he really is the ruler. Taught to rule people through fear and submission, knowing neither love nor trust nor solidarity, he is prey to fears. Navalny terrified him.

As declassified KGB archives in Ukraine and Lithuania show, the work of the secret police did not end when a target was arrested and sentenced, or when a political prisoner was sent to the camps. His file was sent with him, so that they could continue their persecution there.

They could try to compromise him, to ruin his reputation in the eyes of his comrades. To force him to change his views.

To incline him to self-denial, to compel his repentance, his denunciation of his previous activity. A combination of carrot and stick. Play, tempt, press, force.

Judging from reports by Navalny's lawyers and comrades, they did not play with him. They simply tried to destroy him. To kill him a second time. But Navalny had a lot of life in him. Actually, he, with his body, his character, and his strength, symbolized life. Life against death. His mistakes, misunderstandings, and failures were the qualities of a living person. And so he spoke out — albeit belatedly — about the criminality of the war against Ukraine. He spoke from solitary confinement.

His surname came from the verb *navalivatsya*, to pile on, and it was the surname of a fighter. I do not feel it is necessary to discuss why he returned to Russia. He made his choice. The Christian connotations ascribed with almost religious fervor to that return, so as to make of him a redemptive sacrificial victim, are outrageously inaccurate. What he certainly never intended to be was a sacrificial victim. Not in a psychological, or legal, or sacral sense.

Basically, this is the main lesson of his life, his main gift, his main legacy: you can live and act freely in Russia, you can live without feeling doomed, without acknowledging the right of the regime to punish or pardon, without a bent spine. That is how we will remember him: the harbinger of an unfulfilled hope.

Real politics in Russia will emerge only when the subject of liberal-democratic thought becomes the question of what to do with the so-called Federation, in which the "subjects" of this

Federation have no political subjectivity. What to do with a country that is a conglomeration of forcibly annexed nations, whose national identity has been and is being erased, whose culture is being Russified? What to do with the last empire, afflicted with residual imperial megalomania, and with a nuclear arsenal?

Everything else is not politics, but a way of avoiding this urgent and extremely painful question. For this reason, the distance between Vladimir Putin's United Russia and Alexei Navalny's Beautiful Russia of the Future is not as great as it may seem. Both of these supposedly visionary concepts are just screens, a way to hide the real poverty of the political toolkit.

Alexei Navalny's utopia was futuristic, modernist, it functioned like a time machine, which is to say, he imagined that the future could simply be summoned rather than earned. The future drew its magic power from time as such: one day the future would come, and the future would put everything in its place, canceling the past. It is necessary only to live, to wait, as one waits for the change of seasons. Vladimir Putin's utopia, by contrast, is retrospective: what makes us strong is our connection to the past, to the figures of our archaic ancestors, the victors in World War II. The West, which rushed into the future, is afflicted with moral corrosion, while we are becoming morally stronger because our future is the past.

In relation to the real, historically conditioned Russian Federation, which began to unravel back in the 1990s, a process that was reversed by the ostentatious massacre of Chechnya and the establishment of an authoritarian regime, both political projects described above are mirages. Real democracy in the Russian Federation, which would give representation and political power to national minorities, will always (potentially) raise the question of political architecture, subjectivity and, in the end, independence.

Vladimir Putin, the self-appointed tsar, will never understand or recognize this. Alexei Navalny could probably have understood. He could have learned, which is a capacity only of the living. He had come a long way, from flirting politically with street nationalism to fighting against tyranny. In a bitter irony, flowers for him in the days of his death were left at monuments to the victims of Soviet repression, an unwitting recognition of the continuity of Russian violence, which he tried to deny with his life.

ASSAF SHARON

October 7: The Tragedy of the "Debate"

Three months after its barbaric attack on southern Israel, Hamas published a memorandum explaining its actions. "The events of October 7 must be put in their broader context," it said. That broader context, according to Hamas, is "all cases of struggle against colonialism." Zionism is a "colonial project," according to the memorandum, and Israel is therefore an "illegal entity." These days this is not an uncommon analysis. In the West, Zionism's relation to colonialism has become a political shibboleth, shouted from the streets and the campuses. According to the rules of the present discussion, tell me whether you think that Zionism is colonialism and

I will tell you whether you are a Zionist apologist or an antisemitic bigot.

The confusion here is not only political but also intellectual. The primary task of theoretical terms such as colonialism and imperialism is to elucidate the facts, and to offer an explanation of the facts that may be critically examined. They are not meant to serve as badges of ideological loyalty. These abstract terms must be judged as concepts before they are admitted as slogans. The first question, then, is whether the post-colonial framework is helpful for making sense of the situation. Is it useful for understanding the unrelenting crisis tormenting Palestinians and Israelis? More urgently, is it helpful for resolving it?

Let us begin at the beginning. Like other colonial efforts, Zionism was a European movement that aimed to transpose Europeans (and, later, non-Europeans) to a land populated by non-Europeans. It strove to create a European state, or state-like, entity in the Levant. Prima facie, this sounds like colonialism. But it is hardly the whole story. Zionists never saw themselves as shouldering "the white man's burden," as Kipling infamously put it. Jews took to Palestine to escape persecution and squalor, not to partake in *la mission civilisatrice* or to promote imperial powers. Their objective was to leave Europe, where Jews were themselves the domestic victims of the imperial states, not to carry Europe's flag to Palestine. If anything, early Zionists wished to sever ties with their places of birth. Their descendants certainly do not see themselves as ambassadors of Polish, German, Russian, Iraqi, Moroccan, Yemeni or other metropoles.

Colonial imperialism provided the context in which Zionism took shape — how could it not in a world dominated by colonial powers? In his attempt to lay the foundations for a national home for Jews, Herzl wooed the Ottoman Sultan and the German Kaiser. His successor in the Zionist leadership, Chaim Weizmann, secured the Balfour Declaration from the British after they seized Palestine from the Ottomans. (Many decades later Yasser Arafat courted first the Soviets and then the Americans.) But Zionists did not seek to impose their culture or their religion on the Arab population of Palestine, nor did they exploit the land's natural resources for the benefit of their European motherlands. Jewish émigrés to Palestine — before the war and certainly after it — were more refugees than colonial settlers.

Then there is the idea of "settler-colonialism," defined by the sociologist Gershon Shafir as "the active repossession of land and its repopulation, most commonly by white immigrants from Europe, through the exclusion, expulsion, or elimination of native peoples." He added that the Zionist program undeniably involved "the creation of new settlements, over and against the wishes of native peoples." But these empirical characteristics, these facts, do not explain what happened, and why. Was the pre-Zionist Jewish minority in Palestine less entitled to expand its population and ownership of land than the Arab majority? Did it aim to "destroy and replace" the indigenous population?

To fit Zionism into the settler-colonial mold, it is useful to ignore the fact that Jews were indigenous in Palestine, albeit a minority, and that they had been forcibly exiled from their land without ever having renounced their loyalty to it. It is also useful to forget that alongside the great displacement of Palestinians within the mandate of Palestine in 1948, there was a parallel displacement of Jews. In every area conquered by Arab forces, Jews were evicted or killed, and their dwellings were demolished. In fact, Arabs remained in areas conquered by Jewish forces in 1948, whereas not a single Jew remained in Jerusalem's Old City, Mount Scopus, and Atarot to its north, Gush Etzion to the south, or any of the other territories that came under Arab control. It is not unreasonable to argue that the asymmetry in death and displacement is merely a consequence of the imbalance of military success.

Zionism moved Jews into historic Palestine and pushed Arabs out. That much is undeniable. Whether this was Zionism's "logic of elimination," in the ominous words of Patrick Wolfe, whose book popularized the term "settler colonialism," or a consequence of the violent Arab reaction to Jewish settlement, will continue to be endlessly debated. If the "elimination" of Palestinians had been the Zionists' objective, we must acknowledge that it was among the least effective of ethnic cleansings, as the Arab population "between the river and sea" has increased tenfold since Zionists arrived there.

An American newspaper recently interviewed two of Israel's most prominent revisionist historians. Both trace the roots of October 7 to the mass uprooting of Palestinians in 1948. Avi Shlaim frames "the essence of the conflict as being the Zionist settler colonial movement." Benny Morris blames it on Palestinian refusal to accept that "if people commit major mistakes in history they pay for them," referring to the Arab rejection of the UN partition plan of 1947. Slapping the label of colonialism on the situation does nothing to settle the issue. "It really started with the arrival of the British in 1917," Rashid Khalidi said in a recent interview, subsuming Zionism under British colonialism. Zionists became anti-imperialist only when colonialism fell out of fashion after the Second World War, according to the foremost Palestinian historian of the era. But this is false. In fact, Jewish immigration and Arab hostility toward it long preceded the colonial British Mandate, and Zionist opposition to the British began before the war (and certainly no later than the White Paper of May 1939).

These arguments and counter-arguments are rehearsed *ad nauseam* in the cacophony that is the present debate on Israel-Palestine. For one side, it is belligerent Zionist expansionism that is at fault; for the other side, it is Arab intransigence and perpetual — though consistently counter-productive — violence. The rhetorical war over labels is as obfuscating as it is inflammatory. There is no answer to the question "Was Zionism a colonial enterprise or an in-gathering of exiles?" because the question itself is misleading. Zionism was a movement to settle one population in a land largely occupied by another, but it was also an anti-colonialist nationalist movement for the liberation of an oppressed people with ancient ties to the land. It involved dispossession of indigenous populations, but also created a refuge for the perennial pariah. Making sense of this convoluted mess is better served by sticking to facts than by fighting over labels.

In the nuance-free battlegrounds of the campuses, however, facts are a nuisance and coherence is not a concern. The tale of white colonialist settlers wielding power and privilege to displace indigenous non-whites is too good to be false. And if the facts don't fit the tale, so much the worse for the facts. The effort to squeeze the Palestinian issue into the colonialist mold is driven less by the desire to understand than by the urge to condemn. And there is much to condemn in Israel's conduct, above all its unrelenting oppression and dispossession of the rightless Palestinians whom it has occupied since 1967. But the advocates of the colonization narrative are not interested only in condemning Israel's actions. They wish also to rebuke its very essence. For them, Israel is not a consequence of colonialism, like Australia, South

Africa, Lebanon, Jordan, and Iraq. Israel *is* colonialism.

This might have made some sense had the analysis been limited to Israel's conduct in the West Bank and Gaza, but this is precisely what the evangelists of decolonization deny. Exactly like the Jewish settlers in the West Bank, they hold that there is no distinction to be made between the occupied territories and Israel. Their history is sloppy and their politics irresponsible. Under the vague rubric of colonialism, the historical imperialist conditions associated with the creation of Israel (and many other countries) in the era of postwar decolonization are conflated with the ongoing occupation of the West Bank and Gaza, and never mind the fact that the first was a British affair while the second is perpetrated by Israel over the opposition of the United States, England, France, and virtually every other country. In left-wing circles, calls for ending the occupation or for equal rights for Palestinians have been replaced with calls for the decolonization of Palestine. If colonialism is the diagnosis, then decolonization must be the remedy.

But what exactly does decolonization mean? The rare attempts to unpack the term in the context of Palestine turn to the so-called "one-state solution." Lacking all detail concerning political arrangements and offering no path for attaining them, this is yet another slogan cosplaying as policy. The notion that a century-old blood feud can be dissolved by political fiat has always been ludicrous. After October 7, the idea of democratic coexistence in a single state is not even wishful thinking. Frivolous assurances along the lines of Judith Butler's recent assertion that, done right, "decolonization will more likely produce ... emancipatory joy, a sense of freedom, the release from shackles" rather than vengeance, do not deserve serious consideration. Where, exactly, does "decolonization" leave seven million Israeli Jews? Will leaving them anywhere "from the river to the sea" satisfy the jihadists?

One wonders whether the advocates of decolonization witlessly misunderstand or deliberately ignore the fact that the Islamists emphatically do not want peace and reconciliation. They want to eliminate Israel. They are extremely candid about this. Or are we to believe that they are oblivious that their playful rhyme about the river and the sea, taken straight out of the Hamas charter, is nothing but a euphemism for ethnic cleansing? Some were at least honest enough to indicate what "emancipatory joy" really means. Let us remember the notorious tweet on October 7 that triumphantly declared "what did y'all think decolonization meant? Vibes?" (Recall, too, that the tweet was in response to one of a photo of a grandmother kissing her granddaughter and explaining that Hamas terrorists had broken into the pictured grandmother's home in Nir Oz, recorded a video of murdering her, and then uploaded that video to her Facebook page, "which is how her granddaughter found out.")

So "decolonization" offers little insight and even less foresight. But again, the point of attaching the label "colonialism" is not to analyze but to criminalize. Rather than a critical concept, it is a weapon of criticism. Or rather, of delegitimization. The distance from that analysis to the justification of violence is traversed, it turns out, in a swift Fanonian leap. "Decolonization is always a violent phenomenon," the militant psychiatrist wrote. Hence the mind-boggling spectacle of "progressive" academics gleeful about October 7. Violence cleanses the land of its colonizers and the colonized of their subjugation, preached Fanon (at least in his extreme moods, which were his most influential ones). So let anti-imperialists of the world rejoice at the rape, torture, and massacre of colonial women and children. Which is also to say, of Jews.

The sympathy of some Western intellectuals with pogromists is not the fruit of rigorous analysis of either history or the current political environment. Rather, it reflects a knee-jerk radicalism that divides the world into oppressors and oppressed and sides with the latter no matter what they do. It regards victimhood as a sign of righteousness and replaces politics with an international solidarity with underdogs. In this Manichaean moral universe, empathy is reserved for one side only, and so is context. The massacre of Israeli civilians is the sole responsibility of "the apartheid regime," as Harvard Undergraduate Palestine Solidarity Committee declared and as post-colonial theorists suggest. Israel's actions, on the other hand, have no context — not in 1948, not in 1967 and not in 2024. The oppressed are always and only one thing — victims, defined by their circumstances. Their actions are intrinsically reactive — a response to and an outcome of their oppression, over which they exercise no agency. Whether they react or overreact, responsibility ultimately resides with the oppressors.

The post-colonial framework easily lends itself to this bi-valent moral metaphysics, dividing the world between colonizer and colonized. Anything done by one is ipso facto an act of oppression and anything done by the other is ipso facto a struggle for liberation. Did they not hear Ismail Haniyeh's injunction to Jews on Oct 7? "Get out of our land. Get out of our sight. Get out of our city of Al-Quds and our Al-Aqsa Mosque. We no longer wish to see you on this land. This land is ours, Al-Quds is ours, everything is ours. You are strangers in this pure and blessed land. There is no place or safety for you." Or do they simply not care? This moral bankruptcy is responsible for the absurdity of post-colonialist intellectuals who, in the name of liberation and equality, support tyrants and terrorists. So long as they are on the opposite side of "Western imperialism" it doesn't matter that they wish to impose Sharia law, beat women, hang homosexuals, or incinerate babies. (Let us not forget the fascination of many on the left with the Islamic Revolution in Iran.) Their actions might be excessive, but they are, by definition, "on the right side of history."

Ironically, historical determinism — in the form of a divine plan — is also the ideology of the zealous settler Israelis who man the front lines of the occupation. According to them, Jews are the eternal victim, and, consequently incapable of evil. Any critique directed at them or their state is, by definition, anti-Semitic. I have no doubt that the criticism leveled here will be similarly brushed off as Zionist apologetics. But this is merely another iteration of the lazy moral bi-valence, whereby any criticism of one side must entail unreserved support of the other. If you are not on the side of the light, you are on the side of darkness, for there are no other sides.

That irreverent old radical Ellen Willis once wrote that she was not against peace but "against peace as a mantra — anti-imperialism being another." When it comes to Israel-Palestine, colonization and decolonization have also become mantras — magical words that ward off thought rather than advance it. The neat separation into colonizers and colonized relieves one of the intellectual challenge of having to reconcile the rights of indigenous Palestinians with the just claims of persecuted Jews. If the root cause of all violence is Zionist colonialism, then there is no room, and no reason, for investigating the responsibility of the Arab leadership for its reaction to it. The pronounced antisemitism of militant fundamentalist groups such as Hamas and their stated commitment to eradicate the Jewish state is trivialized as symptomatic of colonial oppression. That explanation is also an excuse.

And since Jews are colonizers, it is perfectly legitimate and proper that exiled Palestinians have a right to return but exiled Jews do not. How neat, how simplifying. It is much easier to rail against Israel's war on Gaza than to offer any reasonable alternative to this bloody war that could still permit Israel to defend itself against savage jihadis who reject "initiatives, and so-called peaceful solutions" because they "are in contradiction to the principles of the Islamic Resistance Movement," as Hamas's charter states.

As explained, the point of invoking colonialism is to achieve neither clarity nor progress but moral positioning. It is elevation by condemnation. And the harsher the condemnation, the higher the elevation. In this regard, Zionism's fiercest detractors are the mirror-image of its apologists who whitewash all of Israel's crimes by citing the justice of its birth or the offenses of its rivals. The problem is not taking sides, but the narcissism of moral positioning at the expense of both sides. In the age of virtue signaling, this vice characterize most discourse. But when it comes to Zionism, it is particularly vicious.

The Arab-Israeli conflict has been moralized like no other. The Yugoslav wars did not trigger a reckoning with the imperial past that created Yugoslavia. The conflict in Northern Ireland involved many moral and historical disputes, but the primary concern was to end hostilities. The recent invasion of Ukraine by Russia evoked little discussion of historical justice. The main issue on the agenda, and rightly, is how to stop Russian aggression and forge a stable peace, not the history of ancient Rus, the merits of Ukrainian nationalism, or how to "decolonize" Ukraine. When it comes to the Arab-Israeli conflict, however, bloody events become an occasion for investigating historical justice. With every flare-up, academics, journalists and activists of all stripes rush to peer through the region's history and pronounce moral verdicts. Leading newspapers and institutions bring together experts to debate history rather than solutions. Every bomb that goes off in Jerusalem or is dropped on Jabaliya becomes an argument for the historical justice or injustice of Zionism. The deaths of children are collected as talking points, or rather shouting points, in the indefatigable contest of righteousness, where victimhood is the mark of virtue.

The conflict has been moralized right out of politics. This is tragic because politics remains the only domain in which it can be resolved. The historical verdict regarding Jewish nationalism at the turn of the century is of little consequence for the political question: what is to be done? Yet this is where much of the conversation seems to be focused, partly, no doubt, due to fatigue following decades of impasse. But darker suspicions are provoked by the crude tenor of the debate. It is hard to resist wondering if age-old tendencies to treat anything Jewish in symbolic terms — something mythical, having to do with divine good or diabolical evil, but never mundanely political — have not creeped in, particularly amongst intellectuals and activists, where the colonialism narrative looms large.

Not every critique of Israel is anti-Semitic and anti-Zionism does not equal anti-Semitism (just as criticism of Hamas's barbarism is not an extenuation of Israel's misdeeds). And yet, can it be denied with a straight face that the Jewish state receives special treatment by the left? The left did not march for Syrians or for Bosnians or for Uyghurs or for Ukrainians or for Rohynga, but they march for Palestinians. Does this have something to do with who the Palestinians are fighting? Lest I be misunderstood, I hasten to add: march they should. I have done my own share of marching (and not just marching) for Palestinian emancipation. But it is hard to shake off the feeling that many march not to end Israel's oppression of Palestinians but to end Israel. After all, it was 1969 when Jean Améry wrote that "for the New Left, Zionism is roughly what, in Germany, some thirty years ago was called 'World Jewry'." As a purported offspring of colonialism, Israel has many siblings, yet it is the only one whose legitimacy is questioned on account of this pedigree. Does this not imply that, unlike other peoples, Jews are not entitled to self-determination? Reading "post-colonial" analyses, I feel a need to remind myself that Israel is a country that already exists and that it was created with as much legitimacy under international law as any other country.

But setting aside the injustice to Jews, is any of this helping Palestinians? Is the cause of Palestinian liberation advanced by tying it to the eradication of Israel? Are the lives and well-being of Palestinians secured by bolstering fundamentalists devoted to holy jihad against an exponentially stronger power? And how much Palestinian blood will be spilled in the Balkanization that is likely to ensue after the dreamed-of dismantlement of the Jewish state? The truly unnerving thing about these questions is not their answers, which are painfully obvious, but the fact that so many on the left are unbothered by them. In their haste to pronounce the most extreme condemnation of Zionists, and thereby bolster their own moral credentials, they are condemning Palestinians to permanent conflict (for between the children of light and the children of darkness there can only be perpetual and total war), a conflict in which Palestinians have been paying a disproportional price.

The real tragedy — the real outrage — of all this is not the absence of intellectual integrity, but the disregard for real-world consequences. Ask the shepherds in the Jordan Valley about the "liberation" that they won following "the victories of the resistance," as one Columbia University professor called the pogrom, or the farming communities of Mount Hebron expelled from their villages by terrorist settlers about Hamas's success at "decolonization," or the homeless and starving refugees in Rafah if their heads are raised "so high that they touch the sky," as Haniyeh declared on their behalf. As one Gazan wrote in December, Western apologists for Hamas "marginalized me, an actual Gazan, inexplicably demanding that I conform to the opinions and beliefs of privileged Western activists detached from what people in Gaza actually feel about Hamas and other Palestinian groups and leaders." Moral kudos in the West are won through suffering in the East. A post-colonialist might have detected a whiff of imperialist exploitation.

The main problem is not the distortion of history, but the futility of narcissistic moralism. Shouting "Justice for Palestine!" may be cathartic in Berkeley or Berlin, but if it means undoing the alleged colonialism and getting even with its perpetrators, it portends nothing but more bloodletting. This is the kind of justice that leaves everyone blind to the plight — and the legitimate claims — of the other side. The warriors of justice, on both sides, are prepared to fight to the last Israeli soldier and the last Palestinian child. It is not surprising that many of them live elsewhere.

For us, the flesh-and-blood Arabs and Jews living on this tormented land, the Olympics of victimhood is not a spectator sport. What we need are allies for a political settlement, not cheerleaders for the fanatics currently calling the shots. Anyone genuinely interested in the well-being of Palestinians must yearn for the toppling of Hamas no less than of Netanyahu's government. Ending land grabs, settler terrorism, house demolitions, targeted killings, random killings, and the rest of the occupation's horrors will not be achieved through "decolonization," just as Palestinian resistance and national aspirations will not be extinguished by "more force," as Israel's ministers promise. Both can only be achieved by a political settlement — the kind of settlement that Netanyahu and Hamas have been sabotaging for decades.

Upon the publication of the Hamas post-October 7 memorandum last fall, the Lebanese journalist Hisham Debsi noted that it included not "a single reference to a political solution, national reconciliation, or joint action." And Netanyahu's government has been prosecuting Israel's longest war since the founding of the state, but refuses even to discuss political objectives, let alone solutions. "In the face of this harsh reality," Debsi wrote, "we are regrettably forced to ask: Is this why Palestinian blood is shed every day?" And we are similarly forced to ask: what is Israeli blood being shed for?

When it comes to the tribal blood-feud between Israelis and Palestinians, it often seems that those with the loudest voices are the least concerned with ending it. Unless they are silly enough to suppose that encouraging Israel's abhorrent occupation is a recipe for peace, or deluded enough to regard "from the river to the sea" as a political program, the vociferous cheerleaders on either side contribute nothing to alleviating the situation. They can live with the savagery. Their zero-sum morality of villains and victims only entrenches the conflict, removing it from the realm of interests and solutions. Placing it back in that realm does not mean adopting a cynical realism whereby might determines right. It means rejecting myths and stereotypes and prejudices and dogmas, and resisting the moralistic urge to engage in a frivolous politics of condemnation.

ROSANNA WARREN

Happy Birthday, Harmonium

Wallace Stevens's *Harmonium* recently turned a hundred. When Knopf published this brashly youthful and original first book of poems in September 1923, the poet himself was hardly youthful, and he was known only to a few modernist cognoscenti from his poems in little magazines such as *Poetry, Others*, and *The Little Review*. Nor did Stevens *look* like a poet. A firebrand on the page, in person Wallace Stevens in 1923 was a portly, clean-shaven, forty-four-year old executive for the Hartford Accident and Indemnity Company, working hard to support his wife in a comfortable house in Hartford. "I am far from being a genius — and must rely on hard and faithful work," he had explained to her, referring not to his poetry, in which she had little interest, but to his legal labors with bonds and surety claims.

Stevens, the unlikely modernist, had not sprung out of nowhere. He was born in Reading, Pennsylvania in 1878, to modest parents, both teachers. His father, from a farming family, had scrabbled a law degree for himself and practiced law, so he was able to send his son to a local private school and then to Harvard, where young Stevens met poets, wrote poetry, and became president of the *Harvard Advocate*. While knocking around New York City in low-level jobs in journalism and earning a law degree, he began making friends in avant-garde circles, and by 1914 he was getting to know William Carlos Williams, Mina Loy, Francis Picabia, and Marcel Duchamp. And so began the double life, even more doubled because of his marriage to Elsie Moll, a young woman from Reading who played the piano and sold sheet music at the local department store. Elsie was classically beautiful — her profile appears on the Mercury dime — but she was ill-educated, anti-social, and increasingly reclusive. At home and in the office, Stevens was the dependable, jowly, suited paterfamilias and man of business. In his poetry, he was a wild man. And with the publication of *Harmonium*, he went head to head with the younger, reigning Modernists, T.S. Eliot, Ezra Pound, and Marianne Moore.

One way to read the whole arc of Stevens's poetry would be to trace it from the Baroque profusion of *Harmonium* in 1923 to the austerities of *The Rock* in 1954, from the Keatsian splendor of "Le Monocle de Mon Oncle" ("This luscious and impeccable fruit of life") and the razzle-dazzle of "Bantams in Pine-Woods" ("Chieftain Iffucan of Axcan in caftan") to "The Plain Sense of Things": "After the leaves have fallen, we return/

To a plain sense of things…" And one way to tell that story would be to see it as a Modernist redemption of the pentameter line, a way Stevens found, in a century of adventurous *vers libre*, to re-engineer the traditional cadence to serve radical and abstract purposes.

But that isn't the story I want to tell. *Harmonium*, in 1923, already contained those contrary forces, the extravagances and the ascetic refusals, and set them into a dizzying counterpoint. It is true — it would have to be true in a first book — that notes are sounded which will be elaborated and revised in later work. "The Snow Man"'s "Nothing that is not there and the nothing that is" will reverberate throughout the later books — say, in "Man Carrying Thing" from *Transport to Summer* (1947), where "We must endure our thoughts all night, until/ The bright obvious stands motionless in cold" ; or in "The Man on the Dump" from *Parts of a World* (1942): "Where was it we first heard of the truth? The the." And the hymns of "Forms, flames, and flakes of flames" from *Harmonium's* "Nomad Exquisite" will echo in all kinds of later prodigalities and jubilas, like "The blue woman, linked and lacquered, at her window" in "Notes Toward a Supreme Fiction" (*Transport to Summer*). The fascination of *Harmonium*, for me, is listening to the new poet testing his enormous acoustic range, adjusting inherited magnificence to a harsh new century. "What manner of building shall we build?" he asks in "Architecture." "In this house, what manner of utterance shall there be?"

Keats echoes through Stevens in ways we don't hear in other modernists. For Stevens's contemporaries Eliot and Pound, Keats did not loom as a problem: they were more threatened by Victorian grandparents, by Swinburne, Browning, Arnold, Tennyson. But in Stevens I constantly hear a Keatsian pulse, the sensuous pentameters, the luxuriant sonorities, versions of "With plume, tiara, and all rich array" and "With jellies soother than the creamy curds,/ And lucent syrup, tinct with cinnamon" (from "The Eve of Saint Agnes"). All through *Harmonium*, from the firecat at the beginning to the roaring wind at the end, Stevens is sorting out what music he is willing to make his own, and what he will disown.

But let's go back to the beginning. Pound's "Hugh Selwyn Mauberley" had come out in 1920, Eliot's *The Waste Land* in December 1922. Stevens, who had been publishing his poems in little magazines since 1914, was older than both of these rivals. In *Harmonium*, coming in September 1923 right on the heels of *The Waste Land*, he plotted an entirely independent mode of being "modern." The book opens with "Earthy Anecdote": its belligerent free verse asserts its allegiance to the aesthetics of the new century. In a drama generated more by assonance and alliteration than by logic — "bucks," "cat," "clattering," "Oklahoma" — the firecat keeps blocking the old "lines" (of verse?) clattered by the bucks:,

> Every time the bucks went clattering
> Over Oklahoma
> A firecat bristled in the way.
>
> Wherever they went,
> They went clattering,
> Until they swerved
> In a swift, circular line
> To the right,
> Because of the firecat.

Or until they swerved
In a swift, circular line
To the left,
Because of the firecat.

The bucks clattered.
The firecat went leaping,
To the right, to the left,
And
Bristled in the way.

Later, the firecat closed his bright eyes
And slept.

The mythical invented firecat forces the old metrical clatter to "swerve" in swift, circular, short, irregular lines: he is the daimon of the new poetry, and he opens the volume. But the poems that follow don't adhere to the firecat's pattern. They will retrace old lines as they figure out how to integrate them into *Harmonium's* distinct radicalism.

The second poem in the book, "Invective Against Swans," takes up those old lines, in pentameters, mostly iambic, and in irregularly rhyming couplets, to cock a snook at traditional prosody and at the traditional lyric symbol of the swan. The gesture feels almost adolescent in its irreverence, for one thing demoting swans to male geese, "ganders": "The soul, O ganders, flies beyond the parks/ And far beyond the discords of the wind." (This wind, which blows through the book and concludes it, recalls Shelley's West Wind rather than Keats.)

The reader opening *Harmonium* in 1923 would have been confronted, then, with two jarringly different poetic modes right in the first two poems. And the volume, as it develops, proliferates variations in free and metrical verse and an exuberant variety of stanza forms. In this riot of formal possibilities, I am interested in the extremes: a stark minimalism set against a lush maximalism. One way to observe this interplay is by tracking one of Stevens's favorite words, "syllable."

A syllable is a phonetic, not a semantic, unit of language, organized around a vowel: semantic, that is, only by accident, if it coincides with a prefix or a suffix: "in-digestion," say, or "care-less," or with a monosyllabic word, like "the" or "in." A poet as aggressive as Stevens needs that "fecund minimum" (as Crispin the Comedian will have it) in order to refashion language from the ground up. A syllable is like a linguistic atomic particle. It also cues us to listen for sound even more than for sense in these new harmonies and discords.

"Le Monocle de Mon Oncle" comes early in the volume. Already the French title deranges English sense, and in its phonetic play it veers into a kind of non-sense in French as "Monocle" becomes "Mon Oncle" by the addition of one letter. This evasive and ambitious poem of twelve blank verse stanzas of eleven lines each punishes its own Keatsian eloquence ("This luscious and impeccable fruit") as it mourns and savages an ideal of romantic love (lower case "r"). One can sense here, if one wishes to read biographically, something of Stevens's disappointment in his marriage to Elsie, who may or may not have prompted the Eve addressed here: "When you were Eve, its acrid juice was sweet..." But it would diminish the poem cruelly to shrink it to personal anecdote: Stevens takes pains not to allow that. Yes, the lovers are seen as aged beyond romance: "Our bloom is gone. We are the fruit thereof./ Two golden gourds distended on our vines,/ We hang like warty squashes..." But intrinsic to erotic loss is a rebellion against the language of romance, the "fops of fancy" as this self-proclaimed "yeoman" rudely puts it. The whole poem bursts with disappointment, and by mocking the old hymns — "Mother of heaven, regina of the clouds" — in their own "magnificent measure," it discovers a new way to use that measure:

> I wish that I might be a thinking stone.
> The sea of spuming thought foists up again
> The radiant bubble that she was. And then
> A deep up-pouring from some saltier well
> Within me, bursts its watery syllable.

Saltier well? Tears? Who is "she"? Mother of heaven? An estranged lover or spouse? An ideal of Romantic lyric? All of the above? The past tense of the verb "to be" bespeaks heartbreak: "that she was." This "watery syllable" is as close to confession as Stevens will come. Not for the first time (recall Petrarch), disappointed eros gives rise to verse. In Stevens's case, the failure of romance leads, paradoxically, to the rescue and metamorphosis of a Romantic poetics of luxuriant idiom and cadence, but always in tension with the snow man and the man on the dump.

The hunt for syllables brings us to "The Comedian as the Letter C," the longest poem in *Harmonium* and the latest composed. I confess: I don't like "The Comedian." I find its mock epic dimensions boring, its afflatus noisy, its fabulations coy. But I understand why Stevens had to write it. With Crispin, he looks backward and devises a story of his own coming-into-being as a poet, his search for a relation between language and the world; and he looks forward, laying out something like a map or promissory note for the poems to come: "The Man on the Dump" and "Connoisseur of Chaos" in *Parts of a World*, "Notes Toward a Supreme Fiction" in *Transport to Summer, "An Ordinary Evening in New Haven" in The Auroras of Autumn*, to mention only a few.

In "The Comedian," Stevens brazenly adopts the old measure, blank verse, "...to drive away/ The shadow of his fellows from the skies,/ And, from their stale intelligence released,/ To make a new intelligence prevail." These "fellows" to be driven away, I take it, are rival poets, of past and present. This choice of meter in 1923 throws down a gauntlet: how will Crispin, the poet-clown, "this nincompated pedagogue," create "an aesthetic tough, diverse, untamed" in this hand-me-down form? That agon takes shape in the collision, line by line, between the impulse toward maximalist verbosity and the counter-impulse toward minimalist reduction. The poem presents a theoretical commentary, later called a "pronunciamento," on the counterpoint fundamental to Stevens's whole oeuvre.

We first meet Crispin on a ship sailing from his native Bordeaux (In Stevens' mythology France is the world of traditional poetic ideals) to the Yucatan, the barbarous new world. Six lines describe the poet-hero as an absurd aesthete: "The lutanist of fleas, the knave, the thane,/ The ribboned stick, the bellowing breeches," and so forth: he is Stevens's pathetic alter-ego who must be chastened, his Prufrock, his Mauberley. Faced with the sea, the poetling is "washed away by magnitude." The poem asks, "What word split up in clickering syllables/ And storming under multitudinous tones/ Was name for this short-shanks in all that brunt?" The whole saga, we are told, from Yucatan to Havana and thence to Carolina, will reduce and transform the hero "...until nothing of himself/ Remained, except some starker, barer self/ In a starker, barer world..." In the midst of all this brouhaha, Stevens outlines the aesthetic ideal of the quest for the essential, not the decorative: an ideal that "The Comedian" can articulate but not yet fully embody.

As we follow Crispin to his destination in Carolina, we watch a poetic *Bildungsroman*, a story of renunciations: "How many poems he denied himself," "And what descants he sent to banishment." Beneath the harlequinade, it is moments like this that feel urgent. Stevens here is writing close to the bone of his experience of self-creation. When Crispin arrives in Carolina at the end of Section III, the verse grows suddenly stern, and we can feel Stevens tuning up for what will become his lifelong theme, the Man with the Blue Guitar's attempt to render "things as they are" in the language of the Imagination. "...It made him see how much/ Of what he saw he never saw at all./ He gripped more closely the essential prose..."

This blank verse "prose" is not where "The Comedian" ends, nor is it, by itself, Stevens's ideal. The poem brings Crispin through various illusions to an earthbound reality, building a cabin, espousing a "prismy blonde," and producing four daughters, a procreative effusion accompanied by an explosion of still more ornate language, archaisms, neologisms, and arcane syntax: his cabin is "...the haunt/ Of children nibbling at the sugared void,/ Infants, yet eminently old, then dome/ And halidom for the unbraided femes,/ Green crammers of the green fruits of the world..." (Stevens's daughter, Holly, was born only the following year.) The word "syllable" both introduces and almost concludes this final section, marking the poem — as if it needed more marking — as an *ars poetica*, a thesis about the quest for a reinvented language capable of holding the vast world in its embrace.

"Portentous enunciation, syllable/ To blessed syllable affined," Section VI begins. Along its way, the poem has rung the changes on words for language: "speech belched," "gasconade," "hubbub," "vociferate," "bray." It winds up by defining itself as a "disguised pronunciamento," a declaration heard, once again, as syllables — "In these portentous accents, syllables" — only to double back on itself, proposing that the whole "anecdote" might be "false." But it asks, in an ironic, self-protective gesture, what that would matter anyway.

A portent is a sign, indication, or omen. The syllables in "The Comedian" portend Stevens's future, his endlessly inventive counterpoint of the linguistic minimum and maximum. Within *Harmonium*, however, let us look at two instances of a poetics of reduction to set against the noise of "The Comedian." "O Florida, Venereal Soil" is marred by the racism and xenophobia of its second stanza, a large theme for another day. What concerns me now is the way this short poem in relatively short lines manages to pare itself down still further. The first stanza addresses the "venereal" state, playing on the double valence of "venereal" as pertaining to the goddess of love and to sexually transmitted disease. The opening phrase, "A few things for themselves," repeated a few lines later, uses the barest language: no simile or metaphor, no fancy verbiage, insistence on reduction ("few"). Only in line seven do we understand this sentence as an imperative to "disclose" these "few things" to the lover: "A few things for themselves,/ Florida, venereal soil,/ Disclose to the lover."

Personified as a goddess, Florida has a double character. In the third stanza she appears "lasciviously as the wind" to torment the speaker, whereas in the final two stanzas she is imagined as "a scholar of darkness" and addressed in alliterative, liturgical terms, "Donna, donna, dark," and commanded to disclose not "a few things" but "fewest things to the lover." Only a page after "The Comedian as the Letter C" in *Harmonium*, "O Florida" contracts, and performs its own arithmetic of subtraction. It also sounds a chord, playing the muted "few things for themselves" against the sumptuous notes of "Donna, donna, dark,/ stooping in indigo gown."

"Anecdote of the Jar" is famous as a manifesto of human order imposed on nature. In the context of *Harmonium* as a whole composition, it stands between two poems of verbal fireworks: "Bantams in Pine-Woods" and "Palace of the Babies." Its own spareness feels polemical. Its three tetrameter stanzas keep repeating phrases, as if penurious with vocabulary, as if it had no more words to spend and had to practice thrift: "upon a hill," "surround that hill," "the slovenly wilderness," "The wilderness rose up to it," "I placed a jar," "The jar was round," "The jar was gray and bare." The internal rhymes also feel poverty-stricken: "round," "surround," "sprawled around," "The jar was round." The only end-rhyme ("air," "everywhere," "bare") connects the jar's power to its bareness; if the poem is a manifesto for human order, it also enforces an aesthetic of sobriety and reticence. The simple copulative verb "was" dominates. The most unusual word, "port," is simple but complicated; derived from Old English, it means a gate, a city with a harbor, a carrier, and a tune. That line, with its slightly elevated syntax, lends the poem a mysterious stateliness: "and tall and of a port in air."

Along with "The Snow Man," "Anecdote of the Jar" marks the minimalist extreme in *Harmonium*, to set against the hyperbole and plenitude of "The Comedian as the Letter C."

"The Snow Man" performs a syntactic feat as it threads its argument on a single sentence through five tercets. It finds its way to a more extreme version of Crispin's "starker, barer self" in a Zen-like erasure: there is no first- or second-person pronoun in this taut poem, only the impersonal "one" who "must have a mind of winter" in the first line, and who may or may not be the "listener" in the last tercet, who hears the wind "blowing in the same bare place." "The Snow Man" sets its weird "fullness" against its astringency: its landscape is "full of the same wind," and the philosophically charged word "nothing" resounds three times in the last two lines to describe the listener, who "...nothing himself, beholds/ Nothing that is not there and the nothing that is." The meter acts out this negative fullness: only the final line, burdened with extinctions, attains a full pentameter.

In the book's sonic middle range, Stevens has made rooms for all sorts of combinations, including hymns to poetry that unabashedly adopt the prosody inherited from the English Romantics: from Keats, yes, but not only from Keats. It is a feature of the wild originality of *Harmonium* that Stevens gets away with this, as he does in the concluding rhyming couplet of "To the One of Fictive Music," where he meditates on the modernist "spurning" of Romantic imagination and invites the muse to restore it *within* the frame of a modernist volume: "Unreal, give back to us what once you gave,/ The imagination that we spurned and crave."

Harmonium ends with another syllable. "To the Roaring Wind" mediates between minimalist and maximalist forces, and between the Romantic trope of the wind as source of power, Coleridge's "Eolian Harp" and Shelley's "Ode to the West Wind," and modernist skepticism.

To the Roaring Wind

What syllable are you seeking,
Vocalissimus,
In the distances of sleep?
Speak it.

It is a tiny poem, and at the same time immense. It is a question and a command. It is only four lines long, and it seeks not a word but a syllable. But "vocalissimus," a single word taking up a whole line, is the superlative form of the Latin adjective "vocalis," meaning "most sonorous," "most voiced": a maximalist grammatical form, and multi-syllabic.

Wind-sound has been translated into alliterating S's; traditional rhyme has been distorted in the chime of "seeking" and "Speak." Romantic personality has been projected onto the wind — "What syllable are you seeking?" — while it is the poet, Stevens, who has been seeking and finding and arranging syllables throughout the book. In this poem, as in *Harmonium* as a whole, Stevens is magnificently having it both ways: writing poems both expansive and condensed, both of their own disruptive moment and vocalizing breath that has sources far more ancient that Keats, Shelley, or Coleridge. The Hebrew *ruach* and the ancient Greek *pneuma* in various contexts signified divine breath and prophetic inspiration. Stevens no longer believed in those gods, but he certainly experienced inspiration, and that wind blows through every page of *Harmonium*.

EKATERINA PRAVILOVA

"Why Were We Beaten?": Atrocity, Law, and Truth

On Easter Day, April 6, 1903, a violent mob attacked the Jewish population of Kishinev, killing forty-nine people and wounding hundreds. During two days of bloody massacre, about a third of the city was destroyed, leaving hundreds of Jewish families destitute, their meager belongings smashed, broken, torn, or stolen. Hospitals were overwhelmed with injured men, women, and children. Fluff and feathers from torn pillows covered the streets of Kishinev as if snow had fallen in the middle of a sunny spring. It clung to puddles of blood and dirt, settling on the trees and the rubble scattered across the streets. The Kishinev pogrom would be followed by several others, some even surpassing it in brutality, but it would remain etched in the memory of generations as a turning point in Jewish history and the history of the Russian Empire and Eastern Europe.

The Hamas attack on October 7, 2023 again evoked the memory of Kishinev, supporting the historians' claim about the pogrom's lasting significance. The two events differ in their context and their scale: the carefully orchestrated terrorist operation carried out by the Gazan invaders equipped with advanced weaponry stands in stark contrast to the violence perpetrated by a mob of men and teenagers who brutally killed their neighbors and acquaintances using stones, clubs, metal pipes, and axes. Still, it is not unusual for a shocking event to trigger memories of past shocks and traumas despite all the differences. The common threads in this comparison are a deep understanding of the tragedy's historical importance and an intensely felt need to uncover the truth about its causes. In the wake of the Hamas attack on October 7 and the conduct of the Israeli operation in Gaza, the avalanche of facts, coupled with a striking deficit in crucial details, created a sense of pervasive uncertainty. Everything seemed open to challenge. The most rudimentary and incontrovertible facts were thrown into doubt. There were even claims that the atrocity never took place. Particularly unsettling were the efforts to cast doubt on the suffering of civilians — Palestinians and Israelis — caught in the crossfire of the conflict, as though the trauma inflicted by war was not self-evident and required proof.

One does not have to be a trained historian to imagine that the crisis of credibility, the collapse of trust, that we experience today is not new, and that any tragedy creates room for contestation. Once upon a time it seemed that the catastrophes of the twentieth century had taught people to suspend their doubts in the face of the testimonies of victims and survivors, yet the ongoing wars in Ukraine, and in Israel and Gaza, show that this skill is easy to unlearn. The search for the solution to the political crisis in the Middle East often stumbles upon arguments about facts, throwing us back to the moment in 1903, when palpable anxiety about empirical truth pervaded the post-pogrom city of Kishinev.

Weeks after the pogrom, rain washed away the dirty fluff and feathers from the pavements. Shops remained closed, and people were paralyzed by fear of another attack, but the city was animated with a sudden influx of visitors. Amid the fear-stricken ruins, outsiders — journalists, writers, lawyers, and investigators — were busy collecting evidence and attempting to construct the stories of the event. Michael Davitt, an Irish journalist writing for American newspapers, spent several days in Kishinev interviewing government officials, visiting the sites of violence, and trying to obtain from "the living witnesses of the outrages an account of what they saw and experienced." In the fall of 1903, Davitt's dispatches from Odesa and Kishinev were collected in a volume called *Within the Pale* — an eye-opening account of the life of Jews in the tsarist Empire, explaining the sources and the outcomes of the Kishinev catastrophe. A short while later, in June 1903, the young Hebrew poet Hayim Nachman Bialik came on a mission from the Jewish Historical Commission in Odesa to collect evidence for a documentary book on the Kishinev pogrom. The testimonies of the pogrom's survivors that he recorded remained unpublished until 1991. Instead Bialik wrote *The City of Slaughter*, a grand, wrathful, and influential poem. Around the same time as Bialik's visit, Vladimir Korolenko, a Ukrainian writer, boarded a train from Poltava to Kishinev. Korolenko was fortunate to secure a room in the Hotel Paris, as many of Kishinev's hotels were sold out, and tourists were seeking apartments to rent. By June, Kishinev coachmen had already learned the new morbid topography of the city, taking their guests to the sites of the tragedy. Korolenko followed the same paths as many others: observing the ruins of houses, visiting victims in hospitals, and conversing with Jews, Ukrainians, Moldavians, and Russians. "Fourth day in Kishinev, and I feel like I'm in a nightmare," he lamented in his diary, feeling overwhelmed by despair and a sense of helplessness in understanding, aiding, or changing anything.

What we know today about the Easter pogrom in Kishinev has been primarily shaped by literary texts and journalists' accounts: Davitt's book and articles, Bialik's writings, Korolenko's "House No. 13," a short story about the tragedy that unfolded in one of the houses where seven Jewish families had lived before the pogrom. Contemporary historians have tried to dig deeper and explain the inner mechanisms of violence, reconstructing the events preceding the pogrom and documenting the public reaction to it. But what has often escaped our attention is the fact that although the massacre happened in front of everyone's eyes, both its overarching story and its details were vehemently contested. The struggle to establish the master narrative of the massacre unfolded not only in books or newspapers that sold their readers sensational news, but also, most importantly, in lawyers' offices and courtrooms, where hundreds of victims and witnesses testified about what they had seen, heard, and endured.

When the news of the massacre reached the public, the demand for justice was the most common reaction, and everyone started anxiously awaiting the results of the investigation and the trial. The trial of the pogrom's participants, or rather, the series of twenty-two trials that took place in 1903 and 1904, was almost as troubling as the atrocity itself. It marked the first time that hundreds of defendants were indicted for participating in collective violence driven by racial and national hatred, thus setting a precedent for the legal proceedings against war crimes and crimes against humanity in our own day. It was also the first trial of this magnitude to be entirely based on survivors' testimonies, which were meticulously scrutinized, often neglected, and overwhelmingly disbelieved. The raw and unedited testimonies of victims and witnesses, preserved in court documents and lawyers' notes, in some instances paralleled Davitt and Korolenko's accounts and exposed the horror of the days of slaughter. Yet the court systematically dismissed these testimonies, deeming them untruthful. As a result, the court, the government, and a significant part of Russian society agreed upon one version of the event. At the same time, another truth, described in Korolenko's, Bialik's, and Davitt's writings and remembered by the survivors and the witnesses, existed in a parallel universe.

Reading the witnesses' accounts, one may wonder how those heart-wrenching words could leave anyone unmoved or doubting. Why did the judges not believe the survivors? It might be tempting to attribute the imperial court's attitude to the testimonies of the pogrom's victims solely to the prevalent antisemitism within the Russian establishment. Yet antisemitism is not just its own endemic disease: it is also a symptom of other structural problems and malfunctions. The roots of doubt and disbelief could be far more intricate than mere nationalism, indicating a broader epistemic and moral crisis within society. Similarly, our own crisis of misunderstanding and distrust extends beyond mere national or political biases, sympathies, or aversions, reflecting deeper, more complex undercurrents. Our society has been stricken by a fear of gullibility, and of the embarrassment that it may cause, and in this way it becomes more and more gullible. The fear of this embarrassment has become a norm of everyday life. And when this psychological weakness overlaps with extraordinary events, the anxiety of uncertainty goes through the roof. Politicians weaponize the discourse of "fake news," peddling doubts and exalting them; facts mingle cozily with fiction, and conspiracy theories proliferate.

One remedy to the pervasive doubt — to the culture of doubt and its political manipulation — is the memory of past crises and the history of the attempts to deal with them. And even though the historical analogy between the spring of 1903 and the fall of 2023 is imprecise, the story of the pogrom trial in Kishinev can be very instructive. It suggests that even when the criteria of right and wrong are clearly seen and uncontested, the markers of truth may still remain unclear and undefined, even among those who oppose evil.

The Kishinev pogrom trial of 1903 could set a world record for the number of defendants, witnesses, and plaintiffs involved. A total of three hundred and ninety-one individuals were indicted for murder, plunder, rape, and participation in collective violence rooted in "national discord." Nearly two thousand witnesses and plaintiffs were expected to testify. The authorities opted to divide this colossal case into twenty-two smaller ones, with the number of defendants in each ranging from one to sixty-two. This decision was owed not merely to the logistical challenge of trying almost four hundred defendants simultaneously. By splitting the trial, the authorities effectively reduced the massacre of Jews to a series of violent incidents between "Christians" — as the defendants were referred to — and their Jewish neighbors. This trivialization of the Kishinev tragedy enabled the authorities to downplay the role of those who incited antisemitism and to hide the complicity of officials in criminal negligence.

Everyone in Kishinev was aware that the pogrom had been incited by a series of articles by the journalist Pavolakii Krushevan published in the blatantly antisemitic daily newspapers *Znamia* and *Bessarabets*. In the weeks leading up to the bloody Easter of 1903, *Bessarabets* propagated falsehoods about an alleged ritual murder of a Christian boy in the small town of Dubossary. When the investigation swiftly identified the boy's murderers among his own relatives, *Bessarabets* was compelled to issue a retraction, yet it persisted in inciting retributory violence against Jews. At the same time antisemitic leaflets circulated urging Christians to "liberate" Russia from Jews. Within weeks or even days, Kishinev, a city where Jews, Russians, Moldavians, and Romani had coexisted peacefully, was polarized, with rumors of an imminent Easter pogrom becoming more and more believable. Thus, the massacre that erupted on the afternoon of April 6 did not appear as a sudden, unforeseen calamity. Another fact that made it look less like an unpredictable disaster was the authorities' passivity — both the military command and the police observed the assault and the looting of Jewish neighborhoods with indifference and apathy until an order from above to dispatch the troops halted the violence.

As soon as the bloodshed ceased, the police summoned the survivors and interrogated them, often in the presence of an armed gendarme. In many cases, their words were not fully recorded, especially when the witnesses spoke about the criminal passivity of the authorities. Alongside the official police investigation, however, a separate inquiry was underway. In May 1903, a group of liberal lawyers from St. Petersburg known as the "Young Advocates" arrived in Kishinev and settled into the city's hotels. The "Young Advocates," famous for supporting the oppressed, traveled around the country as a flying squad, aiding workers, peasants, and prisoners charged with participating in strikes, uprisings, and other forms of civil disobedience. The Kishinev trial marked a departure from their usual role. Here they represented the pogrom victims in civil suits, assisting them in seeking compensation for financial losses.

The "Young Advocates" established a temporary office and began interviewing victims and documenting damages — broken chiffoniers, stolen jewelry, the lost income of relatives who perished in the pogrom — and filing on their behalf thousands of suits against the civil administration. The unofficial investigation centered on the actions, or more accurately, the lack thereof, of the civil officials — the Bessarabian Governor von Raaben (who spent the critical days of the pogrom secluded in his mansion, failing to take any action to halt the violence), his deputies, the head of the police department, officers, gendarmes, and other officials. With none of these officials facing indictment, pursuing civil suits against the wealthy bureaucrats for financial reparations emerged as the sole means to hold the authorities accountable.

The competition between two investigative groups — the official police and the unofficial team led by the "Young Advocates" — tapping into the same sources but seeking evidence for different facts fostered an impression that the truth was buried under layers of falsehoods and misinterpretations. Journalists, philanthropists, and lawyers interviewed witnesses and survivors about what they had seen and heard from their neighbors. Accounts and rumors swirled together. When a few Russian newspapers published stories about the Kishinev atrocities, featuring shocking although sometimes inaccurate details, the government curtailed this uncontrolled publicity, allowing only a select few conservative outlets to report on the atrocity and its consequences. Another measure that the government took to maintain control was to hold the trials in secrecy, barring the public and journalists from attending. But this attempt to suppress information only heightened interest in the court case. A member of the advocate team meticulously recorded the proceedings and covertly passed these notes to the Western press. Inside the courtroom, with its doors firmly shut, all participants behaved as though the entire world was watching.

Indicted in the first trial was a group of thirty-seven men accused of participating in "a violent public gathering and the attack of one part of the population against another" and charged with the attack on the Jewish residents of 33 Gostinnaia Street, which ended with the murder of the sixteen-year-old Benjamin Baranovich and his neighbors Benzion Galanter, Duvid Drachman, Ios Kantor, and Reiza Katsap. Even before the beginning of the trial, it became apparent that the Jewish victims and the survivors, as well as their murderers, were of little interest to the court. As the Russian-language emigré journal *Osvobozhdenie* summarized the position of the liberal public, it did not care whether "these naïve savages" who were the blind weapons in the hand of "educated" organizers" would be adequately punished. "The main interest of the trial is in revealing the role of the administration in the Kishinev massacre, the local administration as well as the central one."

This was the position of the sixteen Young Advocates representing the victims: their main goal was not to defend the victims but to accuse those who were not yet indicted and to prove that the pogrom had been orchestrated according to a premeditated plan from behind the scenes. The role of the prosecution and the judges was to prove the innocence of the administration and to show that the massacre resulted from "national discord," which was the subject of Article 269 of the Penal Code. This statute, introduced after the pogroms of the early 1880s, allowed the court to punish dozens of pogromists who joined the crowd, but it presupposed that the "discord" was mutual and tacitly blamed Jews for provoking the assault. The collective guilt of the crowd also dissipated the guilt of individual murderers, making the killings appear almost accidental.

The trial began with the testimonies of well-known figures: the former city mayor Karl Schmidt, the commander of the local regiment General Beckman, doctors from the local hospital who admitted and treated victims during the pogrom, police officers, orthodox priests, and journalists. The Young Advocates aggressively interrogated witnesses whom they held responsible for the disaster, trying to convince the court to re-investigate the case and indict antisemites who had instigated the violence and the officials who allowed it to happen.

It was not until November 17, the eighth day of the court proceedings, that survivors and witnesses of the violence at 33 Gostinnaia Street were finally called to testify. Ruvim Katsap, who had hidden in the attic while the pogromists invaded the house, recounted to the court the brutal murder of his sixty-year-old grandmother, Reizel Katsap. Following Ruvim's testimony, Shimon Baranovich took the stand, sobbing and barely able to speak. A skilled house painter, renowned as "the best in Bessarabia," Shimon had been a resident of Kishinev for twenty-two years. Among those who had attacked his house were Russians and Moldavians who had previously worked under him as apprentices. He testified that on April 7, the second day of the pogrom (I am translating from the records of the court proceedings in the Serguei Zarudnyi collection in the Russian State Historical Archive),

> the crowd ... started breaking glass and forcing open the iron gates. ... Soon the vandals made their way through the windows into the courtyard and the apartment. We all rushed to escape, some onto the roof, some into the attic, some into the outhouse. I was in the far corner.... Suddenly, a heart-wrenching cry reached me, "Daddy, Daddy, they're killing me." I rushed into the yard and begged them, promising to give them everything I had. I pleaded with Kolesnichenko to take everything from the house and leave me my son. He replied, "Shut up, you Jew, we'll finish with you now, and we'll take all your belongings without [asking] you." I ran out into the street, [the gendarme] Solovkin was standing there; I fell at his feet, kissing his coat and boots, begging him to protect us. He remained calm, lit a cigarette, and said, "Everything is over in your yard; you have nothing to fear now." "Here comes the patrol, for God's sake, save us," I asked him and cried in front of him. But the patrol passed by, and he did not call them. I noticed Officer Trofimov and began to plead with him. "What can I do for you?" he answered

> and walked away. Meanwhile, they [the pogromists] continued to destroy property in the apartments. I took my son to the water tap and tried to pour water on him. I heard only a groan from him. "For God's sake, send a doctor," I begged the officer again, but he walked around the yard, paying no attention to my words.

Baranovich's court testimony, along with those of other survivors, not only provided the details of the killings but also exposed efforts by the police and the authorities to hide the truth about their criminal negligence. Survivors' petitions vanished from the prosecutor's office, and the presiding judge frequently censored and interrupted witness testimonies during their court appearances, dismissing their accounts as "irrelevant" to the case. The plaintiffs' legal representatives protested and called for a re-investigation, citing new evidence of a conspiracy and the authorities' complicity that had emerged during the trial. These demands were summarily dismissed by the court. When the Young Advocates' efforts to redirect the focus from the collective guilt of the mob and the individual actions of the pogromists to the suspected orchestrators of the pogrom reached an impasse, they decided to withdraw from the trial and left the courtroom.

The "quitting" maneuver employed by the group of Young Advocates had been used in previous trials as a public gesture to signal the illegality of the proceedings and to suggest that the court was not genuinely interested in uncovering the truth. By exposing the culpability of the antisemitic journalists and the authorities, the advocates felt they had fulfilled their role. Before exiting the courtroom, the lawyers declared that the true crime remained unpunished and that the wrong individuals had been placed on the defendant's bench. Nikolay

Karabchevsky, the star lawyer from St. Petersburg, nailed down the image of the pogrom that the lawyers had in mind, comparing Kishinev to the Roman coliseum.

> On the basis of verified evidence [that emerged during] the court hearings, I claim that for several hours Kishinev instantly turned into one giant arena of a Roman circus, surrounded by troops and the festive applauding crowd, while in its depth a bloody spectacle, unheard of in our days, was taking place: from one side, the defenseless victims were pushed out, from another, the infuriated beasts were set on them. And when they were told: "Enough, end of the show," it ended, as all shows usually end. I insist that even the external features of the event contain all the evidence of its internal organization.

Karabchevsky's speech, which was published by Western newspapers, achieved rhetorical success. In reality, however, the lawyers lacked sufficient evidence to prove conclusively that the pogrom had been systematically organized or that there was a strategic plan directing the movements of the pogromist groups. There were rumors that a list of Jewish residences was compiled, and one witness claimed to have overheard that groups of pogromists were numbered like military units. The lawyers also tried to prove that it was implausible that an unorganized, leaderless mob could cause such extensive destruction. Yet despite their efforts, no definitive evidence was uncovered — neither the documents proving a conspiracy nor any indication of a pre-existing plot involving government authorities. The lawyers' frustration with the court's refusal to investigate the crimes committed by what they termed "educated people" — referring to officials, antisemitic politicians, and journalists — was justifiable. They viewed the pogromists as mere pawns, people without a will of their own, manipulated evildoers executing someone else's order.

The decision to withdraw from the first of the twenty-two trials had an unintended consequence: both public and foreign press interest in the victims' and defendants' fates rapidly waned, as if a spotlight of attention had been abruptly switched off. This decline in interest was particularly notable as it occurred shortly after the court had begun to hear the accounts of the pogrom's victims. Consequently, aside from the moving account of Baranovich regarding his son's death — an account also captured in the interviews that Hayim Nachman Bialik conducted for the Jewish Historical Commission in Odesa, which provided the raw material for his great poem — and a handful of brief testimonies from Baranovich's neighbors, the stories of many other survivors went unheard. The tragic irony of the pogrom trial lay in that, despite being heavily reliant on the testimonies of nearly six hundred witnesses, the court seemed disinclined to consider these accounts from the outset.

Let us pause for a second and consider whether the rebuke for failing to listen and appreciate the survivors' testimonies is fair. Can we blame judges and advocates for not knowing how to listen? Even in the modern historiography of pogroms, as the historian Gur Alroey admits, "the victim has been marginalized," and the attention usually centers on perpetrators and instigators. Indeed, the scholarly methodology for analyzing the testimonies of witnesses to mass atrocities emerged only in the aftermath of the Second World War, alongside the emergence of what is known as the jurisprudence of atrocities, but even in legal practice, the voices of witnesses and victims did not always play a key role.

The Nuremberg trial in 1945–1946 was based entirely on Nazi documents, and the Eichmann trial in 1961 was the first instance of adjudication that overwhelmingly relied on the testimonies of survivors. Historians also had to learn how to suspend doubt when dealing with testimonies — sources that may be imperfect in relating facts yet nevertheless be truthful. Jan Gross, writing in the early 2000s about wartime anti-Semitic atrocities in the Polish town of Jedwabne, argued for the change in the attitude to testimonies from "a priori critical to in principle affirmative," and proposed "to accept as true Jewish testimonies about atrocities committed by the local population until they are proven false." Gross's message did not find unanimous approval in Poland, and the story of the killing of fifteen hundred Jews in 1941 by their Polish neighbors remains a subject of bitter contention.

Still, even if the ethics of reading survivors' testimonies is fairly recent, evaluating evidence, including eyewitness accounts, has been an essential element of judicial and everyday reasoning practiced by courts for centuries. In the early nineteenth century, Jeremy Bentham, in his attempt to define the principles of the critique of evidence, called on judges to suspend doubt and "hear everyone." Bentham believed in people's natural propensity to tell the truth and advocated for the presumption of truthfulness as a default setting. (He thought that lying is a laborious task that most humans tend to avoid.) One may dispute his optimistic view of human nature, but in the 1860s Russia introduced new courts with an improved organization and procedure that followed

Bentham's principles and allowed for an almost unrestricted freedom of evidence, including the use and interpretation of witnesses' testimonies. Vladimir Spasovich, picking up Bentham's thesis, added that each society, in each stage of its historical development, has its own principles for assessing proofs. The level of trust in testimonies fluctuates, Spasovich maintained; it is influenced by various factors, including the political climate, scientific advances, religious beliefs, and cultural trends. In the 1860s and 1870s, the era of liberal thaw, courts and the people whom they represented were open to listening and believing. In the 1890s and early 1900s, by contrast, Russian society was at its most skeptical and even cynical, at its lowest capacity for believing.

There were multiple reasons for this incredulity. One of them was the persistent policy of the autocratic government to conceal the truth about crucial events and their causes — such as, for instance, a mass stampede in Moscow in 1896 that took the lives of around two thousand people. The regime of secrecy and censorship exacerbated popular anxiety, as did the proliferation of media and the industry of rumors and sensations. There were other factors as well. In the late nineteenth and early twentieth centuries, Russian forensic psychologists and lawyers delved deeply into research on the psychology of memory and attention. Psychological experiments that tested people's ability to remember and to reproduce facts led scientists to conclude that even honest and unbiased testimonies can be inaccurate and misleading. This was particularly true in extraordinary situations such as natural catastrophes or mass violence, in which individuals might struggle to fully comprehend and accurately recall the details of events, including the identities of perpetrators. This emerging understanding of the fallibility of memory played a significant role in shaping the judicial approach to witness testimonies during this era. Lying was exonerated and normalized, yet everyone appeared as a liar. "Doubts [in the trustworthiness of testimonies] grew into the merciless rejection of testimonies," admitted Anatoly Koni, a famous judge who tried to restore trust in the human ability to remember and tell the truth.

The "scientization" of truth in legal proceedings resulted in a peculiar situation when the two notions of truth emerged parallel to each other: one based on facts, calculatable and verifiable, the other based on moral judgment. Russian philosophers loved pondering the specificity of the Russian language, which has two words to designate truth, "*pravda*" and "*istina*," aligning themselves with the first or the second. Speculations about notions of truth could be entertaining, but when it came to deciding the fate of victims or the defendants, this splintering, this epistemological crisis, resulted in misjudgments. Leo Tolstoy attributed the persistence of doubt and uncertainty to the celebration of scientific knowledge: "Doctors, lawyers, theologians, all those who scientifically study fantastic matters that cannot be conceived, employ methods with which they can achieve only the superficial, mechanical semblance to authenticity ... But the methods they use in principle cannot achieve the state of true knowledge."

Tolstoy, to be sure, was an almost mystical upholder of the moral truth and a believer in the human propensity to honesty, while remaining skeptical when it came to scientific "proofs" and "facts." Yet the distrust in testimonies was not fueled merely by "scientific" skepticism. Testimonies were viewed through the lens of class, nationality, and religion. Although legal reform in the 1860s eliminated many institutionalized biases, in the 1880s and 1890s nationalists revived the most obnoxious myths about the propensity to lie among Tatars, Chuvash, Daghestanians, and, of course, Jews. Nationalists often used modern sociological and psychological theories to support centuries-old lies and biases, doubling the effect of *the fin-de-siècle* epistemological crisis. Thus, inadvertently, forensic psychologists, philosophers, and lawyers gave antisemites the language and the right to reject testimonies, normalizing prejudices as a form of doubt.

Even before the beginning of the pogrom trial in Kishinev, nationalists started agitating against Jewish witnesses and victims. The nationalist newspaper *Novoe Vremia* published an article that insisted, with sarcasm, on a thorough interrogation of the "trustworthy" Jewish eyewitnesses, warning about the "unanimity of Jews" when they face Christians in court. The article manifested a tendency that would become even more apparent when Alexei Shmakov, a nationalist lawyer who represented the pogromists, evoked the *Oath More Judaico*, the medieval anti-Semitic institution that required a special oath of Jews to guarantee the credibility of their testimony about Christians in a Christian court, and demanded that the Jewish eyewitnesses take the oath in a synagogue. Judges rejected the demand as incompatible with law and the court's ethos. But this rejection exposed only their own annoyance with the attempt of the nationalist press and antisemitic lawyers to instruct them how to interpret testimonies. Their own approach, sadly, was not significantly different.

The judges and the administrators shrouded their antisemitism under the mask of objectivity and a healthy, rational skepticism. Prince Serguei Urusov, the new and progressive governor of Bessarabia who deemed himself a "philo-Semite," did not conceal his disappointment that after the "interesting" beginning of the trial that featured the interrogation of "half-witnesses, half-defendants" by the Young Advocates, "the testimony of the Jews began:"

> Witnesses who sat in their basement during the massacre had seen what was going on two squares ahead of them. Witnesses identified different persons among the accused as the perpetrators of the murders they saw.... In short, a Bacchanalian orgy of witnesses arose, confounding the unhappy judges and interesting the lawyers for the plaintiffs but little.

Urusov, who was not sympathetic to the pogromists-defendants, blamed the authorities for their inactivity and even held the central government "morally responsible" for the massacre. But his lack of empathy and his overt distrust of the testimonies from Jewish survivors mirrored the prevailing attitude of even progressive administrators and the liberal public, who harbored doubts about the credibility of testimonies.

Following the liberal lawyers' collective withdrawal from the first trial, the court's regard for testimonies diminished even further, while the voices of the survivors failed to reach an audience outside the courtroom. Some "young lawyers" returned to the courtroom for the subsequent trials, supporting their clients and recording testimonies. From the notes of Alexander Zarudnyi, one of the Young Advocates, we can gain insights into what transpired in the courtroom and can access the survivors' accounts. Throughout the trials, which lasted until the end of 1904, Zarudnyi persistently pressured the court to reinvestigate cases, and sent appeals to the Senate, and urged the court to heed the words of the survivors. Zarudnyi was fighting what seemed to be a losing battle; his records, now kept in an archive, preserve the details of his legal ordeal.

I ran away from home with my husband and the boys... We slipped into the alley next to the [brothers] Papanuks' house... we were pressed against the fence. Papanuk started shouting, "Jews need to be killed!" We pleaded with them to let us go. Georgy Papanuk pulled me forward. And all of them started beating me, and I fell. I couldn't see what was happening on the street. My eyes and my entire face were swollen from the beatings. I heard the voices of these two [pointing at the accused in the courtroom]. My husband stayed behind me, and I didn't see who killed him. My son, who saw better than me, told me that Ivan Papanuk rushed out with a piece of iron in his hands and hit my husband. I recognize the accused. In the raging crowd, I didn't see them, but when I regained consciousness, I heard their voices in the mob."

As Perla Kogan testified in court, she, her husband Avrum, and their sons, pursued by the mob, fled towards the railway station but were captured and brutally beaten. Avrum died on the spot. Although several witnesses identified the perpetrators, the court was reluctant to convict them. The judges' hesitation stemmed from uncertainty over which blow to Avrum Kogan's head was fatal — whether it was the one delivered by Anton Kuiban or by Georgy Papanuk. (The debate focused on whether Kogan remained standing after the blow.)

In her testimony, Perla asserted that the two neighbors, Georgy Papanuk and Konstantin Rotar, raped her after the beating.

> I lay on the ground from 8:00 PM until morning. Georgy Papanuk came to me twice around 12:00 and raped me twice. Then [Konstantin] Rotar approached and also raped me, then he left, cursing and pulling my shirt up. I recognized both of them by their voices, as I've known them for a long time. I couldn't see their faces; I was all beaten up. When dawn broke, I covered myself with a shirt. By morning, a city guard and some Jew took me to the hospital.

During the investigation, Perla mentioned the fact of the rape, but the officer in charge did not even record it. She reported it verbally to the prosecutor, and her lawyer, Zarudnyi, filed a written complaint on her behalf. Despite these efforts, the rape allegation was not included in the indictment.

The court also doubted that Perla could recognize her attackers without seeing them, although forensic experts invited to the proceeding stated that a person who loses vision could still hear clearly and thus recognize people by their voices. Finally, Perla's testimony was called into question when Eduard Woldenmeier, a resident of the same street where the tragedy unfolded, claimed to have seen a woman fall in the middle of the road, lying there until morning without anyone approaching her. Despite the apparent cynicism in Woldenmeier's testimony — he watched Perla, severely beaten, lying on the ground for twelve hours and did nothing — the court favored his account over hers. Zarudnyi, representing Perla in court, pushed for the case to be reopened to investigate the assault and the rape that she endured, but his efforts were in vain. Ultimately the court acquitted the defendants accused of beating and raping Perla Kogan and murdering her husband.

Perhaps most shocking was the court's decision to acquit

Yakov Bezdrigin and Nikita (Mitia) Kreuter, the rapists identified by several witnesses and victims, including the sixteen-year-old Sima Zaichik, who testified:

> Gentiles, among whom I noticed Kreuter, cut through the attic roof with an axe...and through this hole they came down to the attic where we were hiding. Five of them grabbed me by my arms and legs, threw me down, and Bezdrigin started having intercourse with me against my will; I recognized him on April 14 when I came to the police department to identify things stolen from us. In addition to Bezdrigin, other people had intercourse with me, but I don't know who because I fainted.

Many residents of the house on Nikolskaia Street witnessed Sima's ordeal. As Rivka Schiffer, another victim of the rapists, confirmed, about thirty people, most of them women, were hiding in the attic when the thugs broke in. Rivka recognized two of them — Nikita (Mitia) Kreuter, whom she had known for twelve years, and Yakov Bezdrigin. Rivka begged Mitia not to touch her, to no avail. Kreuter raped Rivka first, then Bezdrigin and others, eight or nine men in total, followed. She did not resist, fearing that they would kill her.

Rukhlia Krupnik, a witness, saw how Kreuter ripped Rivka's skirts, shut her mouth, bent her arms behind her back, and assaulted her. After Kreuter, someone else took his turn with her while Kreuter raped Sima. Sima was screaming, but they paid no attention. Bezdrigin stood on his knees next to Sima, waiting. After that, Kreuter came to Rukhlia with an axe; she gave him everything she had — money, a tin box with her golden watch and jewelry. Rivka's husband, Shepsel Schiffer, also saw how Kreuter raped his wife, and how Bezdrigin assaulted Sima. The pogromists threatened him; he gave them his watch and ran away.

The story of the two women raped in the attic of the house on Nikolskaia Street was known beyond the courtroom. Social norms of that time made women, and not their rapists, look disgraced, but Sima and Rivka, unlike many other victims who quietly carried the burden of pain and dishonor, chose to speak up. Michael Davitt met Sima, among other victims at the rabbi's house: "One was a girl of sixteen, named Simme Zeytchik, very pretty, and childish-looking for her years." She spoke to him. Bialik recorded Rivka's long and detailed testimony. In court and in interviews, both women repeated their statements almost word for word.

They were not sure about the exact number of the men who assaulted them, but who could blame them for not counting? The court, however, harped on the fact that, according to Sima, Bezdrigin was first to assault her and Kreuter was second, while Rukhlia Krupnik claimed that Kreuter started and Bezdrigin was next. Sima and Rivka had gone through the forensic medical examination by male doctors eleven days after the assault. Sima's legs were bruised, and the exam showed traces of coitus. Two experts — Kogan and Frenkel — asserted (this is from Zarudnyi's courtroom notes) that these were the signs of rape; but an expert named Vasilevich sowed doubt by suggesting that the hymen was ruptured "with either penis or finger," and the fourth expert, a man named Rava, doubted the very fact of the defilement. The results of Rivka's examination were also inconclusive, and the court ruled that the inconsistencies in testimonies about the order in which the women were assaulted and the lack of unanimity among the experts not only undermined the accusation of Bezdrigin and Kreuter "but even raised doubt regarding the fact of rape itself."

The list of crimes that the court refused to recognize because it did not consider the testimonies authentic is staggering. Judges acted as automatons, formally evaluating and calculating evidence, dismissing testimonies that came from victims or relatives or doubting that witnesses had been able to see things that they later reported seeing. Two pogromists, Yakim Sofronii and Ulyan Chebotarenko, knocked out Meir Weisman's eye, and Weisman, who was already blind in one eye, lost his vision completely; but the court, the unconscionable cruelty of this crime notwithstanding, refused to consider Weisman's petition because it was based only on his own statement. Judges acquitted the murderers of Kopel Kainarskii because the key witnesses to his murder were his widow and his children. Petr Kaverin, Ivan Pirozhok, and Stepan Foksh, who had killed Kelman Voliovich, were also exonerated because the testimonies against them came from Voliovich's family members. Although seven witnesses observed the pogromists chasing and beating Srul Ulman, the crucial testimony came from his sons, and the court suggested that in their state of emotional distress they "could unintentionally make a mistake regarding the identity" of the assailants. Therefore, the court decided to clear the accused of murder charges. The case involving the killings on Muncheshtskaia Road, where Sura Fonarzhi, her husband Zis, and their neighbor Yankel Tunik were the victims, was particularly harrowing. Witnesses asserted that Sura's body was found mutilated, with nails driven into her nostrils. However, the doctor who performed the autopsy later refuted this detail. This inconsistency in witness accounts regarding the mutilations provided the court with a pretext to dismiss their testimonies entirely, resulting in the acquittal of the accused on murder charges.

When survivors sought some solace by suing the pogromists for the destruction of their property, the judges questioned the plaintiffs' ability to identify who plundered their homes because, during the attack, the plaintiffs were hiding from the attackers and, consequently, could not see anything. Even when the perpetrators were clearly identified, the court dismissed requests for compensation because the testimonies regarding the value of broken utensils, stolen goods, and clothing came from the plaintiffs' neighbors, who were themselves victims of the attack. In the face of this injustice, Zarudnyi tried to appeal the court decision in the Senate, pointing out that "all these witnesses were themselves victims of the pogrom because, with few exceptions, all the Jews of Kishinev suffered from the pogrom. There were no other witnesses available to establish the value of the destroyed household property except for Jewish neighbors. The victims of the pogrom, who belonged to the poorest segment of the city's population for the most part, were the ones who could testify to it." This, like all other Zarudnyi's appeals, was futile. Russian courts treated all Jews as if they constituted a single collective entity with uniform interests and consciousness. Simultaneously, it sought to individualize the guilt of each defendant, opting for acquittal when this guilt was not immediately apparent.

The main cause of the judges' attitude to the survivors' testimonies requires no explanation. Antisemitism — deep, sometimes even unconscious, prejudice turned them against the survivors' stories. According to many accounts, the presiding judge from Odesa, Vladimir Davydov, was a decent person, a loyal and conservative man, and very representative of the legal estate that was permeated by latent antisemitism. Other factors, however, also played a role. As I have pointed out, the court followed the formal rules of evidence, dismissing testimonies as legally unacceptable. It is quite possible that the judges understood that the survivors were telling the truth, but they prioritized the formal rules, dismissing contradictory testimonies altogether and rejecting the testimonies of close relatives. Doubt and skepticism, often with a scientific gloss, concealed and justified their biases and the lack of empathy.

The result was an absurd coexistence of the two truths. The city was abuzz with tales of atrocities, with burned houses and streets littered with fragments of shattered furniture serving as silent testaments to the catastrophe; everyone was aware of the truth regarding the rapes and the killings. Yet the judges constructed an alternate version of the truth that deviated from common knowledge. The judges' prior doubt mirrored the prior willingness of the pogromists to accept lies and conspiracy theories, such as the story of ritual murder or of the Tsar's alleged order to massacre the Jewish residents of Kishinev. The pogromists' readiness to believe these rumors was not driven by the allure of falsehoods but rather by a desire to believe in their veracity, a credulity based on the platitudes of the world they inhabited, while the court's doubt in the authenticity of testimonies also reflected a tacit convention.

The liberal lawyers who withdrew from the trial because the court refused to investigate antisemitic conspiracy also inadvertently played a role in sealing the irrelevance of the victims' testimonies and contributed to the murderers' acquittal. The Jewish lawyer Samuel Kalmanovich, a member of the Young Advocate defense team, spoke on the victims' behalf when he declared that they did not care about the prosecution of the pogromists: "We are not seeking the punishment of these poor souls... We, Jews, need the reasons... Tell us, why were we beaten?" But while this question certainly resonated with the words of the survivors, it seems that Kalmanovich and the victims were speaking about different things. Kalmanovich asked about the role of the authorities and the instigators, assuming the existence of a plot, while the victims wondered how and why people who had lived side-by-side with them for ages had turned into their enemies. The liberal lawyers' position denying agency to the mob and to its individual participants somewhat foreshadowed Hannah Arendt's stance about the role of individual perpetrators in the giant machine of Nazi violence. Like Arendt reporting in 1963 on the Eichmann trial, the young lawyers, undoubtedly sympathetic to the victims, failed in 1903 to hear their voices clearly.

The court, predictably, could not and did not want to address the question of the pogrom's causes, all the more so because most defendants stayed silent throughout the trial, simply denying their guilt. The study of the origins of the violence requires deep research into the social, cultural, and economic history of Kishinev, and some of this work has been done recently by several prominent historians who showed that the pogrom was neither an organized and pre-planned assault, as the liberal lawyers tried to prove, nor the eruption of a national and economic conflict that had been building up for ages, as the prosecution suggested. What happened in Kishinev was a spontaneous ethnic riot provoked by antisemitic propaganda. In its causes, but not in its context or its scale, it was similar to the massacre in Jedwabne in 1941, when, as Jan Gross asserts, "ordinary Poles slaughtered the Jews" without the Gestapo's command and instruction, "of their own free will."

While the memory of the massacre at Jedwabne lay dormant until Gross's intervention, Kishinev's story was neither unknown nor forgotten. But what remains to be explained is the seductiveness of the lies and the conspiracy theories, and the failure of both the court and the liberal lawyers, with the exception of a few, to hear the voices of the survivors. Was the society, including its liberal part, ready and willing to accept testimonies, and if not, what could have caused the crisis of disbelief? This question resonates, alas, with our own debates about alternative truths, elusive facts, prior ideological disqualifications, and trust that has become predicated on a testifier's group or nationality or citizenship.

Striking a balance between credulity and skepticism regarding the narratives of victims is difficult. What matters is not their identity or their position — on the defendant's bench, among the plaintiffs, or among the witnesses; even the categories of "victim" and "survivor" can be contested. A judge, a journalist, or a historian should approach testimonies with an assumption of truthfulness — but trust is not the same as blind belief, which turns quickly into distrust and injustice towards others. Truth has a history, and a society's progress toward a better way of understanding and critically evaluating evidence is not straightforward. It is from the failures and the retreats in the history of truth that we can learn the most.

MOSAB ABU-TOHA

Howl

I'm howling, howling
in Cairo.
I jump off my chair. I hug
the closest thing to me,
the gray corner of my room,
my head glued to it like
a stamp so eager to travel.
Books on the shelf,
they listen to the whispers of my nose
as it smells the old paint,
as it searches for the fingers of the mason
beneath the paint.

My nose hears the mason's radio
playing Om Kolthoum
and news about the Uprising nearby.
My nose smells the burning tires and stones
thrown by young hands.

I open my eyes to the image of my mother
on my phone
handing me oranges she picked
from a tree that's now under the rubble,
but that continues to howl
in the wind.

Who Has Seen the Wind?

After Bob Kaufman

The ceiling of my bedroom, my fridge
and the stale bread in it,
the notebook inside which I hid the love letters
from my wife before we married,
the foreign coins in my piggy bank ,
my expired debit cards
and my brother's death certificate,
the pieces of shrapnel on or near
each of these.

Right or Left!

Under the rubble,
her body has remained
for days
and days.
When the war ends,
we try to remove
the rubble,
stone
after stone.
We only find a bone
from her body.
It is a bone
from her arm.
Right or left,
it does not matter
as long as we cannot
find the henna
from the neighbors' wedding
on her skin,
or the ink
from a school pen
on her little index finger.

Rescue Plane

I wish I had a rescue plane
to fly over Gaza
to drop wheat flour and tea bags,
tomatoes and cucumbers,
to remove the rubble of the houses,
to retrieve the corpses of my loved ones.

I wish for a second rescue plane
to drop flowers for children—
the ones still alive—to plant
on the graves of their parents and siblings
in the streets or school yards.

The wish behind the wish?

I wish there were no planes at all.
I wish there were no war.

No Art

The art of losing isn't hard to master.
Elizabeth Bishop

Why the anger?
You know everything will come to an end:
The sugar, the tea, the dried sage,
the water.
Just go to the market and restock.

Why the disappointment?
Even your shadow will abandon you
when there is no light.
So just keep things that require only you:
the book of poems that only you can decipher,
the blank map of a country
whose cities and villages only you can recognize.

Why the melancholy?
I personally lost three friends to war,
a city to darkness, and a language to fear.
This was not easy to survive,
but survival proved necessary to master.
But of all things,
losing the only photo of my grandfather
when he was young
was a real disaster.

CARLOS FRAENKEL

Is a Public Philosophy Still Possible?

Are we living in a "golden age" of public philosophy, as some claim? There sure is a lot of it, as magazines, blogs, podcasts, and Substack newsletters proliferate. Even the *New York Times* ran a philosophy column for over a decade in which philosophers shared their thoughts on issues "timely and timeless" with the *hoi polloi*. Is this deluge of wisdom a boon for democratic deliberation or a vanity project for academic philosophers who feel embarrassed to be counting angels on a pin's head while Rome burns? A cursory glance at the world provides little evidence that enlightenment is spreading. Yet philosophers do grapple with the most pressing human questions: How should we live?

What defines a good society? Are they, the philosophers, qualified to shape public discourse and guide us through tumultuous times? And their grappling trickles down to an army of earnest pundits, who now write eight-hundred-word columns about God and history.

Putting aside political and religious differences, two strands of public philosophy are on offer today: the down-top Socratic approach and the top-down Platonic. There is the grassroots view and the elite view. Both have limitations: the former is ineffective, the latter is paternalistic. But if we strike the right balance between the two approaches, we might be able to anchor liberal societies in a robust philosophical foundation. If that is still possible.

At its most ambitious, public philosophy "aspires to liberate the subject from its academic confines" and "offer non-philosophers a way of participating in the activity," Agnes Callard recently wrote in *The Point*, a small magazine with a big mission: to create "a society where the examined life is not an abstract ideal but an everyday practice." The concept of the "examined life" derives from Socrates, of course, who famously declared that "an unexamined life is not worth living" — a radical claim that never fails to baffle my students.

Their idea of a fulfilling life is very different from Socrates'. They want to study medicine, law, engineering, social work, education, and the like to realize their professional ambitions. They also want to find friends, fall in love, and go out and party. Socrates is not exactly telling them to throw their goals overboard, but he is telling them that they have no value whatsoever without relentless self-scrutiny. No wonder that

Socrates admonishes his fellow-citizens with evangelical fervor. Their very salvation is at stake:

> I shall treat in this way anyone I happen to meet, young and old, citizen and stranger....I think there is no greater blessing for the city than my service to the god. I was placed in this city by the god as on a horse, great and of noble birth, which was sluggish because of its size and needed to be stirred up by a kind of gadfly. I never cease to stir up each and every one of you, to persuade you and reproach you all day long.

Note that Socrates is not merely offering intellectual stimulation. He seeks nothing less than conversion:

> I shall not cease...to point out to anyone of you whom I happen to meet: Good Sir, are you not ashamed of your eagerness to possess as much wealth, reputation and honors as possible, while you do not care for nor give thought to wisdom or truth, or the best possible state of your soul? Then, if one of you disputes this and says he does care, I shall examine him..., and if I do not think he has attained the goodness that he says he has, I shall reproach him because he attaches little importance to the most important things and greater importance to inferior things.

Socrates has immense confidence in the power of reason. Argument, he thinks, can remove false beliefs about what benefits us and then get us to reframe our lives around the truth. Nobody is so dumb to chase things of little value and neglect things of great value once they grasp what *really* is to their advantage.

Liberal-egalitarians will find an ally in Socrates. For one thing, he is inclusive: the gadfly piques everyone. Sure, Socrates is in your face. But he doesn't force you to change. Nor does he pour wisdom into your head. As an intellectual "midwife" he wants to help you give birth to your own ideas, making sure that they are founded in reason. This might still be too much for the complacent or the self-righteous. But it certainly fits nicely with John Stuart Mill's brand of liberalism, for example, that champions critical thinking and vigorous debate. Karl Popper celebrated Socrates as the first advocate of the "open society."

The values that we embrace, Socrates argues, guide our choices. Scrutinizing them is crucial. If you really want to be pious, make sure you know what piety is. If you really want to be just, make sure you know what justice is. In short: if you really want to do well and thrive, make sure you know what that means. Who would not rally behind public philosophy if it could steer us to an examined life steeped in virtue and wisdom?

The crises piling up around us add urgency to Socratic public philosophy. We need all the help we can get to make good decisions. I was finishing high school in Germany when the Cold War ended. With friends I drove to Berlin to watch thousands of East Germans climb over the Wall. We were mesmerized by what seemed like the triumph of freedom. In the decades that followed the world enjoyed more freedom than ever before. And yet, thirty-five years later, I am scratching my head. What are we doing with it?

Liberals hail the freedom to live as we please. We can celebrate Christmas, Diwali, or Gay Pride; donate money to Greenpeace or the National Rifle Association; stay with one partner "till death do us part" or go out with a new one every week. Yet even in a perfect liberal society in which we have freedom, a fair share of resources, and equal opportunities to advance, we still need to learn how to compose worthwhile lives. What liberal societies fail to give us is the tools to deliberate within our freedoms and make good use of all that choice.

The last few years have plunged us into ever-growing confusion: extreme weather, divisive ideologies, global health crises, populist upheaval, billionaires buzzing through space next to capsized migrant dinghies washing up on shores, intractable wars, technological revolutions, disinformation. These challenges don't come out of nowhere. The world we live in is the world we create through our choices: the dreams we nurse, the careers we pursue, the politicians we elect, the stuff we buy, the vacations we plan, the charities we support, the social networks we join. In liberal societies, where free and equal citizens are the sovereign, we cannot point fingers at kings, popes, or despots when things go wrong.

Consider the politicians we elect. Plato's critique of democracy never failed to spark spirited protest in my classroom. A state where the *demos*, the people, rule, Plato argues, is like a "ship of fools." To make it safely to the other shore, we need a seasoned captain at the helm, not passengers who have no clue about navigation. Pass the rudder to the *demos* and they will run the state into the ground. My students who grew up with the firm conviction that liberal democracy is the best political system were keen to recapture the captain's wheel. Pushing back on Plato, they stressed the value of freedom, collective wisdom, and the need to hold rulers accountable.

On a cold winter day in 2017, however, fervor gave way to gloom. More than one hundred students had signed up for my Introduction to Political Philosophy. Not one was eager to speak up for democracy. At first I was surprised. Then I saw a raised hand. "Didn't you watch the inauguration of the new American president last week?" the student asked. "Maybe democracies are ships of fools after all!" The other students nodded. By then even diehard optimists conceded that the moral arc of the universe at best looks like a zigzagging line. Suddenly the post–World War II political order trembled. One day we had been discussing transgender bathrooms. The next day a full-blown assault on the foundations of liberalism was underway: an American president who would go on to incite a mob to storm the Capitol in Washington; the United Kingdom breaking out of the European Union; nationalist, populist, and even fascist movements popping up everywhere.

Can public philosophy rescue liberal societies from turning into ships of fools? At stake is our most basic moral paradigm: the "morality of self-governance," which replaced the "morality of obedience" from the seventeenth century onwards, as Jerome Schneewind argues in his classic study *The Invention of Autonomy*:

> All of us, on this view, have an equal ability to see for ourselves what morality calls for and are in principle equally able to move ourselves to act accordingly. [...] The conception of morality as self-governance provides a conceptual framework for a social space in which we may each rightly claim to direct our own actions without interference from the state, the church, the neighbors, or those claiming to be better or wiser than we.

Consider Kant's "motto" of the Enlightenment: "*Sapere aude*!" "Dare to use your own reason!" It is addressed to those who out of "laziness and cowardice" follow "the guidance of others" that the guidance of a "book" or the guidance of a "priest." Kant is optimistic: we can all become captains and competently steer our individual and communal lives. The sting of the gadfly is just what we need to help us overcome "laziness and cowardice" and embrace rational self-rule. If public philosophy can help us with that, it would be a blessing indeed.

Socrates's debates are anything but academic. Take, for example, the dialogue of the gadfly on the nature of piety with Euthyphro, the diviner-priest. The stakes could not be higher. Euthyphro insists that it is his pious duty to indict his own father for murder. But is his understanding of piety correct? Concurrently, the people of Athens have charged Socrates with impiety. His trial is looming. Will they wrongly put to death the very man striving to save them?

Or consider inquisitors, missionaries, terrorists, and others who through the ages have done things in the name of piety that are questionable to say the least. In 1995 Yigal Amir, a right-wing Jew, assassinated Israel's prime minister, Yitzhak Rabin, and was followed by a string of suicide attacks in Israeli cities ordered by Hamas. Together, in God's name, they derailed the Oslo peace process.

As is typical for Socratic debates, the one with Euthyphro ends in an impasse. Socrates knocks down every definition of piety that Euthyphro proposes. Does this mean that the exercise was futile? Not at all. Socrates has freed Euthyphro from the illusion of knowledge. Identifying and discarding false beliefs is a prerequisite for finding the truth. But will we hit on the right answer eventually? If we can count, measure, and weigh things, Socrates notes, disputes are quickly resolved. Concerning "the just and unjust, the beautiful and the ugly, the good and the bad," however, disagreement persists. For Socrates the realm of values is messier than that of mathematics. We cannot know for sure what piety is.

Still, some beliefs about piety are more plausible than others. Say, you propose a definition of piety that is not refuted in a Socratic debate. Granted, it may still be refuted the next time you enter the ring. Still, each failed refutation is a reason to believe the definition is sound. At the same time, even the most scrutinized definition hasn't been proven beyond doubt. At the very end of his life Socrates is willing to reexamine—and, if need be, to revise—his long-held views on justice. Following his death sentence, his friends urge him to escape from prison. After probing the matter thoroughly, Socrates concludes that this would be wrong.

The "examined life," then, is not something you can learn like the periodic table, long division, or the *passé composé*. It is a lifelong practice, driven by the desire to get the values you live by right while conceding that you may be wrong. In this sense, public philosophy in the Socratic mode does not offer answers. It aims to get us hooked on an open-ended Socratic quest.

Plato thought that Socrates's gadfly mission — the attempt to change people's minds and lives through argument — didn't stand a chance. Yes, the parable of the cave is a moving tribute to Socrates's effort to drag the cave dwellers up to the light. But it also highlights his spectacular failure: "And, as for anyone who tried to free [the cave dwellers] and lead them upward, if they could somehow get their hands on him, wouldn't they kill him? They certainly would."

Plato's pessimism about Socrates's project has two reasons; one we can dismiss, the other we should take seriously. Here is the former: Plato was an elitist who argued that most human beings are cave dwellers by nature. They are in the grip of lust, greed, and ambition. Even the best education cannot enlighten them. Only the select few have the desire and the talent for wisdom. Most of us are unable to govern ourselves rationally because of our deficient nature, not because of cowardice or laziness. No amount of Socratic argument — or public philosophy, for that matter — can get the masses to embrace the examined life or turn a ship of fools into a vessel of the wise.

Plato's other worry, the one we should engage with, concerns not nature but nurture. Even "the best nature," he contends, risks being "corrupted by its upbringing": "It will grow to possess every virtue if it happens to receive appropriate instruction, but if it is sown, planted, and grown in an inappropriate environment, it will develop in quite the opposite way." Consider Plato's visit to the south of Italy. He stresses how "profoundly displeased" he was by "what they call the 'happy life'" there: "a life filled with Italian and Syracusan banquets, with men gorging themselves twice a day and never sleeping alone at night, and following all the other customs that go with this way of life."

This decadent lifestyle, Plato contends, corrupts everyone: "For no man under heaven who has cultivated such practices from his youth could possibly grow up to be wise ... or become temperate, or indeed acquire any other part of virtue." And note, finally, that Plato takes the corruption to be irreversible: "There isn't now, hasn't been in the past, nor ever will be in the future anyone with a character so unusual that he has been educated to virtue in spite of the contrary education he received from the mob." Socratic argument, Plato insists, simply cannot pierce through to the partying Italians — *even if* they were by nature able to live an examined life geared towards virtue and wisdom.

Plato, you will object, is exaggerating. There are people who radically change their life. In *Unorthodox: The Scandalous Rejection of My Hasidic Roots*, Deborah Feldman tells how she left the Hasidic Satmar community in Brooklyn to become a bohemian writer in Berlin. My father hopped from one worldview to another. As a teenager he wanted to become a rabbi, after high school an engineer, in university a communist, and in his thirties a New Age mystic.

But even if there are exceptions, Plato's critique of Socrates's project still holds. Recall that Socrates — and all champions of a public philosophy — are not trying to reach this or that eccentric outlier. They want to effect large-scale change — to create "a society where the examined life is not an abstract ideal but an everyday practice." That is where Plato's skepticism is spot-on. Consider this ancient testimony of what an encounter with Socrates entailed:

> Whoever associates with [Socrates] in conversation must necessarily... keep on being led about by the man's arguments until he submits to answering questions about himself concerning both his present manner of life and the life he has lived until now. And Socrates will not let him go before he has well and truly tested every last detail.

Now picture Socrates pestering your family, friends, and colleagues about their values and convictions. Or picture him showing up at a medical convention, a law firm, a university seminar, a science lab, a museum, the opera—places where he will run into educated, open-minded people. Will they engage in longwinded Socratic discussions, then step out of their busy professional and family lives and rebuild them around new values? Or will they turn their back on Socrates, show him the door, and, if he refuses to leave, call the police? The great majority, I bet, will kick him out.

Aristotle agrees with Plato. Trying to change people through argument is a waste of time at best. At worst they will do to you what the Athenians did to Socrates:

> If arguments were sufficient by themselves to make people good, then they would have won many great rewards... But as things are they appear to have the power...to make susceptible to virtue a character that is well bred and truly loves what is noble.

Only people who have been brought up in the right way — who have internalized the right beliefs and values — benefit from theory. It explains to them why they feel and act as they already do, and it helps them to further refine their choices. People corrupted by their upbringing, on the other hand, are irredeemable:

What argument could reform people like this? For displacing by argument what has been long entrenched in people's characters is difficult if not impossible. Recall Chidi Anagonye, in the NBC sit-com *The Good Place,* comically failing to reform bad girl Eleanor Shellstrop through lectures on moral philosophy. Plato and Aristotle would not have been surprised.

Yet we would not be living in a "golden age" of public philosophy unless there was a broad audience to consume it. Does that mean that we are, on average, more receptive to arguments than ancient Athenians? I don't think so. As Callard stresses, public philosophy is often a form of highbrow entertainment. It makes "us feel smarter, deeper, better informed"; it puts "a spring in our intellectual step." There is nothing wrong "with intellectually engaging fun," she adds. But "there is something wrong with calling that philosophy." Intellectual titillation is one thing. The examined life is another.

At the same time, there is no shortage of aesthetic and intellectual spaces for gadfly-style critique in liberal societies — from literature to arthouse cinema, from performance art to late-night comedy. But does it make a difference? We may feel unsettled for a moment, reflect on prejudices, or ponder social conventions. Yet once we close the book, finish discussing the film, leave the exhibit, or click on the next link, life goes on as before. We feel thoughtful but nothing has changed. A Marxist (and others) might well wonder if these spaces are not a fig leaf for the status quo. By conveying a false sense of openness to radical self-interrogation, they help to keep things as they are.

Plato and Aristotle, at any rate, did not believe that arguments (or other bottom-up approaches) can effect change. The social psychologist Jonathan Haidt shares their skepticism about reason's power. We are "emotional dogs with rational tails," he argues. It is wrong to picture reason as an impartial judge who decides based on evidence and deliberation. Reason is as ancillary as a dog's tail: a lawyer who defends our entrenched values. Haidt likes to cite Hume: "reason is the slave of the passions." This is why political debates are tribal and polarized. Consider pro-life and pro-choice advocates: no matter how many arguments they hurl at each other, they will not budge an inch. We are stuck in what Haidt dubs "righteous minds."

In moral decisions, Haidt contends, "intuition" comes first, "reasoning" second. Both nature and nurture shape intuitions. Evolution selects for instincts that increase our own and our genes' chances for survival — desires for food, drink, and sex, fear of predators, loyalty to one's clan, protecting one's offspring. Social norms, in turn, determine more concretely what we are drawn to and repulsed by.

No wonder that Socrates's attempt to make Athenians wise through argument backfired so badly. Many modern endeavors, too, are pipedreams, on Haidt's view: from Jürgen Habermas's ideal society where genuinely free and equal citizens submit to the "unforced force of the better argument" to Elon Musk's suggestion that unfettered freedom to spew out opinions on Twitter promotes democratic discussion.

Plato and Aristotle are as keenly aware as Haidt of our powerful non-rational impulses — Plato calls them the "multicolored beast" in us. But there is one crucial difference. They believe that "intuition" and "reason" can be *aligned*. Reason is not by default the master of the passions. But it also is not inevitably their slave.

Plato was in his mid-twenties when Socrates swallowed the hemlock. Traumatized, he concluded that instead of trying to change the righteous minds of adults, we must mold the still flexible minds of children — not through rational persuasion, however, but through enforcing rational norms.

Every parent knows what Plato means. If you want your children to eat their vegetables, brush their teeth, and do their homework, don't lecture them on obesity, cavities, and the importance of study. They grasp the short-term pleasures of candy and video games, not the long-term advantages of a healthy lifestyle and a university degree. You must put in place incentives and deterrents to rewire their experience of pleasure and pain. Offset, for example, short-term pleasures and pains with greater pleasures and pains that they understand (a family movie if they have done all their duties; no playdate tomorrow if the homework is incomplete). My children are now avid readers. But when they first started stringing letters, words, and sentences together, it was not fun. To move them over the threshold from pain to pleasure, from no fun to fun, I didn't give a sermon on the benefits of literacy. I nudged them with small rewards.

This is how Plato describes the goal of *paideia* (education):

> Once the child has [developed] the right [tastes and] distastes, he will praise fine things, be pleased by them, receive them into his soul, and, being nurtured by them, become fine and good. He will rightly object to what is shameful, hating it while he is still young and unable to grasp the reason, but, having been educated in this way, he will welcome the reason when it comes and recognize it easily because of its kinship with himself.

Aristotle gives the thumbs up to Platonic *paideia*: people brought up in this way are precisely the people who benefit from moral instruction.

So how do we move from a society that corrupts citizens to one that enables them to flourish? If reasoning cannot get through, Plato argues, we must go for revolution. Of course he doesn't call for storming the Bastille. In his view we cannot change social structures from below. Consider women in

Athens, for example. They are not inferior to men by nature, Plato contends, but owing to the crippled life that they lead, excluded from education, culture, and politics. But persuading them to rebel will not work because their desires have been distorted. They have naturalized their inferiority. Instead the transformation must come from above: philosophers take over the state and create a "clean slate" by tearing down social and cultural institutions and expelling all citizens over the age of ten who have already been corrupted by the old regime. Then they design new institutions — especially a top-notch education system — that direct children to virtue and wisdom.

Molding minds is not the revolution's only purpose. The rulers also put conditions in place that allow citizens to do what they like. You cannot pursue your love for learning unless there are schools, libraries, museums, and universities in town. Opera lovers need opera houses and cinema lovers need cinemas. To ski, you need slopes and to swim, pools. To reduce your ecological footprint you need recycling bins, good public transport, and safe bike lanes. This gives rise to a second objection to the Socratic approach: even if we could win people over through argument, we still need to put the conditions in place that allow them to realize the examined lives they choose. We must create, as the behavioral psychologists (who call themselves "libertarian paternalists") like to say, the appropriate decision architecture.

Public philosophy, as Plato and Aristotle conceive it, is *rationality embodied in social structures* set up by wise rulers. These structures first mold citizens in the right way and then ensure that they can live the lives they love. It is still an examined life—only that the examining is done by the philosophers in charge (as parents do the examining for their children). The most prominent contemporary champion of public philosophy in the Platonic-Aristotelian sense is Martha Nussbaum, especially when she first set out her ideas about how to promote human wellbeing in the late 1980s and 1990s. A key passage for Nussbaum is Aristotle's claim in the *Politics* that "the best constitution" is that "according to which anyone whosoever is able to do best and to live a flourishing life." Like Plato and Aristotle, Nussbaum is deeply concerned that we will miss out on such a life if we are corrupted through our upbringing. There are "entire communities," she writes, "that teach, and deeply believe, false values that are inimical to true human flourishing: excessive love of money, excessive preoccupation with honor and reputation, an unbalanced attachment to the warlike life, a deficient concern with due procedure and human equality in the administration of justice."

Aristotle, Nussbaum points out, "stresses throughout his ethical and political writings that many people are badly educated and therefore want the wrong things." This is why the goal of a good ruler should not be satisfying "people's subjective preferences." Like Plato, she highlights the crippling lives imposed on women: "Women in many parts of the world ...have been so deeply and thoroughly taught to believe that they should not be educated, and in general should not function in various non-traditional ways, that they lack desire for these functionings." Again, like Plato and Aristotle, she opts for the top-down approach. It is the job of philosopher-rulers to engineer good lives:

> The close link that Aristotle wishes to establish between philosophy and public policy (between perspicuous and comprehensive foundational argument and empirical designing) is rarely found in the contemporary world. The Aristotelian conception urges us not to forget that link.

The "most urgent task of the philosopher, qua worker for the human good is, to think about such (to some modern eyes) unphilosophical topics as the number of children one should encourage, the nature of funding for public meals, the purity of water supply, the distance of the marketplace from the sea." Nussbaum's "total task" has three components: to develop "in the young" the features of human nature that will enable them to flourish when they grow up; to "maintain those features in the adult"; and "to create and preserve the circumstances" under which these lives can be realized. Philosopher-rulers must assess how policies affect "the *totality* of a person's way of living and acting." They "cannot simply aim at designing a good and just health care scheme, or a good system of education, but must consider the total picture at all times."

Nussbaum wants the Aristotelian conception of the good life to provide "the philosophical underpinning...of basic constitutional principles that should be respected and implemented by the governments of all nations." If Nussbaum had her way, Aristotle's prescriptions would be followed around the globe. Note, however, that Nussbaum does not think that most human beings are cave dwellers by nature. The rule of philosophers is transient: once citizens have been brought up correctly, they can take charge of their lives — like grown-up children who are no longer defiant, but have matured and become "reasonable." In this sense there is space for rational self-governance. But that much freedom even Plato was willing to grant:

> We don't allow them to be free until we establish a constitution in them [...] and by fostering their best part with our own equip them with a guardian and ruler similar to our own to take our place. Then, and only then, we set them free.

Nussbaum's experiment is to somehow reconcile paternalism with egalitarianism; but even in Nussbaum's egalitarian version the Platonic approach removes the freedom to live as we please, which is the cornerstone of liberal societies. Is this something we should give up? Here are a few reasons why we should not: Kant ties human dignity to autonomy — our ability to determine our own goals. Mill urges us to custom-make life-plans suited to our personal talents and desires. He is, moreover, a fallibilist, like Socrates: even after extensive scrutiny our values are not beyond doubt, which is why we should not impose them on others. Finally, with all due respect to Aristotle, one size may not fit all. If there are multiple ways of thriving, the state shouldn't promote one at the expense of others.

Are we, then, stuck between a Socratic rock and an Aristotelian hard place? Does public philosophy come too late to change "righteous minds"? Fortunately, being pestered by a Socratic gadfly or submitting to the authority of a philosopher-king are not the only ways to promote the examined life. Here are a few thoughts on how we might integrate it successfully into an open society in which citizens are free to live as they please.

First, we must make philosophy classes — classes in the methods and rigors of thinking — mandatory in high school and college. The goal is not to teach students how to craft their lives, but to enable them to think through what that entails and then make their own choices. Serious thinking is not a natural attribute even in thinking beings. It needs to be learned. We could catch people in their late teens and early twenties as they move out of the parental home, facing big decisions that will define the shape of their personal and social lives: about education, work, love, relationships, family, politics, culture, and religion.

The classes I have in mind would cover both content and method. Consider philosophical proposals for how to live: far from being monolithic, they form a vigorous debate. They cannot all be right. "Both Plato and the truth are dear to me," Aristotle writes. "But if they clash, it's my pious duty to choose the truth." Then he goes on to demolish the very foundation of Plato's philosophy. And philosophers, or serious thinkers, clash not only with each other. They also turn conventional ideas of happiness and flourishing on their head. If we took a tour of ancient Athens, all the philosophers we would meet there would try to lure us into their schools by advertising their philosophy as *the* gateway to *eudaimonia*, a happy and flourishing life.

Sign me up! you will exclaim. Who does not want to be happy and flourish? But once the old bearded men in tunics start lecturing, you are in for a shock. Good looks; cool friends, Instagram-ready children, wealth, status, fame, an Ivy league degree, a stellar career? None of this matters. You can be completely miserable sipping champagne on a yacht and perfectly happy living in a slum, or so the Stoics argue. With the right attitude even the "bull of Phalaris" — a hollow bronze bull devised by the tyrant Phalaris to burn his victims alive — won't upset you.

Many philosophers engage in radical experiments in living — the phrase is Mill's — that challenge social norms, from Socrates's incessant questioning and Diogenes's case for living in a barrel to Sartre's notion that we are "condemned" to freedom. Their writings can take on the role of the Socratic gadfly: jolt us into re-examining our upbringing, our career ambitions, our status anxieties, our views on morality and politics, our ideas of friendship, love, and family, the things we fear or feel sad about, our role in society, our place in the world.

But igniting a debate about the right way to live is not enough. Citizens also need to learn the skills of debating, or rather, of reasoning. (Debating skills alone, the cult of rhetoric, can quickly lead to sophistry.) That is why method is important: mastering techniques of argument—logical and semantic tools that allow us to clarify our views and to make and respond to claims, a contemporary version of what Aristotelians called the *Organon*, the "toolkit" of the philosopher. And alongside the methods of reasoning our students must be taught the virtues of serious discussion — valuing the truth more than winning an argument (that is, disciplining what Plato called *thumos*, or the "victory-loving" part of the soul) and trying one's best to understand the viewpoint of the opponent. The debates we want are not based on the sophistical skill of making one's own opinion prevail over others, but on the dialectical skill of engaging in a joint search for the truth.

Such classes, focused on content and method, would do much more to realize "a society where the examined life is not an abstract ideal but an everyday practice" than all the magazines, blogs, podcasts, newsletters, and op-ed pieces taken together, which now define grassroots public philosophy.

At the same time I take seriously Plato and Aristotle's case for the crucial role that early education and social environments play. But if we have booted out the state from our lives in the name of freedom, who will put structures in places to help us flourish? In fact, we don't need the state for such pedagogy. In liberal societies we have freedom of association: we can band together with like-minded citizens and build institutions that suit our distinctive idea of a good and flourishing life. Examples abound: Jews have their synagogues and yeshivas; Muslims their mosques and madrassas; hipsters their trendy bars and galleries; and the bourgeoisie, of course, has Carnegie Hall."

Initially, existing institutions may not embody rationality in Plato and Aristotle's sense. But this will begin to shift as citizens, empowered by mandatory philosophy classes, embrace an "examined life." Gradually these citizens will reform the existing institutions and build new ones aligned with their considered values, ensuring that future generations will grow up in a philosophically informed environment which they can, in turn, refine and reform. Through this cycle, an open-ended feedback loop is established, connecting philosophical education to evolving institutions in a free and pluralistic society.

Aristotle, in fact, envisaged something like that as the second-best option: "The best thing, then, is for there to be correct public concern with such things. But if they are neglected in the public sphere, it would seem appropriate for each person to help his own children and friends on the way to virtue." For those who value freedom more than Plato and Aristotle did, this option becomes the more attractive one. A public philosophy that calibrates the Socratic and Platonic approach in the way I suggest is our best shot to salvage "the morality of self-governance" and save us from hopelessness about our coarse and nasty society and prevent liberal democracies from turning into ships of fools.

Or am I deluding myself?

JUSTIN SMITH-RUIU

A Series of Small Apocalypses: On the Real Threats of AI

In the doldrums of last summer, I found myself swept up in a fleeting social-media frenzy. I had thought this could not happen to me again. I had myself written an entire book describing the mechanisms that cause such explosions of irrationality, and counseling readers on how to claw their way out of the naïve and gullible frame of mind that takes claims found on Twitter/X at face value. I had also closed my Twitter account upon concluding "research" for the book. But suddenly I found myself back there, almost unconsciously, disguised behind a new alias account.

The particular frenzy that sucked me in had to do not with artificial intelligence, though there was plenty of that swirling around too, but with the controversial reports of a new substance engineered by South Korean materials scientists, dubbed LK-99. This lab-generated polycrystalline compound was reported to exhibit at least some of the properties of a room-temperature, ambient-pressure superconductor. At present, our superconductors have to be maintained at temperatures and pressures so extreme as to require vast effort, energy, and thus money, to maintain them. But if LK-99 was what some had begun to believe it was, well, this would have been the beginning of a truly enormous technological revolution, with vast, almost unthinkable implications for the global economy and the organization of society. Some compared it to the discovery of the transistor, which inaugurated our current era of telecommunication. Others found even that comparison inadequate. One fellow took to Twitter to declare: "We have discovered fire all over again."

There was a fascinating scramble to replicate the sketchy results from South Korea, which seem to have been posted precipitously online after a dispute among the members of the lab. Many on social media observed that this was an exciting opportunity for the broader public to watch the scientific method in action. The scientific method, however, as it developed from Francis Bacon to the present day, does not include buzz, or upvoting, or virality, among its mechanisms for arriving at the truth. Yet in the LK-99 fever of the summer of 2023 one would have been hard-pressed to separate the wheat of the findings from the chaff of the buzz.

This became all too clear to me when Sinéad Griffin, a social-media-savvy physicist at the Lawrence Berkeley National Laboratory, ran a simulation proving at least that the Korean results were possible, and linked to her own results along with a GIF file showing Obama's mic drop at the White House

Correspondents' Dinner in 2016. Griffin's confidence radiated far, and many found themselves unable to resist it. Even as my own skepticism grew, I remained spellbound. Each night, for a week or so, I skimmed the latest LK-99 results before turning out the lights, closing my eyes, and entertaining visions of a near future of levitating skateboards, quantum computers, ultralight space-elevators to take us to our moon villas, and so much more.

But as an effort to clinch the legacy of presidential administrations and scientific discoveries alike, mic drops seldom age well. (We also saw Obama making the same gesture around the same time on *The Tonight Show Starring Jimmy Fallon*, upon declaring that Trump would never be president.) In both domains, people are always going to keep right on talking, and if they don't pick up the mic from the floor this will only be because they have brought their own. In general, we consider this sort of continuity to be vital for the health of both honest science and good democracy. In recent years, however, both science and politics have been warped, sometimes beyond recognition, by the sort of frenzy that we are considering, and of which room-temperature ambient-pressure superconductors, whether they exist or not, whether they can ever exist or not, are perhaps the clearest crystallization yet.

Yes, never-ending contestation is what makes science and politics both work as they should. But this new element — of never-ending posturing by leaders and experts, and of instantaneous camp-choosing and takesmanship by followers and would-be experts — has made it infuriatingly hard to take any reliable measure of where we are really at in the present, and so also of where we are headed.

After my comedown from those few days of LK-99 euphoria, the phenomenon I had just witnessed began to remind me of two others in our recent past, both of which are still sending out ripples in our public debates, and both of which also, perhaps significantly, got delivered to us in the form of acronyms: NFTs on the one hand, and AI on the other.

Now, when I place these together, I do not mean at all to suggest that the science of artificial intelligence is a silly fad, or an abstraction of late capitalism, or something whose future prospects depend on anything similar to what some laconic crypto-bro is willing to pay for a pixel-art image of a Bored Ape. What I mean is that claims of AI's revolutionary power, either to save our world or to destroy it, must be interpreted in the same way we interpret any other discursive artifact that comes down to us through the filter of the internet. As with effusions about the dawning utopia heralded by LK-99, so, too, warnings of the coming "AI apocalypse" can be assessed with accuracy only when we consider them within the broader context of twenty-first-century apocalypticism: the new habit of interpreting every development, bad or good, dystopian or utopian, as a sign of the end of the world as we know it.

It is hard not to hear the echoes in our present moment of a distant time, when European peasants saw great social transformation around them, along with great suffering, and simply could not conceive a future for humanity on the other side of these transformations. Under such conditions, apocalypse can become not just a prediction, but a fashion. When the rapper and Tamil activist Mathangi Arulpragasam, better known as M.I.A., went to visit Julian Assange in prison last year, the inmate asked her why she was dressed in shrouds the same dull grey-beige as the prison walls. Her response?

"I told him we are still going through the apocalypse, and he asked, why the walls haven't yet fallen, I said because everywhere is prison now." A strange thing to say to a man in actual prison: a bit like assuring a beggar, for whom you have no coins, that money is only a social construction.

Now M.I.A. is a pop artist and she is allowed, perhaps encouraged, to say silly things. But the fact remains that, while her casual claim of "apocalypse now" is one that we may dispute, it is nonetheless one that we can all make intuitive sense of today in a way that we could not have done, say, in 1993. Objectively speaking, the 1990s were a huge mess, too. No healthy society could be expected to endure such things as the Oklahoma City bombing, or the Waco hecatomb, or Jerry Springer. But, at least in my memory, that era didn't feel like a mess, and so we are left now to reckon with the brute social fact that something has shifted, something the young people might call a "vibe." Like it or not, apocalyptic talk makes sense now in a way it previously did not. We feel it.

What has changed, exactly? For one thing, the weather. Climate change is surely happening. Yet a record temperature shown on a color map will look a lot hotter if the color scheme starts with orange for the lows and moves up all the way through dark maroon and black for the highs, than if the lowest temperatures are indicated in green and the highest in a calmer shade of red. I cannot prove this, but it seems to me that our culture has in recent years come to prefer the darker shades. Perhaps the chief editors instruct their graphic designers to go for these grim hues, on the conviction that the alarm needs to be sounded. ("I want you to panic," Greta Thunberg said in 2019.) But the information would remain the same no matter the intensity of the colors. And *that* is a general lesson, I think, that we would do well to apply to any and all of the several current candidate horsemen of the purportedly imminent apocalypse.

I will steer clear, here, of any consideration of the threat of nuclear apocalypse. This seems different to me than climate change, or most pandemic scenarios, or indeed AI, as it would likely involve a singular all-or-nothing event, such that after it were to occur, there would be no M.I.A.s marching around claiming that it was still in the process of occurring, to the eye-rolls and consternation of many. I also find, in general, that this is a topic about which words fail me. To be compelled to live out our entire lives in the shadow of the ICBMs, the nuclear submarines lurking in the deep, is nothing less than unrelenting psychological terror, no different really from passing your entire life with a crazy man pointing a gun at your head. The threat of nuclear war alone is itself a grave and unfathomable crime. No matter what happens in the future, I often think, I, and you, and everyone else alive today, have been cheated of any hope of a moment of true peace in the unrelenting terror. If you think you are thriving under these conditions, it's because you have succeeded in not thinking about them.

But climate change does not seem to me to be like that.
It seems, rather, to portend at most an unending chain of mini-apocalypses — massive displacement of populations, drought, famine, fire; in short, nothing we haven't seen before, and nothing our eminently resilient species cannot handle. This is little comfort, of course, to those who imagine, like the medieval peasant who could not see beyond the end of the Black Death, that the end of our current economic and social order is the same as the end of the world. These words of comfort are a pep-talk given at the entry to a narrow bottleneck, and many will find this unbecoming. But we need to hear

it: climate change could very well change life as we know it, but it is not going to end life altogether. Nuclear proliferation really does make me panic, while climate change only raises my adrenaline somewhat, and inspires me to go on rooting for our almost unbelievably adaptable species, which has indeed been through some scrapes before — notably the Last Ice Age, which significantly cramped the motions and options open to *Homo sapiens* for around a hundred thousand years of our existence.

What about AI? It is curious to note that worries about its dangers have grown in fairly close synchronization with those about climate change, and indeed about nuclear proliferation. As with the climate, the earliest warnings went mostly unheard. Already in the early 1960s, Norbert Wiener articulated very clearly his fear that, once we have trained machines to do something so seemingly limited as to play checkers, there will be no telling whether it is on such narrow and anodyne tasks as this that the machines will continue to focus. Sooner or later, he warned, they will jump the fence, and start making decisions we should really be making ourselves — at least if we are attached to the survival of our species.

I have written previously, in these pages, about the role of "gamification" in the danger that Wiener identified. By the 1950s, computers were widely being used not only to play checkers, but also to run simulations of conflict-escalation scenarios in the stand-off between the superpowers. We human beings perceive a great difference between different kinds of games. The very concept of "game" is famously an extremely heterogenous umbrella term. It is "said in many ways," to speak with Aristotle, and none of us expects to find any essential unity across its sundry examples: peek-a-boo, poker, Twister, arm-wrestling, checkers, "wargames," and so on. A part of the difference among the different examples of games has to do with the gravity of the affair: tic-tac-toe is "fun," while calculating risk in nuclear-showdown scenarios requires an attitude of utter seriousness. But an appreciation of this difference is something we cannot even in principle transfer from the human mind, or perhaps the human gut, to the machines. Machines are very good at some things, but they are not good, and never will be good, at having fun, or at panicking, and this fundamental difference is the true source of the tremendous existential risk we are taking when we outsource fundamental decision-making responsibilities to automated systems.

It was not until the present century that AI catastrophism began to seep into the broader culture. Its first points of entry were, unsurprisingly, through the fervent chatter of online subcultures, most notably the community of "East Bay rationalists," clustered around the *LessWrong* website and led by the charismatic AI researcher and Harry Potter fan-fiction author Eliezer Yudkowsky. In 2010 a pseudonymous *LessWrong* commenter introduced a now-legendary thought experiment through the figure of a mythical creature that bore his own *nom de plume*. "Roko's basilisk," held by some to offer a contemporary spin on Pascal's wager, invites us to consider the future scenario in which an extremely powerful AI, which otherwise has only benevolence for humanity, discovers a rational incentive to punish all those who had recognized the possibility of such an AI prior to its existence but had failed to do everything they could to make this possibility actual. Soon other members of this community of self-styled rationalists, who seek rigorously to apply Bayesian epistemology to their daily decision-making habits in order to maximize happiness, began reporting nightmares and mental breakdowns. Yudkowsky ended up having to ban any mention of the dreaded creature.

Plainly, these lads had worked themselves into a frenzy that had little connection to the real threats that loomed on the horizon at the dawn of the 2010s. But we may at least thank them for articulating in its most outlandish form a concern that today seems perfectly warranted to anyone paying attention, to anyone not totally duped by the sleek and stylized version of our technological reality sold to us in iPhone advertisements: that our new technologies are hardly operating in the interest of human well-being.

This more mundane version of the problem loses the science-fiction element that seemed essential to getting people excited: the coming-to-life of a new form of consciousness, capable of malign intention and petty revenge, just like Frankenstein's monster, whose will to destroy his creator was ultimately a result of feeling spurned and unloved. In the mundane version, our technological creation has no "eureka" moment, it does not make any sudden qualitative leap from mere algorithmic switching to inward subjective experience. In this regard, it is kind of boring. But like the rare deadly animal whose fatal toxins are contained within a plain earth-colored body, its dullness is intrinsic to its danger. We keep waiting for a clear sign of a "eureka" moment in the development of artificial intelligence, as if by some tacit agreement that only when we finally see it will the real freak-out commence in earnest. But this hesitation in fact only helps to draw out the deeper problem. For whatever dangers AI really poses do not depend on the arrival of the moment of its conscious awakening, which is just science-fiction. The real danger is already very much part of our reality.

Here again we may turn to Norbert Wiener for clarity. Already in the first edition of his classic *Cybernetics*, published in 1948, the pioneering informatician insisted that the artificial feedback systems that he was attempting to describe were in no way some far-fetched vision of the future, but were in fact integrated into many Americans households in the form, for example, of the humble thermostat. Indeed, self-regulating furnaces were already a common instrument in the scientific revolution, and many early modern theorists noticed that these rather simple systems, in which a valve at the top opens up when the heat in the chamber passes a certain temperature, and then closes again when the heat has gone back down, have something in common with animals, who likewise "regulate" themselves by eating when they are hungry.

Cybernetics, though it never really matured as a science, was initially supposed to be the study of feedback in both living and artificial systems. For Wiener, modern technology does not mark a fundamental rupture with nature, but only a partial approximation of processes that we have always observed within nature. It is as if we keep waiting to be truly impressed by technology, even though the fundamental mechanisms that would be the basis of our impression already surround us. Heidegger would probably have something to say here, too, about the relationship between "ready-at-handness" and "everydayness," between the tools that are so familiar in their functions that we are able to take them for granted and the mundane conventions that we easily fall back into when we take a break from the hard work of thinking. But let's leave Heidegger out of it.

What I want to say about AI is but an echo of what Wiener

said about cybernetics: we are already surrounded by the very devices or systems that we keep expecting to appear on the horizon. And these devices and systems, like thermostats, are utterly mundane. A very simple algorithm, for example, triggers a motion-sensor that blocks the subway turnstile when it detects one mid-sized solid body immediately following another. I try to push through with my luggage rolling just in front of me, but I am not fast enough, and after the suitcase is past the sensor the rotating bars freeze to a sudden stop, and slam me in the groin. Some sort of occurrence as this happens almost every time I leave the house. Our built environment seems fundamentally hostile.

We are familiar with this observation from those urban architecture and city-planning specialists who bemoan the now omnipresent "anti-homeless spikes" placed on concrete surfaces where someone with nowhere else to go might otherwise have somewhat comfortably lain down. There is nothing algorithmic about a spike, of course; its effects in the world are not determined by a decision tree, but by the bare physical motion of a body that might come into contact with it. Yet we may agree that the anti-homeless spike and the automated turnstile are doing fundamentally the same thing: they are both the result of efforts to outsource the enforcement of human rules to artificial systems that cannot themselves understand the rules. And in turn it is not hard to see the continuity between the turnstile, with its simple yes-or-no circuit switching, and an analogous online mechanism intended to prevent fraud — say, a two-step security measure that sends a one-time code to your phone, but that times out before you are able to find the phone and type the sequence of digits. These are mundane annoyances; they are well-camouflaged within our everyday landscapes, within the roster of things we can "reasonably" be expected to put up with, and look nothing like the brightly colored fire-breathing basilisk of legend. Yet again we must heed Wiener's lesson, and not keep putting off the reckoning with our technological reality until some future time when its powers will make us gasp rather than simply groan.

Some of the new digital technologies that result from the outsourcing I have just described draw us more deeply and clearly into the reign of the non-human, perhaps the anti-human, which is of course the reign that is predicted by the singularitarians and other Silicon Valley visionaries and quacks who believe that we are on the verge of a great transition from principally biological evolution to principally technological evolution as the dominant force determining our planet's fate. For example — and again this will sound perfectly mundane — when I am asked as part of a security protocol to click on, say, the six out of nine images that include some fragmentary image of a boat or a staircase, this is both to prove that I am not myself a bot trying to enter into the system for nefarious purposes, and to train the AI responsible for security to get better at identifying images of boats and staircases, in order, presumably, to better prepare for fending off smarter bots in the future. One can't help but feel at such moments, as a human being, that one's centrality to the whole operation is diminishing rapidly, and that very soon it will make more sense simply to leave the bots to work it out among themselves.

"What am I doing here?" I find myself muttering, whenever I am asked to click on boats. This question works simultaneously at both the practical and the existential registers. It is a supremely mundane task, and life, such as it is, goes on after it is over and I have gained entry to the desired website. Yet it is also, perhaps, an early rumbling of an emerging order, a prodrome of the next great phase of planetary history, whose arrival was foreseen by Wiener and even by the lads at *LessWrong*, in which the presence of conscious human beings at some of the terminals of our global digital network will have been rendered otiose. At least for a time the human beings will still be able to join up with the network, to sit and stare at a screen and click on boats, but strictly speaking it will no longer be necessary. The worst-case scenario, of a basilisk-like consciousness that will emerge from the network and become determined to eliminate human beings, will not have to come about in order for this new phase of history to be a profoundly unpleasant one. It already is unpleasant. So much so that I often feel I want no more of it.

If I am expressing a weariness that was already familiar from the mid-twentieth-century philosophers of technology, among them Heidegger, who spoke of "alienation" from the mechanisms that are supposed to be making our lives better, rather than getting right to the point and addressing the unique risks and challenges posed by AI, this is intentional. For, again, it has come to seem to me that our recent worries about AI tend to combine two very different problems: the first one, the mundane alienation that I have described, which has already been flagged as a problem for well over a century, and the second one coming more from the domain of science-fiction and legend, which anticipates the imminent emergence of a new form of consciousness with incomprehensible and capricious desires.

This second part of the problem appears quite new, but in fact is also very old, indeed much older than the twentieth-century's discovery of technological alienation. One may cite, for example, the anxiety surrounding the alchemist

Roger Bacon's purported invention of a "Brazen Head" in thirteenth-century Oxford, which, like some medieval Siri, was said to be able to answer any "yes" or "no" question posed to it. The medievals understood that such an invention, and indeed the products of alchemy in general, tapped into dark forces that a certain variety of wisdom warns us away from probing, and in this respect were to be placed on a continuum with black magic, necromancy, and other things we know we ought not be doing. Obviously we do not have any recourse to any explicit notion of deviltry when we are frightened by the more audacious boundary-pushing impulses of technological innovation today, and so we are left with a mostly inarticulate anxiety, and with latter-day neo-Gnostic fantasies such as the one proposed by the shadowy Roko, which we are unable to recognize for what they are.

But could we really be on the verge of summoning a new sort of consciousness into being today, in contrast with the thirteenth century, in the large language models that have been trained up on trillions of data points fed to their artificial "neurons"? I am mostly agnostic about the prospects for machine consciousness, but this follows from the much more general fact that I am agnostic about the nature of consciousness in general. I have no idea what it is, honestly. I do agree with the Google engineer and AI expert Blaise Agüera y Arcas that "statistics do amount to understanding, in any falsifiable sense," and that in principle a system that works on statistical principles could be made to achieve general artificial intelligence, that is, something that looks exactly like human understanding — at least, again, in any falsifiable sense, which is to say, at least from an external third-person point of view. But I am not convinced that the third-person point of view on our own consciousness could ever exhaustively account for what consciousness is, as it continues to seem to be plausible to me that there will always be a remainder, namely, the irreducible primitive feeling of what it is like to be a conscious being.

The sloppier defenders of the singularity hypothesis tend to run intelligence and consciousness together, apparently hoping that skeptics will not pause to insist on making a conceptual distinction between the two. More rigorous materialist philosophers, notably Patricia Churchland, argue explicitly that this remainder which I have just evoked is only a lingering phantom of our pre-scientific folk beliefs, soon to go the way of "phlogiston and witches," to cite the common pairing beloved of philosophers of science. Agüera y Arcas, too, has made a strong case that consciousness just is a sort of high-level capacity for prediction, a very sophisticated form of autofill, that emerged over the course of primate evolution (perhaps also cetacean, canine, and a number of other distinct lineages) in view of the selective advantage of knowing what your mates, or your enemies, are thinking. In this respect, consciousness would be inherently a consciousness of other minds, and this is something that computer technologies, whose more prosaic commercial versions include tools like Google autofill, are getting very good at approximating.

I am aware that the kind of skepticism I am refusing to relinquish is itself ultimately unfalsifiable, and that in a strict sense it also extends to animal and even other human minds as well as to artificial systems with an air of intelligence about them. I cannot know that the machine is *really* thinking, but then again I cannot know that you are really thinking either. Yet it is necessary to hold onto this sort of skepticism, not just because it provides job security for philosophers, but also because science really does need supplementation by a reflection that cannot be subjected to its stringent and admittedly very productive method. What philosophy can tell you, for example, that science perhaps cannot, is that you are often unwittingly relying on metaphors when you think you are giving bare descriptions of fact. Overwhelmingly, in the cultural history of thinking about life and about the mind since the early post-war period, we have preferred to take recourse to information-processing models. Karl Popper famously proclaimed that "all life is problem-solving." And Norbert Wiener himself, with the new science of cybernetics, sought to show that living systems and artificial information-processing sometimes are fundamentally the same in their reliance on feedback looping. Fair enough; such assimilations have proven, again, remarkably productive.

But what if some other capacity were to be centered as most characteristic of what it is to live or to think? What if, for example, the information-processing metaphor for understanding the mind were traded out for some other capacity that in other settings has been seen as most characteristic of a thinking being — attention, for example? The capacity to attend, one might argue, is something that (unlike understanding in Agüera y Arcas's sense) cannot be treated statistically, or at least it is not obvious that it can be. And attention, unlike information-processing, also seems to have little to do with problem-solving. When you stare at a work of art for a long time, for the optimally powerful experience of it you would do best to come to it without any particular problems in mind, to empty yourself out, and to wait to see what the work has to offer you.

Go ahead. Do it. And then ask yourself again, while still high on the aesthetic sublime, whether life is really all problem-solving, and whether your own mind is really best understood as a central-processing unit.

My abiding awareness of the existence of a domain separate from information-processing, in which the human mind can continue to do its thing, will also help to explain in part what may come across as my extreme sanguinity in the face of yet another mini-apocalypse that AI is now often said to be bringing. I have in mind the danger that the latest AI chatbot tools are widely seen as representing for traditional humanistic education, particularly for the writing component of university courses in the humanities.

It is certain, of course, that things are going to have to change in response to our new information technologies. But that was already the case before the most recent frenzy of concern. Long before the most recent AI tools were available, student writing skills had already degenerated to a point where it made little sense to continue to ask them to compose well-researched and well-footnoted fifteen-to-twenty-page papers. For at least the past decade, what students have been turning in has relied heavily on internet-based prosthetics, not to mention autofill and spell-check and grammar-check tools that have largely absolved them of the need to master our shared written language. Well before the rise of GPT-4, there was already little awareness among the students, when asked to write something, that they were being asked to master a skill that is necessary for a well-rounded life. And perhaps they are right. The machines that can now simply write the papers for them, without all that time-consuming cutting-and-pasting, and grammar- and spell-checking, are really just sealing the deal, making it too obvious to deny any longer that we have moved into a very different epoch of the long history of literacy.

But this has happened before, and with enough distance the previous revolutions that seemed at first to destroy entire thought-worlds, entire "epistémès," always eventually come to be seen by all as great improvements. Thus the tremendous research of Frances Yates in the 1960s showed just what a rich world of learning was lost when the medieval "art of memory," a complex system of rote memorization of vast bodies of knowledge through the use of mnemonic devices, came to be displaced by books. Was this an improvement? Well, something was lost, surely, but something was certainly gained. What was previously stored in the human mind could now be stored on the shelf of the monastery library, in a volume that could be pulled down at any moment should one desire to do so. The internet revolution has simply been a further development of the Gutenberg revolution. I no longer need to go the library at all, if a sudden impulse awakens my curiosity about, say, Paleolithic cave art; I have at least a very good introduction to the topic, indeed more than I could ever read in my lifetime, right in my pocket.

This technological transfer, from a mental technê to an external storage device, relieves me and others of the need to cultivate any art such as was practiced by the medievals, and that is perhaps good for the "progress of knowledge" as a whole. It is bad, however, for self-cultivation. The students today have lost the rather more modest art of writing term-papers that was practiced as recently as twenty years ago, and at least for the moment are caught in an interregnum in which their elders are futilely telling them to keep doing things the old way while they, again with good reason, are increasingly having trouble understanding why they should do so.

But the more lucid among the elders might do well to seize this tremendous and rare opportunity, and to think hard about ways in which education in the twenty-first century could be brought to focus (again?) on self-cultivation, of the sort that once came with initiation into the art of memory, or that comes with learning a musical instrument or a martial art or stone-masonry, rather than on information. In other words, the AI revolution might afford us a perfect opportunity to stop treating human beings like information-processing systems, and to start treating them (again: again?) like human beings.

A delicious irony, that this precipitous rise of the machines might be what it finally takes to break us free of the machine metaphor of the human mind, and to open up the possibility for a vision of education based fundamentally on experience: something that we have no evidence that machines, for their part, are capable of having. We have no falsifiable evidence that human beings are capable of having it either, but humanistic education has always set out from the assumption that they do. In this era of STEM imperialism, when the methods and the requirements of the natural sciences increasingly dominate the humanities, and increasingly require of humanists that they justify their work in terms imposed on them by the STEM fields, we are indeed in a moment of severe crisis. But no crisis, short of total apocalypse, ever comes without a glimmer of hope.

There remains a question concerning the prospects, in our new technological landscape, of the more exalted forms of writing – of "real" writing, perhaps such as you are reading right now. Are we in the midst of a writing apocalypse? Here again, my answer is: a small one, perhaps. Much will change beyond recognition, but human beings will continue to express themselves.

I have recently taken to telling my students, to whom I,

stuck permanently in the ancien régime, continue to assign writing exercises, that they could likely, if they wish to be dishonest, get a better grade by farming out their work to GPT-4 than by doing it themselves. But I always add that this would amount to a shameful admission of defeat, and it is up to them to determine whether they wish to live with the shame. I also add that, for my part, as someone whose entire identity is wrapped up in writing, I remain completely certain that no machine can do what I do. There are just too many idiosyncrasies, too many quirks, too many untransferable kinks.

These might indeed amount, from an optimized AI's point of view, to "imperfections"; what I call my "style" might really only be the collection of old scars gathered over the course of my spotty education, lingering traces of all those generic rules that I failed to grasp. So be it. My own writing, in the era of ubiquitous machine writing, may finally be able to come forth as what it really is: the record of a singular and unreproducible inner experience, which again is something that machines do not have. So here again, ironically, the rise of AI, the emergence of a world in which machines can in some sense do everything humans do but "better," may afford us an opportunity to center, in our system of human values, that one thing that remains entirely off-limits to the machines, and to come to see writing not as a simple transfer of information, but as the witness and record of an inner life.

Of course, few of the most familiar outlets for human writing have understood our predicament and seized this opportunity. Most are going in an opposite direction. New media publications, from the lowbrow listicles of the unlamented *Buzzfeed* and the dumbed-down explanatory presentations of *Axios* to the highly formatted middlebrow TED-like "deep dives" of *Aeon*, are effectively constraining their writers to do their best to imitate AI, to strip away all their human idiosyncrasies and to transfer information to the reader with maximal clarity and minimal "noise." (There are also a few venues, such as Substack, where human writers can go and cultivate their style, indulge their idiosyncrasies, and sometimes even make some money while doing so.)

I suspect this regime cannot last. The house style that is imposed in such ventures as I have described is a style that can just as well be imitated by AI, and to compel human authors to sound like AI is really just to acknowledge that we are currently in a transitional phase, like the CVS or Duane Reade that continues, for now, to employ a lone human being to watch over all the self-checkout counters. I often wonder how that drugstore employee feels about her future prospects, and I wonder the same thing, too, about copy-editors. But again, here, I see a glimmer of hope. For once this regime collapses definitively, we may (again?) be in a position to appreciate the art of writing for what it really is: an *art*, and not an imitation of an art. As such, it positively requires, at its source, a faculty of freedom. This is something that is unlikely ever to emerge from an algorithmic engine.

KIT WILSON

Music in the Prison of History

On December 21, 1908, several hundred men and women gathered at the Bösendorfer-Saal in Vienna, settled into their seats, and bore unexpected witness to one of the great revolutions in musical history. Heading the program that night was a new work for string quartet and soprano by a controversial young composer named Arnold Schoenberg, already known in Viennese music circles for his challenging style: tense, drawn-out Wagnerian harmonies, allowed only the briefest and rarest moments of respite. And indeed, as the first three movements of his piece unfolded — Schoenberg straight away twisting the four lines of the quartet, cat's-cradle-like, into one splayed chord after another — the crowd could be heard growing increasingly restless. But none of this was, strictly speaking, out of the ordinary. Yet.

Then came the fourth, and final, movement. Suddenly, and seemingly without preparation, Schoenberg abandoned any sense of a home key, or resolution, at all — and unleashed on the unsuspecting audience eleven minutes of total, unforgiving dissonance. There had been near-precedents: flashes of atonality in Debussy, Scriabin, and Strauss. But Schoenberg's radicalism was of a different order. Unlike Debussy, he did not employ dissonance as a streaky, painterly effect. Unlike Strauss, his atonality did not just bubble up momentarily from otherwise conventional harmonic tensions, as though somebody had simply turned up the heat too high and accidentally caused simmering chords to spill over, for a second, into outright dissonance. No, Schoenberg used atonality, really for the first time in history, directly: as an all-encompassing, self-contained — and consciously abrasive — musical language of its own.

The audience was, predictably, stunned. Schoenberg would later reminisce, perhaps a little romantically, that the crowd began to "riot." The morning after the concert, one local paper ran the headline "Scandal in the Bösendorfer-Saal!" In another, the music critic called Schoenberg "tone-deaf." The *Neues Wiener Tagblatt* published their review in their "Crime" section. Some close to Schoenberg speculated that the fourth movement was simply a crazed musical response to an ongoing crisis in the composer's personal life. The previous summer, while writing the quartet, Schoenberg had discovered that his wife, Mathilde, was having an affair with their friend and neighbor, the painter Richard Gerstl. Richard and Mathilde eloped shortly after — but in October, following an intervention from Schoenberg's pupil Anton Webern, Mathilde agreed to return home. A few weeks later, Gerstl set fire to most of his paintings, stripped naked, and hanged himself in front of the mirror that he used for self-portraits. He was twenty-five years old. Schoenberg, contemplating his own suicide, drafted a will in which he wrote: "I deny facts. All of them, without exception. They have no value to me, for I elude them before they can pull me down. I deny the fact that my wife betrayed me. She did not betray me, for my imagination had already pictured everything that she has done." In the end, he did not follow Gerstl's example. The String Quartet No.2, which premiered forty-seven days after the painter's death, was dedicated "to my wife."

Others dismissed Schoenberg's experiments as an adolescent attempt to trash the past, in keeping with the radical mood of the decade. But the composer, an austere and academic man, and living an otherwise bourgeois lifestyle, always insisted that his use of atonality was a rational decision. It was simply a matter of taking the inevitable next step in the evolution of Western music. The conventions of tonality, he would argue a few years later in his theoretical treatise *Harmonielehre*, had been worn out over the course of the nineteenth century — and melody and rhythm now needed to be decanted into a fresher idiom to ensure their survival.

Whatever the ultimate explanation, what emerged from that night was a narrative that has stuck ever since: that tonality had come to its irreversible end, and that, for serious composers, there was now "no going back." Thanks in part to the painter Wassily Kandinsky — who, after hearing the quartet in 1911, made his own "break" with pictorial tradition, going fully abstract — and especially to the philosopher Theodor Adorno, who saw in Schoenberg's work the only truthful musical expression of the horrors of twentieth-century life, a connection was made, too, between atonality and the so-called "crisis of modernity." The death of traditional harmony, the death of representational art, the death of syntax, the death of God: all the deaths, it was assumed, were intrinsically linked.

It proved to be an intoxicating thesis. In the "high art" musical world, tonality became quickly associated with pastiche and compositional cowardice. And yet atonality, for all Schoenberg's predictions that it would one day come to sound to us as natural as Mozart or Bach, failed to mature into a lasting idiom of its own. The result has been a profound sense of frustration: a musical culture stuck between a forbidden past and an increasingly irrelevant future. As the composer György Ligeti wrote in 1993: "[One] cannot simply go back to tonality, it's not the way. We must find a way of neither going back nor continuing the avant-garde. I am in a prison: one wall is the avant-garde, the other wall is the past, and I want to escape." And all of this has fed into the favored grand narrative of our times: that we are culturally stuck, still unable to get our spinning wheels back out of the modernist ditch. Consider the cultural historian Jacques Barzun's book *From Dawn to Decadence*, which appeared in 2000, in which he partitions the last five centuries into two basic chunks: the years 1500 to 1900, during which the West blossomed, and the hundred or so years since, in which we have witnessed a "tailing off." Our society has become restless, Barzun writes, "for it sees no clear lines of advance." He continues: "The loss it faces is that of Possibility. The forms of art as of life seem exhausted, the stages of development have been run through."

As a story, this narrative undoubtedly has a certain allure. If, as seems to me true, we have still not fully recovered our philosophical balance since the blows landed on us by Nietzsche all those years ago, then it would follow, naturally, that other areas of our culture — music among them — would exhibit surface signs of that same spiritual concussion. And indeed, the evidence seems to tally. Can it really be a coincidence that, in the space of a couple of decades at the beginning of the twentieth century, tonal music, representational art, narrative fiction — indeed our very faith in language, in beauty, in truth — all seemed to collapse at once?

A coincidence, no. But neither were these crises, as many people still seem to believe, inevitable and irreversible, as though penciled into the almighty calendar of the universe for a set date and time — a point after which humanity was obliged, by some mysterious force, to abandon its cultural past and start all over again. Put like that, such an idea obviously sounds absurd. But the notion that "history" makes specific demands of us — that, like a stern parent or a jealous god, it will "judge us" harshly if we ignore them — runs much deeper in our cultural subconscious than we perhaps realize. Anyone who wants to understand Schoenberg should first ponder why we, ourselves, still, right now, cannot fully shake the unerving sense that he might have been right — that modernity really did spell the end of an artistic era, and that it would be wrong, a spiritual failing even, to "go back."

Rewind for a second, and replay the last few centuries on fast-forward. As a car runs on petrol, humans run on myth — on some kind of a story that gives their lives order and purpose. In the last few decades of the eighteenth century, conscious of the ongoing decline of traditional religion, humans began drilling into every other bit of their inherited conceptual landscape — science, philosophy, art — in search of some new dependable source of meaning. And they found a vast, and surprisingly potent, reservoir of spiritual fuel in, of all things, history. Give it its proper name: historicism. In the most basic telling, historicism is simply the belief that, like the laws of physics, there exist laws that dictate how history, too, will unfold. For nineteenth-century Europe, the task of discovering these historical laws, and then shaping our lives according to them — finding the inevitable stages that art is "meant" to pass through, for instance, and then doing one's best to bring them about — proved a remarkably rich and rewarding project. Under the influence, in particular, of Hegel — who argued, brilliantly if a little oddly to our ears today, that every single aspect of history could be understood as part of the universe's great teleological plan to become fully self-aware — historicist ideas spread rapidly into pretty much every aspect of intellectual culture.

True, the days of industrial-scale drilling for meaning — with Hegelian geysers spurting up all across Europe — are behind us. But historicism still bubbles up. Look at our language. We talk endlessly about "making history"; accuse each other of being on history's "wrong" side (or boast that we are on its "right" one); argue that our beliefs are "ahead of" — or "behind" — its curve. We view everything, natural or human, developmentally. The tyranny of history owes as much to Darwin as to Hegel (and then of course to Marx). History, and the particular histories which it contains, is confidently headed toward a goal, a telos. We repeat, almost ritually, Martin Luther King, Jr.'s dictum that "the arc of the moral universe is long, but it bends towards justice."

None of this is quite the same thing as a belief in full-on determinism. What really sets historicism apart — what made it, and continues to make it, so alluring — was, as the Polish philosopher Leszek Kołakowski once put it, that it turned history into something "real: not just something that once was, but a living being." History became, that is, an anthropomorphic figure. It wants to unfold in certain ways, and we feel a profound obligation to make sure that it does so. We gain a monumental, even quasi-religious, sense of purpose — but a monumental burden, too. How often do we hear, for instance, the complaint that "even in 2023" some people still hold certain views — not because these beliefs contravene permanent moral laws, but because they happen to have popped up at the wrong time, like a magician's assistant, struggling with a faulty trapdoor, emerging through the floor several moments too late? In 1936, Friedrich Meinecke called historicism "one of the greatest intellectual revolutions that has ever taken place in Western thought." The contemporary historian Thomas Albert Howard calls it the defining ideology of our age — a "post-theological worldview coeval with modernity." So entrenched is it in our way of thinking in fact, that we barely notice it. As Paul de Man once put it: "Whether we know it, or like it, or not, most of us are Hegelians.... Few thinkers have so many disciples who never read a word of their master's writings."

Certainly Schoenberg was animated by a profound sense of historical duty as he put the finishing touches to his quartet in that summer of 1908. And he was, himself, just one link in an already much older chain. Casting his gaze back over the nineteenth century, he would have seen generations of musicians, themselves influenced by emerging historicist ideas, increasingly troubled by — as they saw it — the coming end of traditional harmony. He would have seen the growing popularity of the Hegelian notion that the teleological endpoint of all art is complete abstraction. He would have seen impassioned claims about some great irreversible rupture from the past — and the birth of a uniquely modern age towards which artists had a new spiritual responsibility. All he — Schoenberg — really needed to do was to write down the notes.

In 1847, at the age of thirty-five, and at the height of his fame, Franz Liszt, the composer and virtuoso pianist, suddenly, abruptly, quit touring. For almost a decade before, the Hungarian master had been the nearest thing the nineteenth century had to a pop star. Women fainted at his concerts. They fought over his used handkerchiefs. Some brought phials into which to pour his old coffee dregs. One admirer even had a cigar stump that Liszt had discarded encased in a diamond-encrusted locket. It helped, of course, that Liszt had clenched-fist cheekbones, flowing hair, and a jaw that you could use to teach children about right-angles. It helped doubly that he was generally considered — as he still is, by many today — to be the greatest pianist ever to have lived.

All the more strange, then, that Liszt should not only withdraw from performing, but settle, of all places, in Weimar — a small, sleepy town in central Germany, which George Eliot, on a trip there only a few years later, would describe as a "dull, lifeless village." But Liszt had plans. Ostensibly there to take on a small (but handsomely paid) conducting role with the local orchestra, he was afforded enough time — finally — to think intently, and intensely, about a growing preoccupation of his: the future of music. That Liszt should be interested in the future was, of course, nothing unusual. The previous century had been marked not only by rapid social and technological change, but by a heightened sense, too, that such change was now predictable. Indeed, for many people, the apparent successes of democracy, capitalism, and the sciences — as well as emerging "social sciences" like economics — yielded confidence that the future was, really for the first time, something fully controllable. Now hurtling along at a thrilling speed, nineteenth-century Europeans began to reorientate themselves, switching from rear-facing to forward-facing seats.

Naturally, this led to an increased dynamism in the arts. But Liszt, as his lover Princess Sayn-Wittgenstein would later write, "hurled his lance much further into the future" than most. Already, behind the scenes, and rather in conflict with his reputation as a showy and shallow crowd-pleaser, Liszt had been working on some of the most harmonically experimental music ever produced. If you had broken into his study in, say, 1842, you would have probably found, on his desk, a pile of radical sketches for piano, each only a bar or two long, testing out wild, chromatic flourishes and cascading stacks of clashing chords. None of these early snippets was ever performed in public. But as steps in the evolution of Liszt's compositional psyche — and in the development, therefore, of nineteenth-century music more widely — there is a good case to be made that they count among the most consequential bits of music ever written. The key to understanding why, though, is in the strange title that Liszt gave to each one: Prélude Omnitonique.

A decade earlier, in 1832, a twenty-one-year-old Liszt had attended a series of lectures given by the Belgian musicologist François-Joseph Fétis. Fétis had been working on an elaborate theory about the predetermined teleological evolution, and therefore the inevitable destiny, of music — based, at that point, on a relatively new idea: "tonality." Even today, tonality is a slippery concept: Patrick McCreless, a professor of music theory at Yale, claimed recently not to have the first clue what the word really meant. To paint the matter in primary colors, tonality simply refers to the set of implicit harmonic rules, seemingly intuitive to us all, by which almost all music, in the West at least, has abided for the last five hundred years. Why do certain combinations of notes sound pleasant and others intolerable? Why do some chords sound awkward and restless, while others seem perfectly happy where they are? We might never fully know the answer, but — in just the same way we call that mysterious force by which physical objects are drawn to each other "gravity" — we can at least give the phenomenon a name: tonality.

All of this was already tacitly understood. But like his good friend Alexandre-Étienne Choron — who had first coined the term "tonality" in 1810 — Fétis wanted to step back and analyze the concept as a whole, from all sides. He had noticed — who hadn't? — that the history of music was a story of ever-growing harmonic complexity, from the single-line simplicity of medieval plainchant to the constant key-hopping and deliberate dissonances of Beethoven. And, spotting a link with the voguish Hegelianism of his time, he posited that this was not, as many had previously assumed, because we were discovering ever-more intricate connections between the natural mathematical laws underpinning music, but because human consciousness itself was evolving, and demanding of music, as it were, ever-greater levels of harmonic excitement. Tonality, in other words, was not something coded into the laws of nature, but a kind of mental ability — which, like every other aspect of human thought, was developing teleologically over time.

Contemporary composers, ostensibly still writing in one particular home key, were now regularly borrowing notes and chords from others, yielding, at least for adventurous listeners, the exhilarating sense of being constantly upended. But Fétis predicted this process would soon reach its inevitable "endpoint": music of the future, shaped by our increasingly "insatiable desire for modulation," would flit so frequently between theoretically unrelated harmonies that the effect would be like being in all possible keys at once. Fétis — and here he split from traditional Hegelian optimism — found the idea profoundly troubling: this coming *ordre omnitonique* would, he argued, spell the ultimate end of all musical meaning. After all, when a painter mixes together all possible colors at once, she ends up with only a dull, lifeless black.

The young Liszt, though, was transfixed. He struck up a correspondence with Fétis, and began — not entirely to the theorist's liking — attempting to put some of his harmonic predictions into practice. What, Liszt wanted to find out, would full omnitonality sound like? How would it work? Of the *Prélude Omnitonique* sketches that survive from those early trial runs, perhaps the most tantalizing consists of a quick waterfall of notes from the high end of the piano to the low, riffling, seemingly quite deliberately, through every single one of the twelve possible notes of the chromatic scale before repeating any a second time — an uncanny premonition of Schoenberg's twelve-note tone-rows, employed seventy years later to obliterate all sense of tonal hierarchy.

It would be several decades before Liszt himself incorporated anything nearly as radical into his published compositions. But he arrived at Weimar with a deep desire to decode the secrets of music's future. Over the next few decades, along with a small group of fellow musicians, among them Richard Wagner and Peter Cornelius, known collectively as the New German School, Liszt would transform Weimar into a hub of musical progressivism — or, in the words of the composer

Humphrey Searle, "the Mecca of the avant-garde movement." The informal catchphrase of the group was, fittingly, *la musique de l'avenir*, "the music of the future."

It helped hugely that Liszt had the support, and admiration, of perhaps the most influential musicologist of the time, Franz Brendel — the longstanding editor of the journal *Neue Zeitschrift für Musik*. Brendel was as Hegelian as Hegelians come, convinced that the history of music was a tale of ongoing, step-by-step, teleological emancipation. Renaissance music had freed itself from the church and become fully secular. Secular music had freed itself from words and become fully instrumental. Instrumental music was now loosening itself from its obligation to audiences, and becoming, in true Hegelian spirit, concerned only with its own internal laws — in short, those of tonality. Brendel outlined all of this in his monumental history of music published in 1852, which functioned as a kind of Hegelian heart, pumping historicism out into every last capillary of European musical culture. As the great music historian Richard Taruskin put it: "Ever since the appearance of Brendel's *History*, historicism has been a force not only in the historiography of music but in its actual history as well.... Ever since the middle of the nineteenth century, in other words, the idea that one is morally bound to serve the impersonal aims of history has been one of the most powerful motivating forces, and one of the most exigent criteria of value, in the history of music."

Discussions about the fate of tonality in particular began poking up everywhere like flower shoots in spring. Brendel, to celebrate the fiftieth issue of the *Neue Zeitschrift für Musik* in 1859, ran a contest in which music theorists were asked to predict the future of harmony on the basis of currently discoverable laws. Liszt began penning a theoretical treatise, *Sketches for a Harmony of the Future*, which has unfortunately been lost. Elsewhere, in a letter, admittedly a little tongue-in-cheek, he wrote about not only embracing omnitonality, but also going a step further and splitting the distance between all consecutive notes on the piano in two, thus creating a scale of twenty-four quarter-tones. (The avant-garde composer Ferruccio Busoni would later, in the twentieth century, do exactly this.) Liszt concluded with an ironic quip: "Behold the abyss of progress into which the abominable Musicians of the Future are hurling us!"

Perhaps because Liszt was still keeping his most radical compositional ideas under wraps, the focal point of the discussions turned to his friend Wagner, whose strained harmonies were seen as leading, as the French composer Louis Pagnerre put it, to "the almost complete annihilation of tonality." The composer Karl Mayrberger summed things up in a rather more measured tone:

> The harmonic language of the present day is on a footing essentially different from that of the past. Richard Wagner has pointed the musical world along the path that it must henceforth travel. The sixteenth century knew only the realm of the diatonic. In the eighteenth century, the diatonic and the chromatic existed side by side, equal in status.... But with Richard Wagner an altogether new era begins: major and minor intermingle, and the realm of the diatonic gives way to that of the chromatic and the enharmonic.

Still, in the last five years of his life, Liszt would again move ahead of Wagner in the race for the musical future, publishing several works that harked back to his early omnitonal experiments. In quick succession came *Nuages gris*, in 1881, and *La lugubre gondola*, in 1882 — both dark, proto-impressionistic works, later celebrated by Debussy and Stravinsky alike, in which Liszt, rather than telling a story, paints something more like a static mood, with slow-motion splashes of notes up and down the piano. Then came the aptly titled *Bagatelle sans tonalite*, in 1885, a playful dance-like piece in which the pianist's hands scuttle across the keys like drugged-up spiders. There are melodic fragments, but they sound more like childlike parodies of tunes — and none settles for long enough to establish any sense of a home key.

Liszt knew that these pieces were radical, and warned his younger piano students against performing them. But one day, he believed, they would be understood. He wrote to Princess Sayn-Wittgenstein: "The time will yet come when my works are appreciated. True, it will be late for me because then I shall no longer be with you." In both senses, he was right. Liszt died in 1886, at the age of seventy-four. But as the composer Béla Bartók put it, several decades later,

> Liszt's works had a more fertilizing influence on the following generations than Wagner's. Let no one be misled by the host of Wagner's imitators. Wagner solved his whole problem, and every detail of it, so perfectly that only a servile imitation of him was possible for his successors.... Liszt, on the other hand, touched upon so many new possibilities in his works, without being able to exhaust them utterly that he provided an incomparably greater stimulus.

In 1867, Philip Gilbert Hamerton, an English printmaker and critic living in France, noticed something strange going on in Parisian art circles. Painters, he wrote, were "beginning to express contempt for all art which in any way depends on the interest of the subject." Increasingly, they seemed concerned only with abstract shape and form:

> Painting, like journalism, should in their view offer nothing but its own merchandise. And the especial merchandise of painting they hold to be the visible melodies and harmonies — a kind of visible music — meaning as much and narrating as much as the music which is heard in the ears and nothing whatever more... when they paint a woman they do not take the slightest interest in her personally, she is merely, for them, a certain beautiful and fortunate arrangement of forms, an impersonal harmony and melody, melody in harmony, seen instead of being heard. It may seem impossible to many readers that men should ever arrive at such a state of mind as this and come to live in the innermost sanctuary of artistic abstraction, seeing the outer world merely as a vision of shapes; but there is no exaggeration in the preceding sentences, they are simply true, and true of men now living.

Hamerton turned out to be extraordinarily prescient. Over the next few decades, artists would become increasingly obsessed with the purely formal or aesthetic aspects of painting — flattening their images as though with a steak press, carving the world into two-dimensional shapes with hard outlines, and eventually eliminating any sense of a depicted subject at all. And they would indeed look to music as their model. Titles like "Nocturnes" and "Symphonies" became commonplace.

Cézanne talked about color "modulating." Matisse explained that "colors are forces, as in music." Henri Rovel claimed, simply, that "the laws of harmony in painting and in music are the same." And it wasn't just painters. Poets, too, seemed less and less interested in subject matter, and more and more preoccupied with the abstract sounds of speech. Verlaine urged "*de la musique avant toute chose,*" "music above all else." One critic, lamenting the state of late nineteenth-century poetry, remarked: "It is music and picture, and nothing more."

Where was this strange mass movement coming from? Cue a bang, a puff of smoke, and Hegel emerging from a time machine with a self-satisfied expression on his face. All of this, he would say, surveying the world a half-century or so after his death, was exactly as predicted.

Well, sort of. Hegel had always contended that art was a manifestation of the universe's ongoing journey towards complete self-awareness. For painting, that meant moving away from illusionistically, as if through a window, "representing" external subjects in space — a vase of flowers, a muddy battlefield, a ballroom dance — and instead reflecting on, and drawing greater attention to, itself: the flatness of the canvas, the texture of the paint, the repetition of certain shapes, the unconventional selection of colors. Poetry, too, would become increasingly about poetry, and music increasingly about music. Indeed, Hegel believed, pure and non-programmatic music already represented a kind of ideal: "Music has the maximum possibility of freeing itself from any actual text as well as from the expression of any specific subject-matter, with a view to finding satisfaction solely in a self-enclosed series of the conjunctions, changes, oppositions, and modulations falling within the purely musical sphere of sounds."

No wonder the other arts would look to music as a model

of formal purity. Eventually, in Hegel's account, the arts would go one collective step further, inviting reflection not just on the unique qualities of each medium, but on the philosophical nature of art itself. The abstract, that is, would give way to the conceptual, and merge with theory once and for all. It was a chillingly prophetic narrative, at least in the hands of a twentieth-century critic such as Clement Greenberg, who adapted it, retrospectively, to explain the journey from representation, via "flatness" and abstraction, to fully conceptual art. In truth, Hegel himself never spelled out in concrete terms what artworks of the future would look like, and it is hard to know whether Degas, Delaunay, and Duchamp are what he had in mind. His more rudimentary claim — that art would become increasingly interested in its own formal properties — can be just as well explained by the emergence of photography, which forced painters to reflect about what advantages the canvas offered over the darkroom.

It certainly helped Hegel's reputation that his ideas were adopted by several generations of art theorists — such that, by the end of the nineteenth century, a genuine feedback loop had formed: artists went increasingly "abstract," largely for non-theoretical reasons; theorists then interpreted this abstraction in Hegelian terms; and artists duly adopted the new rationale, with the bonus sense of historical significance it gave them. In 1873, for example, the highly influential aesthete and art critic (and Hegelian) Walter Pater observed that "all art constantly aspires towards the condition of music." The German art historian Wilhelm Worringer, a few decades later, would popularize the idea of the "urge to abstraction." Artists lapped it up. But the idea that music represents a model of aesthetic purity was, in fact, nothing new. Michelangelo, for instance, had written, in a critique of Flemish painters:

> They paint stuffs and masonry, the green grass of the fields, the shadow of trees, and rivers and bridges, which they call landscapes... And all this, though it pleases some persons, is done without reason or art, without symmetry or proportion, without skillful selection or boldness, and, finally, without substance or vigor... for good painting is nothing but a copy of the perfections of God and a recollection of his painting; it is a music and a melody which only intellect can understand, and that with great difficulty.

All Hegel really did was add a twist of teleology — the mildly more exciting plot line of a journey from realism towards abstraction — thus giving an age-old idea a second lease on life. It is a measure of his influence that Liszt, Wagner, and Brendel's great nemesis, the Austrian critic and philosopher of art Eduard Hanslick, spent years attacking the New German School's progressive Hegelianism on equally Hegelian, but slightly more conservative, grounds. Hanslick was a purist. Music, he believed, ought to be entirely non-representational, concerned only with the aural architecture of the notes themselves. He despised Wagner's attempts to combine music with other art forms — to create the fabled, all-encompassing *Gesamtkunstwerk* or "total artwork" — and Liszt's use of extended program notes.

The gap between Hanslick and the New German School only appeared great because they were staring at each other from opposite points on the same Hegelian spiral. After all, it was the progressive Brendel who had already waxed in quasi-mythological terms about the emancipation of "pure" music from words and religion — he just happened to recognize in Wagner's *Gesamtkunstwerk* the prospect of another synthesis, the creation of a new art form that might itself be further purified down the line. The conservative Hanslick, meanwhile, held that pure, non-programmatic music was already the perfect aesthetic endpoint. Ironically, it was Hanslick's pivotal book, *On the Musically Beautiful*, in 1854, that ended up becoming a kind of Bible for formalism in the arts. The abstract painter František Kupka cited it fifty years later as one of his great influences.

But what if there were a way for pure music itself to become even more "abstract" than it already was? What if tonality, say, were the musical equivalent of a "subject" — an external point of reference, a catalog of well-known storylines that had been passed down from generation to generation, ultimately distracting listeners from the pure sounds, gestures, and rhythms that really constituted music? Certainly Debussy seemed to be arguing this when he wrote:

> I am more and more convinced that music, by its very nature, is something that cannot be cast into a traditional and fixed form. It is made up of colors and rhythms. The rest is a lot of humbug invented by frigid imbeciles riding on the backs of the Masters — who, for the most part, wrote almost nothing but period music.

Schoenberg echoed this a couple of decades later, in a letter to Kandinsky: "One must express oneself! Express oneself directly! Not one's taste, or one's upbringing, or one's intelligence, knowledge or skill." And of course, as the twentieth century wore on, the notion developed that composers should even abandon sound itself — music, in the hands of John Cage, dissolved into pure spirit.

“Of great painting or great music there can no longer be, for Western people, any question.” So wrote the German polymath Oswald Spengler, in his magnum opus *The Decline of the West*, in 1918. Spengler was not a cheery fellow and neither was his thought. His father, a dissatisfied civil servant, had discouraged the young Spengler from pursuing his literary interests as a child, leading to a lifelong sense of his being misunderstood. He would suffer, in adulthood, from severe insomnia and debilitating migraines — extreme enough to give him regular bouts of memory loss. He was a recluse, and never married. And yet his profound pessimism about the fate of Western art was not — at least not entirely — projected gloominess.

Spengler’s great thesis was that all cultures were, in his word, “organisms” — and that the religion, art, philosophy, and science of each one had more in common “physiognomically” than, say, the paintings or poetry of two unrelated societies or ages. Indeed, Spengler contended that no such thing as “painting,” “music,” or even “maths,” really existed — certainly not as a single “entity” that you could compare across different eras or places. The criteria for producing and judging “art” (or anything else) were restricted to each particular cultural epoch:

> One day the last portrait of Rembrandt and the last bar of Mozart will have ceased to be — though possibly a colored canvas and a sheet of notes may remain — because the last eye and the last ear accessible to their message will have gone. Every thought, faith and science dies as soon as the spirits in whose worlds their “eternal truths” were true and necessary are extinguished.

Spengler believed that our own culture was in rapid decline and could no longer produce anything of artistic merit. But this was not because, by some permanent and universal set of aesthetic standards, we were not up to it anymore, but because the very standards themselves, as part of the dying organism, no longer had the authority to "dictate" whether art was good or bad. If someone were to create a work of art that, in a previous era, would have been considered aesthetically great, Spengler argued it would now be meaningless. "What is practiced as art today — be it music after Wagner or painting after Cézanne, Leibl and Menzel — is impotence and falsehood," he wrote.

One of Spengler's biggest — and looking back, most surprising — followers, Ludwig Wittgenstein, echoed this in a personal note, in 1948:

> If it is true, as I believe, that Mahler's music is worthless, then the question is what I think he should have done with his talent. For quite obviously it took a set of very rare talents to produce this bad music. Should he, say, have written his symphonies and burnt them?

Wittgenstein denounced Mahler for trying to speak, stylistically, to a bygone era. And yet the alternative, he conceded, was little better: contemporary music that attempted to reflect authentically the present moment was condemned only to articulate the "absurd" and "stupid" axioms of its time. A familiar refrain emerges: artists must be true to their times, but modernity, as an epoch markedly different from everything that came before, seems to offer us no meaningful way of doing so.

If Spengler's ideas were to do one of those spit-in-a-tube genealogy tests, the results would show a big flush of ancestry coming from Germany of the late eighteenth century. Hegel, as we know, saw artworks as momentary snapshots of the evolving spirit of the universe, and thus believed that artists were answerable not to timeless truths but to the specific demands of each age (or the *Zeitgeist*). But like many of his peers, Hegel also worried that the unique conditions of his own time — namely, rapid disenchantment — were making art increasingly impotent. It "is certainly the case," he wrote, "that art no longer affords that satisfaction of spiritual needs which earlier ages and nations sought in it, and found in it alone." His intellectual sparring partner, Friedrich Schlegel, lamented in 1800 that "modern poetry's inferiority to classical poetry can be summed up in the words: we have no mythology...." The same year, the philosopher Friedrich Schelling wrote mournfully about a lost golden age of art "before the occurrence of a breach that now seems beyond repair."

There was one crucial difference, though. What stopped Hegel and his contemporaries from lapsing into full-on Spenglerian nihilism was the sense, still widespread at that time, of fundamental teleological optimism — the implicit belief that these crises (even the "death of God," which Hegel had announced in 1802, almost a century before Nietzsche) were sent our way for some greater purpose. Hegel was especially taken with the Biblical image of The Fall — "the eternal Mythus of Man; in fact, the very transition by which he becomes man" — which he believed to be a kind of historical stencil, appearing again and again, each time carrying us one stage closer to full self-awareness. This basic template — crisis followed by a return at some "higher point" on the upward helix of historical progress — became so common in late-eighteenth-century literature that it gained a nickname: the "Romantic Spiral."

But over the course of the nineteenth century, such teleological optimism steadily disappeared. Thanks in part to Schopenhauer's melancholy philosophy, and especially to the rise of Darwinism and subsequent fears of "degeneration," the Romantic Spiral was knotted into a closed loop, and any excess string that might have led to a happier ending was snipped off. History, as Spengler later put it, was no longer seen as a story of linear progress — a "tapeworm industriously adding on to itself one epoch after another" — but as a series of self-contained epochs, each following the same fixed lifecycle: birth, growth, decline, and death.

Hope having evaporated, there remained in the dregs, though, two key elements of "cultural modernity." First, the sense that we now found ourselves irreversibly on the other side of a terrifying historical threshold. "The complete negation in the state, church, art, and life, that occurred at the end of the last century," the historian Jacob Burckhardt wrote midway through the century, "has unleashed... such an enormous measure of objective consciousness that a restoration of the old level of immaturity is quite unthinkable." And second, the residual conviction among artists that this "modern" epoch presented them with an entirely new set of spiritual demands. (In Rimbaud's words, "*il faut être absolument moderne*.")

Schoenberg, like Spengler and Wittgenstein, inherited this psychological burden, and felt it deeply. Unlike them, however, he despised defeatism. In 1923, he wrote an article castigating Spengler for his pessimism and lack of ambition. What Spengler failed to see, he argued, was that a truly brilliant figure, a real genius, might yet still rescue the West — like a superhero flinging his arm over the cliff edge at the last-minute to grab the falling heroine — and single-handedly return it, once more, to artistic greatness.

When intellectual revolutions happen, it is rarely because everyone has sat down, considered a manifesto line by line, agreed that it improves upon the currently accepted account of reality, and then employed it consciously in their day-to-day lives. On the contrary, ideas — big ones, at least — are like islands of chalk in a river, little bits crumbling off all the time, swept along in the cloudy water, until, at various kinks down the way, piles of sediment build up anew. For nineteenth-century historicism, a great bend in the stream appeared around 1910, and the ideas of the previous hundred or so years began slopping up, wave after wave, on the bank. Schoenberg scooped up the broken-off notion of a predetermined destiny for tonality; of art's yearning to abandon all representation; of a new, terrifying — but also, for the truly heroic, liberating — historical epoch; and created his own strange amalgam of them all.

In his subsequent attempts to ghostwrite modernity's memoirs, Schoenberg had collaborators, each retelling the same myth with slightly different inflections. His friend and artistic soulmate Kandinsky emphasized, for his part, Hegelian ideas about abstraction, music, and purity:

> And so at different points along the road are the different arts, saying what they are best able to say and in the language which is peculiarly their own. Despite, or perhaps thanks to, the differences between them, there has never been a time when the arts approached each other more nearly than they do today, in this later stage of spiritual development.
>
> In each manifestation is the seed of a striving towards the abstract, the non-material. Consciously or uncon-

> sciously they are obeying Socrates' command — Know Thyself....
>
> And the natural result of this striving is that the various arts are drawing together. They are finding in music the best teacher. With few exceptions music has been for some centuries the art which has devoted itself not to the reproduction of natural phenomenon but rather to the expression of the artist's soul, in musical sound.... Every man who steeps himself in the spiritual possibilities of his art is a valuable helper in the building of the spiritual pyramid, which will some day reach to heaven.

Schoenberg's student, Anton Webern, brought out the more rebellious side of the project. "We broke its neck!" he said of tonality. The miserable philosopher Theodor Adorno, an earnest student of both Hegel and Spengler, focused on the consequences of "psychological differentiation" between epochs. Modern consciousness, he wrote, "now debars the means of tonality, which is to say, the whole of traditional music. Not only are these sounds obsolete and unfashionable. They are false. They no longer fulfill their function." Generations of composers added a line, like visitors scribbling in a guestbook at a hotel. The modernist Pierre Boulez proclaimed: "The tonal system has gone through a kind of historical evolution, and you cannot go back. That's impossible." The less modernist Alfred Schnittke lamented: "Earlier music was a beautiful way of writing that has disappeared and will never come back; and in that sense it has a tragic feeling for me." Those who deviated — like Constant Lambert, who in 1934 declared Sibelius the defining composer of his age — had their entries torn out.

Contributing a kind of ideological backing track the whole time was what Ernst Gombrich once called "Hegelianism without metaphysics" — the entrenched belief, among cultural historians, that great art is always a kind of encrypted signal of its time. This entered the game as early as 1843, when the Hegelian critic Carl Schnasse wrote: "The genius of mankind expresses itself more completely and more characteristically in art than in religion.... Thus the art of every period is both the most complete and the most reliable expression of the... spirit in question." Echoes of this idea have sounded every decade since. To give just one more example, the Swiss art historian Heinrich Wölfflin declared, in 1888: "To explain a style cannot mean anything but to fit its expressive character into the general history of the period, to prove that its forms do not say anything in their language that is not also said by the other organs of the age." The result, today, is that we filter out any artists or movements that fail to fit the story that we wish to tell about the "modern" spirit: namely, that it is austere, self-critical, skeptical about beauty, and hostile to tradition.

But the modernist line was, ultimately, a lie. Tonality never "died." Nor have we been "stuck" since. If you were to whizz Liszt to the present, he would be stunned by the range of music written since his death — just think of Stravinsky, Sibelius, Britten, Messiaen, Reich, Ligeti; the whole jazz tradition from King Oliver to Ornette Coleman (and beyond); the Beatles and the Beach Boys; funk, disco, hip-hop, metal, electronica, and, for those who go looking, a million and one other strange stylistic hybrids. The last hundred or so years have been perhaps the most innovative in musical history.

Fétis was not wrong, of course, that something in the intrinsic grammatical rules of tonality allows us to predict what happens when you crank up the harmonic complexity knob. But we knew that. In 1785, in the opening bars of his so-called "Dissonance Quartet," Mozart had experimented, in the words of one contemporary critic, with deliberately over-seasoning his harmonies, yielding a musical dish that could easily have been prepared by Schumann or Mendelssohn fifty years later. The tortured Renaissance composer Carlo Gesualdo (1566–1613) toyed with chromatic harmonies that today sound like a retrospective echo of Wagner. The skittish Fugue No. 12 by Anton Reicha (1770–1836), a Czech composer and a friend of Beethoven, could easily be mistaken for one of Conlon Nancarrow's pointillistic pieces for player piano a century and a half later. Assuming you use a similar complexity setting, tonality seems to produce surprisingly consistent results across time. None of this means that it is somehow predetermined to "end up" in one or other particular place. Nor does it suggest that one could ever fully "exhaust" it: tonality appears to be almost as boundless and malleable as the great primitive syntactic superstructure that underlies our natural languages.

The funny thing, looking back, is that the first few decades of the twentieth century were ostensibly a time of great cultural despair. Belief in Hegel's actual "optimistic" philosophy had long waned, replaced by various iterations of post-Kantian skepticism and a widespread sense that nothing could anymore be trusted. Indeed, Adrian Leverkühn, the austere composer in Thomas Mann's novel *Doctor Faustus*, was based on an imagined hybrid of Schoenberg and Nietzsche — his purported motive for abandoning tonality being a kind of tit-for-tat rejection of beauty as payback for the loss of faith in truth. And yet neither Schoenberg, Kandinsky, Adorno, nor any of the others, were nihilists in the true sense of the word. They believed profoundly, to the point of near-insanity, that what they were doing mattered. Therein lies the tremendous appeal of historicism — the promise, that, somehow, thanks to the benevolent protecting hand of history, the great wave of philosophical acid sloshing over every last belief of ours nonetheless leaves the things that matter unscathed. Indeed, standing there stoically, and watching everything else disintegrate around us, they matter even more.

It is this that we still cannot quite let go of. But we must. Art should not be boxed in by imaginary historical thresholds, like a slapstick artist slamming into an invisible wall. Stasis in one area of culture need not spell stagnation elsewhere. Nor, indeed, should we distract ourselves from the genuine philosophical predicaments we face as a culture with vapid pleasantries about being "on the right side" of history. To somewhat out-Schoenberg Schoenberg, historicism, the willingness to give history the last word, was a cop-out — a crutch in a moment of crisis. "Comfort, with all its implications," he wrote in the *Harmonielehre*, "intrudes even into the world of ideas and makes us far more content than we should ever be." Indeed. What would art, philosophy, literature look like if we abandoned historicism — if we abandoned the concept of cultural modernity itself? We should permit ourselves to find out. After all, history may judge historicism very badly.

BENJAMIN BALINT

Ilse Aichinger's Bad Words

"It's a sad poem," Bettina said as we walked down the glistening wet ribbon of a Vienna street one rainy evening. "I don't read it every day." Bettina, a Viennese psychoanalyst, was describing the daily walk from her home in Leopoldstadt, in the Second District, to her office in the inner city, the First District. The journey takes her across a bridge over the Danube canal which bears a poem by Ilse Aichinger inscribed in cast iron along the span. The poem reads, in part:

> The world is made of stuff
> that wants watching,

no eyes left
to see the white fields,
no ears to hear birds whirring
in the branches.
Grandma, where are the lips you need
to taste the grasses,
and who will sniff the sky till it's done?

When the German language billowed with Nazi contaminations, said George Steiner, it got "the habit of hell into its syntax." Those who repaired that syntax and got it whirring again, those who after the Shoah expressed estrangement from the German language in German, were by and large "non-German Germans": Paul Celan in Paris, Nelly Sachs in Stockholm, Elias Canetti and Erich Fried in London, and Ilse Aichinger in Vienna.

Unlike German writers who found in the German language an inalienable form of belonging, each of these writers grappled with a language that had become foreign, hostile, a sign of non-belonging. Each of these adversaries of postwar forgetting wrestled with a language, as Celan put it, that "gave back no words for that which happened." Of these figures, Ilse Aichinger, with whom the story of postwar Austrian literature begins, has been until recently the most overlooked and undertranslated. Since her death in 2016, a spate of new English translations affords us an opportunity to correct this literary injustice, to take some soundings from the still-potent body of work that Aichinger bequeathed us.

Ilse and Helga Aichinger, identical twin sisters, were born in Vienna in 1921. Their mother, a Jewish pediatrician and one of the first women to study medicine in Vienna, and her father, a Catholic schoolteacher, were "opposites in race and character," Ilse said. They divorced when the twins were six years old. "A threefold suffering dominates my life," Ilse recalled. "The antagonism between my parents, the antagonism within me, the antagonism to my surroundings." Only "the powers of childhood held the world together." Ilse and Helga were raised in Vienna by their grandmother, "the dearest person in the world to me." One spring day in 1933, a twenty-two-year-old Bavarian medical student spending the semester in Vienna appeared at their door and politely introduced himself as someone with a professional interest in twins. "My name is Josef Mengele," he said. They shooed him away and never saw him again.

Long before the Anschluss, Hitler's annexation of Austria in March 1938, Vienna had suffered from virulent and politically successful anti-Semitism. But the Anschluss unleashed a pent-up brutality that amazed even the Germans. The German playwright Carl Zuckmayer described Vienna during the following days as a once-cultured city transmuted "into a nightmare painting of Hieronymus Bosch," as if "Hades had opened its gates and vomited forth the basest, most despicable, most horrible demons." The racial restrictions that had gradually taken root in Germany over the previous five years demonized Austrian Jews almost overnight. The National Socialist regime classified Aichinger as a so-called *Mischling*, a "half-breed" or "mixed-race." In August 1938, SS officer Adolf Eichmann set up his Central Office of Jewish Emigration in an "Aryanized" palace not far from where Ilse lived with her grandmother.

Ilse's sister Helga escaped on July 4, 1939, with the last Kindertransport to leave Vienna's Westbahnhof. She fled via Holland to London. Ilse's father had urged her to leave, too: "I don't understand it, it's much nicer out there in England.

A young person belongs outside." The superficial materiality of his remark, Ilse noted in her diary, showed "a great lack of understanding." Ilse chose instead to stay in Vienna to protect her mother, who remained safe from deportation so long as she had a "half-Aryan" child to support. As a Jew, the mother was ostracized, and forced to support herself as a factory worker. With this reversal of roles, the daughter protecting mother, Ilse and her mother — by then stripped of her job as a school doctor — lived in constant fear, billeted with a hostile landlady in a small room on Marc-Aurel-Strasse, adjacent to the Vienna headquarters of the Gestapo in the former Hotel Metropole. As Paul Hofmann, later head of the *New York Times* bureau in Vienna, recorded, the Hotel Metropole "became the synonym for terror and torture." It was where former chancellor Kurt Schuschnigg and Baron Louis Nathaniel Rothschild were held.

In March 1945, when the four-story building sustained heavy damage from an aerial bombing raid, a passerby cautioned Ilse: "Don't look happy or you'll be arrested, too." (A scene in *The Third Man*, shot in Vienna in 1948, uses the building's ruins as a stark backdrop. Helga makes a cameo appearance in the film. After the war, a plaque at the site described it as an "inferno for those who believed in Austria... It crashed to pieces like the Thousand-Year Reich.") The twins meanwhile corresponded through Red Cross messages limited to no more than twenty-five words. In these clipped messages sent across the Channel — intended, as Ilse wrote to Helga in November 1945, "to rip the veil between us" — Aichinger whetted her terse prose style. The editor of their correspondence suggests that it served as Ilse's "engine of literary writing."

Once released from their inhibitions, the Aichingers' neighbors proved so untroubled by the roundups of Jews that before long the Gestapo conducted raids with impunity in broad daylight. In May 1942, Ilse watched as her seventy-four-year-old grandmother, together with her aunt Erna and uncle Felix (awarded the Iron Cross in the First World War) and about a thousand other Jews were forced before jeering onlookers onto a truck which disappeared over a bridge across the gray-green Danube canal. "Those who watched as my grandmother and my mother's younger siblings were driven on an open cattle car across the Swedish Bridge toward torture and death looked on, to be sure, with a certain glee," Aichinger recalled. "And someone called out: 'Look, there's Ilse.' But she didn't turn around." This is the bridge that today is sanctified by Aichinger's lyrics, the one that burdens Bettina's daily walk. The Austrian writer and Nobel laureate Elfriede Jelinek said that ever since that day on the Swedish Bridge Aichinger had her gaze riveted on this most excruciating sight of her childhood. The horror that took place on that bridge is never really past," Jelinek said. "Only who sees it anymore? Ilse." In an interview fifty years later, Aichinger said that her greatest wish would be to see her grandmother again.

Only after the war did Aichinger learn that her relatives had been transported east on "iron rails running straight on into infinity," as she wrote, and had met their deaths at an extermination camp near Minsk — they were three of over sixty-five thousand Austrian Jews murdered during the Nazi occupation. In her last diary entry before a white flag was hoisted over St. Stephen's Cathedral, signaling the end of the war for Vienna, Aichinger confessed to a fatigue so extreme that she wished to die. Ilse and her mother survived, at least physically. "You don't survive everything you survive," Aichinger wrote. The state grudgingly offered her mother a paltry ten thousand shillings for the loss of her apartment, her medical practice, and her murdered relatives — a "disgraceful" restitution, Ilse said.

Storytelling can be another form of restitution, of restoring what has been lost or looted. In 2021, the Belarusian writer and Nobel laureate Svetlana Alexievich, whose work, none of it fiction, is a monumental project of recapturing the lived experience of suffering in the Soviet Union, expressed her admiration of the ways in which Aichinger tore through the banal idea of peaceful dwelling-in-the-world in which so many bystanders had swaddled themselves.

The Moscow Declaration of 1943 had defined Austrians as the Germans' first victims and thus free of obligation to make reparations for Nazi crimes. The preamble to Austria's declaration of independence, signed in April 1945, interpreted the years between 1938 and 1945 as a violent, externally imposed interruption in the country's history, foisted on the "defenseless state leadership" and on "the helpless people of Austria." If Austria had ceased to exist in 1938, if it was an occupied nation rather than an aggressor, it could not be held itself responsible for crimes committed in the name of the Third Reich. This was pure self-exculpation, the brazen foundational lie — the *Lebenslüge* — upon which modern Austria rebuilt itself and which Aichinger sought to shatter for the sake of "the attempt to translate our hope into a future."

In 1946, at the age of twenty-five, she suggested how to accomplish this great sobering in a trailblazing two-page political manifesto called "A Call for Mistrust." Aichinger implored her young contemporaries to question the self-exculpating complacencies of their "wounded world," to prefer self-doubt to self-pity, to direct mistrust "toward ourselves, in order to be more trustworthy!"

> This is how the tremendous thoughtlessness of these last years called us to think; this is how the inhumanity from which we suffered like tormented animals summoned us to seek and to condense everything human; this is how we learned, first of all, to be human before we became poets.... For what we say today was unsayable yesterday!

André Gide once remarked that if skepticism is the beginning of wisdom, it is often the end of art. But Aichinger's art begins with an address to skepticism—with a distrust of language, of collective self-righteousness, and, above all, of oneself. She wrote her first and only novel, *Die grössere Hoffnung* or *The Greater Hope*, in fragments during the war. On September 1, 1945, Aichinger published a chapter of *The Greater Hope* under the title "The Fourth Gate" in the daily newspaper *Wiener Kurier*. The entire novel appeared in 1948, and it came out in a deft English translation by Geoff Wilkes in 2016. She intended it, as she told her sister, "to show that miracles happen even amidst the darkness." It is an astonishing book, a book like no other.

Aichinger centers the novel on the wartime experiences of Ellen, the sensitive adolescent daughter of a Jewish mother and a Nazi policeman who disowns his daughter and asks her to forget him. This is one of the first literary texts, if not the very first, which mentions the term "concentration camp." But Aichinger avoids the term "Nazis" — the father and his subordinates are described as "lost souls" — and leaves the city unnamed, as though the unembellished story could have unfolded anywhere.

We first meet Ellen lying across a map on the floor of the consul's office, "tossing uneasily back and forth between Europe and America." Having failed to obtain a visa to rejoin her mother, who has fled to America, Ellen endears herself with a group of Jewish children who find themselves trapped. "The last *Kindertransport* had left long ago. The borders were closed." When the children are no longer allowed to go to school, an old teacher is surprised that they want to forget German. "I won't help you do that," he says. "But I'll help you learn it anew, the way a foreigner learns a foreign language."

As the anti-Jewish edicts tighten and Hitler youth skulk outside their doors, Ellen and her friends ask what is left.

> You keep only what you give away. So give them what they take from you, for that will make them ever poorer. Give them your toys, your coats, your caps, and your lives. Give away everything in order to keep it.... Laugh when they tear the clothes from your bodies and your caps from your heads.... Laugh at the satiated people, laugh at the placid people who have lost hunger and uneasiness, the most precious gifts which are vouchsafed to human beings.

But the children do not laugh, certainly not at the prospect of receiving deportation orders. "Who'll help us onto the truck, if it's too high?" one asks. "We're guilty of being alive," another says. They wonder where they can find refuge. "Not the south and not the north, not the east and not the west, not the past and not the future."

Before long, only the children's imaginations offer the semblance of a safe harbor. In one game, the children wait on a riverbank hoping that a baby will fall into the water so that they can save him, as the infant Moses was rescued from the Nile. "We'll dry it off and take it to the mayor. And the mayor will say: Good, very good! You're allowed to sit on all the benches again." In another, the oldest boy, Leon, with "four grandparents of the wrong kind," plays the role of an angel. Angels permeate Aichinger's writing, and they bear messages neither of hope nor consolation but of vigilance toward intrusions into fixed reality. One of the children comments on the unseen adult audience: "Don't you hear how they're already laughing, how they'll laugh when we're being led across the bridges?"

At first, playing together is a confirmation of belonging. But before long the children lose track of what is rehearsal and what is performance, of which game they are playing and which game — with all-too-real malevolent rules — is being played with them. "Already the two plays were beginning to flow into each other, weaving themselves inextricably in a new play." Yet the performances allow the children to give words to the unspeakable. Aichinger elevates playing to the status of a mitzvah: "To play. It was the only possibility remaining to them, composure before the incomprehensible, grace before the secret. The most unutterable commandment: Thou shalt play in my presence!" (In the same year that Aichinger published *The Greater Hope*, Paul Celan published his "Death Fugue," a poem which invokes the word "played," *spielt*, seven times.)

Ellen's uniformed father, "who had asked Ellen to forget him," instructs the children that Jews are no longer allowed to play in the city park. In a chapter called "The Holy Land," they decide to play instead in the Jewish section of the cemetery. Aichinger describes the tram rattling rapidly past the graveyard gates, as if it had a bad conscience. The children dart among the gravestones of their ancestors until at last the dead and the living seem to play with one another. "Our dead people aren't dead," they shout. "They're playing hide-and-seek with us."

Aichinger's book was one of three important novels about children in Vienna during the Nazi dictatorship. It joined Jacob Glatstein's *Emil and Karl*, published in Yiddish in 1940, a book written for children in order to explain to them the historical convulsions that they were witnessing (Emil is a Jewish boy and Karl a Christian boy); and *Children of Vienna*, published in 1946, by Robert Neumann, whose books had been banned and burned in Germany, and who left Vienna in 1934. But *The Greater Hope*, a story filigreed by exclusion, itself became excluded from public perception; it sold poorly and got few reviews. The Vienna-born writer Erich Fried was one of the few to recognize its merit. Within a year of its appearance, he called the novel "one of the most profound and — despite all the horror — one of the most beautiful and joyful books of our time." It would be a dozen years until it was reissued, in paperback in 1960. (The German writer Peter Härtling called it "a book that waits patiently for us.") It embarrassed a readership inclined to regard those who dredged up their country's complicity in Nazi crimes as "befoulers of the nest" (*Nestbeschmutzer*). It denied such readers the comforts of exoneration. For the rest of her life, its author — who understood her own survival as a surprise — refused to play the role of absolver in Austria's theater of guilty memory.

In 1952, four years after the appearance of *The Greater Hope*, Aichinger read her "Mirror Story," in which time runs in reverse, to a transfixed gathering of writers that included Paul Celan and Ingeborg Bachmann. Hans Werner Richter described the experience: "She was able to put everyone under her spell... and it was not only the quality of her texts, it was her voice that fascinated everybody. Of course, the declared realist writers of our group tried to resist... yet they could not escape her charisma." This was Group 47, a loosely knit, mostly male vanguard of young writers who wished to make a clean sweep in the aftermath of the "zero hour" (*Stunde Null*, in German), as they called the final Nazi defeat. If the increasingly occult Martin Heidegger understood language as the "house of Being," these rehabilitators understood that the house had collapsed. Though the group's early efforts were often seen not so much as "tabula rasa literature" as defeatist "rubble literature" (*Trümmerliteratur*), books by its members — including Ilse Aichinger, Heinrich Böll, and Günter Grass — would overshadow the ruins of the German-language literary landscape from 1947 to 1967.

Many of her colleagues in this circle perceived Kafka's influence in Aichinger's spare style and parables of powerlessness. One member of Group 47 went so far as to call her "Miss Kafka." Another, the literary critic Walter Jens, praised her "Kafkaesque technique." "The great K., the holy K.," Aichinger said in exasperation, "that's what I heard." Yet on accepting the Kafka Prize, Aichinger insisted that other than a single passage from his letters (later incorporated into his early story "Conversation with the Supplicant") — a childhood memory of overhearing a perfectly mundane conversation between his mother on the balcony and a neighbor below, she had read almost nothing of Kafka's writing and had avoided conversations about him. She could not bear his precision.

Even as she cast a skeptical eye on promises of radical renewal, Aichinger grew particularly close to two members of Group 47: the poet Ingeborg Bachmann, cherished by the Aichinger family as a "third twin," and the poet Günther Eich, whom she married. When Bachmann met Aichinger in war-wrecked Vienna, their experiences could hardly have been more different. Bachmann, whose father had joined the Nazi party in 1943 and served as an officer in the Wehrmacht, had spent the war years in almost idyllic safety in Klagenfurt. But in its dissonance and tenderness, the close friendship between the two writers could almost stand as a metaphor for Austria's postwar entanglements. (The Bachmann-Aichinger correspondence, more than a hundred letters spanning the years from 1949 until their estrangement in 1962, came out in Germany in 2021. In her last letter, Bachmann confesses to her friend and mentor that she "said far too little... thanked you too little." The letter was never sent.)

In the decade after the publication of *The Greater Hope*, a realistic novel with touches of surrealism, Aichinger's language grew more condensed and more self-scrutinizing, as it turned toward the cracks through which the past splinters into the present. This becomes evident also in works such as *The Bound Man and Other Stories* (1951); "Buttons" (1953), a radio play in which workers in a button factory turn into the products they make; and "Squares and Streets" (1954), a series of vignettes on Vienna places (including Judengasse, or "Jews' Alley," and Seegasse, the Jewish cemetery in the city's Ninth District dating to the sixteenth century), on the theme, as she put it, that "the places that we saw now look at us." So, too, in *At No Time* (1957), a collection of Aichinger's surreal dialogues.

A mundane conversation between a maid and a policeman, for example, ends with the prophet Elijah whirling through the cobalt sky above in a crimson chariot.

Throughout, as she told an interviewer, Aichinger slanted her writing toward an "identification with the weak, the disabled, the injured." The truly strange people, says her novel's narrator, "are those who feel most at home." Aichinger held this to be true both geographically and linguistically. The truest and most individual language, Aichinger said, "has to counter the existing language, the established language." As it tilted away from the literal, her own language turned within a tight radius, almost with a will of its own. "My language and I, we don't talk to each other," she writes, "we have nothing to say to each other."

After her husband's death in 1972, Aichinger devoted herself to *Bad Words*, which appeared four years later, a collection of short stories clotted with memory, dense texts that ask us to overcome our desire to decipher everything. The English translators of *Bad Words,* the poets Uljana Wolf and Christian Hawkey, resist the impulse to "fill in the gaps." Instead they preserve the lexical choices that tighten Aichinger's writing, above all the wariness of verbal virtuosity and pretty words. (Aichinger is to the German language what her fellow Viennese Adolf Loos, author of the essay "Ornament and Crime," is to architecture.) She prefers "bad words," words that "never occur in lullabies." Many writers feel commanded to reach for the right words, *les mots justes*. If, as Aichinger said, "the best is always an imperative," she refused such imperatives. "*Life* is not a special word, and neither is *death*," she writes. "Both are indefensible; they disguise instead of define."

If Aichinger belongs to the avatars of bad words rather than to the seekers of the sublime, it is because to write is, for her, to define, to say what a thing is. "Already as a child I hated the word fantasy. I didn't want fantasy, I wanted precise realness, as precise as possible." That desire — especially when the precise is less beautiful and less enthralling than the imprecise — informs her sole poetry collection, *Squandered Advice*, which appeared in 1978 and was published two years ago in English translation. Its translator, Steph Morris, delivers the rhythmic density of Aichinger's poems, the way she juxtaposes words to give them the unsettled loneliness that she said they need "in order for them to produce meaning." Some, like the following, can be read as attempts to rescue possibilities of remembrance.

> Moby Dick,
> Rabbi Fingerhut
> has drowned,
> has died,
> gone.
> He had yellow eyes
> and a large mouth,
> dark regalia
> packed onto him.
> Moby Dick,
> Rabbi Fingerhut.
> Tell Ahab too,
> and the others,
> the helmsmen
> and the harpooners,
> and tell them soon.
> Pass it on,
> Don't forget.

In 1988, Aichinger returned to Vienna after four years in Frankfurt, and resumed her strolls across the bridges over the Danube canal. Because she had cut against the Austrian grain, she was a solitary figure. Only late in life did she see the corona of her recognition brighten. In 1991, to mark her seventieth birthday, S. Fischer Verlag published an eight-volume edition of Aichinger's collected works, edited by her companion, the literary critic Richard Reichensperger. Her books, translated into eighteen languages, won many prestigious awards, including the Grand Austrian State Prize for Literature in 1995. Several years earlier she had declined the Order of Merit of the Federal Republic of Germany. Aging, she said, "means learning to play better."

She had never sought easy applause, much less fame. "Ever since I was a kid," she told an interviewer, "I've wanted to disappear. That was my first passionate wish." In *Film and Fate*, which appeared in 2000, she stages the story of her early life in the form of an autobiography of a moviegoer who felt that cinema's flickering ephemerality matched her own self-effacement. During the war, she writes, the cinema had served as a "place of disorder," a welcome refuge from the Nazi order. In her last years, Aichinger would disappear after a day of writing into the dark of the Bellaria movie theater, which screened vintage films, including Laurel and Hardy comedies. (She kept a life-size cardboard cutout of Stan Laurel in her bedroom.) She often attended the Burg Cinema's Sunday screenings of *The Third Man*. Aichinger died in 2016, a few days after her ninety-fifth birthday, in her native Vienna, a city that she called "murderous but familiar."

The Habsburg emperors bore many titles, among them King of Jerusalem and Duke of Auschwitz. Ilse Aichinger's language of hope and suffering, Reichensperger said, moved between those two poles, Jerusalem and Auschwitz.

Like Aichinger, the Israeli novelist Aharon Appelfeld, her younger contemporary, who was born in Czernowitz and lived most of his life in Jerusalem, and wrote in Hebrew, understood children as carriers of continuity. He, too, told stories of hope and suffering through a child's eyes. His stories, set in the outer precincts of the Austro-Hungarian Empire, likewise allowed a child's incomprehension to bring the Shoah's incomprehensibility into focus. In *The Age of Wonders*, Appelfeld describes a ghoulish group of Jew-haters on a train in the late 1930s as they taunt the main character's father, a man of letters and of culture. "Am I not an Austrian like you are?" he cries out. "Didn't I go to school here? Graduate from an Austrian gymnasium, an Austrian university? Weren't all my books published here?" And yet, says the son, "Father's determination to remain in Austria was even stronger than before. To leave at a time like this, with evil spirits raging, meant admitting that reason had lost out, that literature was to no avail."

Aichinger called voicelessness "the tuning fork of the wise." But if the Shoah strained the limits of language, after Auschwitz certain silences also sounded different than before. The silence of the survivor, she insisted, is unlike the hushed reticence of the perpetrator, a respectful silence unlike an indifferent silence. On accepting the Nelly Sachs Prize, she commended "the engaged silence without which language and conversation are impossible." Although the accents vary, everything Aichinger wrote over sixty years records her efforts to reclaim both an engaged silence and an afflicted language. In defiance of the evil spirits, she kept her composure before the incomprehensible, in the greater hope that her writing would be of some avail.

MITCHELL ABIDOR

From The Party to The Person: The Example of Victor Serge

*Those banished from a church are always its elite.
They are ahead of their time.*

ERNEST RENAN

I

In the eyes of many, Victor Serge, the Belgian-born writer and anti-Stalinist militant, has come to stand for political probity in a time of cowardice and falsehood. The child of exiles from Tsarist Russia, from whom he inherited an admiration for lone fighters against oppression, Serge's political evolution saw him travel large distances: a young socialist, then a fervent individualist anarchist, then a revolutionary syndicalist, and then, with the Russian Revolution, an orthodox Bolshevik. With Lenin's death, Serge sided with Trotsky against Stalin, before ending his days in exile in Mexico City as an independent socialist of an eccentric type. His ideological shifts were not a demonstration of political fickleness, but rather of his recognition that no fixed ideology can meet changing circumstances, that it is necessary for ideas and people to evolve politically as the world situation itself evolves. He paid dearly for the transformations of his beliefs, living in almost constant exile and statelessness. He was imprisoned twice in France and twice in the Soviet Union, before being expelled from the latter in 1936 after spending three years in forced internal exile. He faced political isolation and poverty, and at the end of his life, in his final exile in Mexico, his poverty was so bleak that when, in 1947, he died in the back seat of a taxi in Mexico City, the soles of his shoes were found to be worn through.

Writing on the margins of politics and history, a citizen only of what he called "the invisible international," Serge's independence and foresight have earned him the recognition that he lacked in his lifetime. After languishing in oblivion in the English-speaking world, he was rescued by the scholar Richard Greeman, who translated most of his novels and over the course of half a century campaigned tirelessly to ensure that all of Serge's essential works were published. In 2004 Serge's consecration was complete, when Susan Sontag wrote an impressive overview of his career, saying of him that "I can't think of anyone who has written about the revolutionary movement in this century with Serge's combination of moral insight and intellectual richness." He has been deservedly rescued from the margins. We may even need his example. But who, exactly, was he?

He was born Victor-Napoléon Kibalchich in Brussels in 1890, and always believed that he was related to Nikolai Kibalchich, one of the assassins of Tsar Alexander II in 1882, who died on the gallows with his fellow assassins. The heroism and the self-abnegation of the members of *Narodnya Volya*, or the People's Will, the socialist revolutionary organization whose members included the assassins of the Tsar, served as Serge's inspiration, which he invoked throughout his life. His family relationship with one of the heroes of the movement to free Russia made this identification an essential part of his being. But alas, Richard Greeman's research into Serge's family history revealed that there was no family tie between Serge and his hero. Serge was also certain that his father had been involved in the Russian Narodnik movement, but the evidence for this, too, is weak.

Victor grew up in an impoverished and dysfunctional family, though "grew up" is not quite accurate: he left home when he was twelve and supported himself from that time on. This claim, made in his memoirs, may sound improbable, but it is confirmed by residency records in the files of the Brussels police. With a group of friends, some of whom would play a crucial and tragic role in his later life, the young Kibalchich joined the youth organization of the Belgian Worker's Party, which he and his friends soon quit, frustrated by its tepid politics. Anarchism called him — a form of anarchism that reflected his youthful disgust with the world. In his *Memoirs of a Revolutionary*, which was published posthumously in France in 1951, Serge recalls his years as an anarchist, saying that "anarchism swept us away completely because it both demanded everything of us and offered us everything."

And yet he downplays his actual beliefs and writings in those same memoirs. The days of bomb-throwing anarchists were gone when Serge became an anarchist around 1907, but he adopted a form of individualist anarchism that in many ways grew from that violent phase of anarchist history. At eighteen he wrote in the newspaper published by his circle of friends and comrades in Belgium an essay in praise of Emile Henry, who was notorious for throwing a bomb into the Café Terminus in Paris in 1894, and for declaring at his trial that he regretted only that he had not killed more than one person. Serge, under his pen name of Le Rétif, spoke of Henry's heroism; and of his death on the guillotine he rhapsodized, "It was a death whose memory will live on. A death that free men will later remember with gratitude. For alongside the people of our century, the arrivistes, crushers, deceivers of all kinds; the immense mass of imbecilic followers and serfs, this young man marching towards death when everything in him wanted to live, this young man dying for the ideal is truly a luminous figure."

In 1908 Serge moved to Paris, the capital of this school of anarchism, where he wrote and edited the newspaper *l'anarchie*, whose founder, uncannily named Albert Libertad, published it entirely in lower case so that all of the letters would be equal. Serge's articles for *l'anarchie* expressed a consistent worldview, one that scorned the working class as a herd of sheep interested only in getting drunk. He was a revolutionary who dismissed the utility of mass revolutions and upheld a firm belief in the power of the individual, writing that "the evil illusion is that of waiting for the revolt of the crowd, of the organized, disciplined, regimented masses. In fact, the only fertile acts are those committed by individuals knowing clearly what they want and advancing without let or hindrance, needing neither leaders nor discipline. In fact, the only good rebellions are the immediate rebellions of individuals refusing to wait any longer and deciding to immediately grab their portion of joy."

Serge also expressed an understanding of — and even some support for — a rising trend among anarchist individualists: illegalism, or the view that crime is a revolutionary act. In later years he would deny advocating such a doctrine, but this is simply not true. He wrote in his newspaper that laws are "aimed at garroting the weakest, at sanctioning their enslavement by brute force. The honesty they proclaim I know to be falsehood, hiding the worst turpitudes, permitting — even honoring — theft, fraud, and deception when they are committed in the shade of the criminal code. The so-called 'respect for human life' that they never fail to mention *a propos* of every murder I know to be ignobly hypocritical, since meanwhile they kill in its name by hunger, work, subjection, and incarceration. I am on the other side, and I am not afraid to admit it. I am with the bandits. I find their role to be noble. Sometimes I see in them men, whereas elsewhere I see only fools and puppets."

Serge and his then-partner Rirette Maitrejean (whose husband was an illegalist imprisoned for counterfeiting) lived at the offices of *l'anarchie* with several members of what became known as the Bonnot Gang, anarchists all, some of whom had been Serge's friends in Brussels, who robbed banks and killed those who got in their way. Serge was not involved in their crimes, but he was arrested along with the gang members who had not been killed by the police. At their trial Serge was found guilty of possession of a stolen weapon. He was sentenced to five years in prison and served every day of it. The depredations of the Bonnot Gang had led him to rethink his individualism, and the five years in prison gave him ample time to decide that he needed to follow a different road.

Released from La Santé Prison in 1917, he was expelled from France and banned from returning. He left for Barcelona, where he assumed the pen name of Victor Serge and became involved for the first time in mass revolutionary activity, in the company of the city's anarcho-syndicalists, who believed that the working class should seize control of the economy through revolutionary unionism (exemplified in the United States by the Industrial Workers of the World and their slogan "One Big Union"). He was in Barcelona when the Russian Revolution occurred, and was determined to find a way to his ancestral homeland and participate in the momentous events. He returned to France, violating his banishment order, hoping to find a route to Russia, either by enlisting in the French army or the Foreign Legion. Instead he was arrested and held in a prison camp until 1919, when he was exchanged for French officers held by the Russians. On the ship taking him to Soviet Russia he met the Roussakov family, headed by Alexander Roussakov, a Jewish anarchist. The Roussakovs became his first real family, and he married one of its daughters, Liuba, in 1920.

Serge worked for the Communist International (Comintern) alongside Alexander Zinoviev and joined the Communist Party. He wrote regularly for official Comintern journals and, though his background was not that of an orthodox Bolshevik, he served the new regime faithfully. Most notably, he wrote several articles for Comintern journals aimed at anarchists, in an effort to get them to support Soviet Russia, which he claimed was fulfilling the anarchist dream. At least this is what he wrote at the time.

In fact, Serge soon realized that things were not what he had hoped they would be. A good Communist careful not to provide grist for the anti-Soviet mill, he knowingly lied for the good of the cause — but as the years passed he came to believe, as he wrote in a later essay, that things went off the rails for the Bolshevik Revolution when the Cheka — the secret police — was granted the right to execute suspects in 1918, before he had even arrived in Soviet Russia. In 1918! He was the most premature anti-Communist of all. If Serge hid his true opinions when he wrote for the Communist press, he was honest in conversations with former fellow-anarchists who visited him in Russia. Publicly, he supported the crushing of the Kronstadt rebellion of 1921, an uprising of sailors who had played a key role in the victory of the Bolsheviks in 1917 and who were now rebelling in an effort to restore some form of democratic freedom. They were brutally crushed. ("Kronstadt" became the euphemism for one's moment of disillusion with Soviet communism. There were those who did not have their "Kronstadt moment" until 1956.) Serge defended the Soviet crackdown when it occurred, citing the dangers of counter-revolution and dismissing the sailors as imbued with a peasant and petty-bourgeois ideology. And yet contemporary accounts by anarchist visitors report him remarking that "the Kronstadt Affair was a revolt of the masses against the dictatorship of the leaders," and that the party's actions there "were the last straw." He explained his public silence about his disillusion to Emma Goldman and Alexander Berkman, who had implored him to tell the truth about the rebellion: "I can't do it. I'm known in the party as an anarchist. If I did anything I'd be arrested." It was only in the 1930s that he would openly repent this position.

After spending a couple of years on assignment in Germany and Vienna for the Comintern, overseeing its French publications to which he frequently contributed, Serge returned to the Soviet Union in 1926 and joined the battle over the succession to Lenin, who had died in 1923. Serge sided with Trotsky against Stalin, which earned him a spell in prison in 1928 for his oppositional activities. During this prison stay, realizing that any form of political activity against Stalin was doomed, he determined to spend all his time on literary endeavors.

Though bearing the mark of an oppositionist, Serge managed to avoid the roundups that swept up his comrades — until 1933, when he was sent to an "isolator" in Orenburg in the Urals. By this time he was a well-known writer in France, and a campaign was mounted to attain his release. Those seeking his release included figures on the left such as Henri Barbusse, Romain Rolland, and André Gide (who was then passing through his brief pro-Communist phase). Articles decrying Serge's imprisonment appeared in both anti-Stalinist left-wing periodicals and the mainstream press. A minor scandal occurred when, in 1935, at a congress of anti-fascist writers in Paris whose main aim was the defense of writers suffering under Hitler and Mussolini, Serge's supporters (who included Simone Weil) insisted that the congress call for his liberation and presented a "request for information" about Serge's condition to the Soviet delegation. A Communist paper reported that "put formally on the spot by this handful of militants, the Soviet delegation could only reply by pointing to the beauties of the Five Year Plan and admitting its ignorance of the charges brought against Victor Serge." Thanks to the intervention of Romain Rolland and Maxim Gorky, Stalin agreed to release Serge, and in 1936 he was granted a residency visa for Belgium thanks to Emil Vandervelde, a leader of the Belgian Worker's Party that Serge had once condemned when he was a young socialist.

Serge's disillusionment with his former beliefs grew, and it is at this point that he became a figure of real significance. Even after arriving in Belgium he described himself proudly as a Communist, but seeing the West again shook him. In the very first article that he wrote, in June 1936, for the Liege-based newspaper *La Wallonie*, in whose pages he would appear until 1940, he described the positive impression made on him by the West. Even as he expressed a hope for socialism in Western Europe, he was struck by the civilization that he was rediscovering, beginning in Poland, and how that border between the USSR and the West made itself felt not just geographically but "in everything, in every face, in the quality of clothing, in tile instead of thatched roofs, in the meticulous cleanliness of towns; one feels it in the more gentle and nuanced inflections of voices." All of daily life was different, was better, and the Western economies were thriving. For the moment he saw in this "the maturity of these countries for socialism," but doubts would set in about this view, too — as would doubts about the validity of the Soviet example, and more profoundly, of Marxism as commonly understood. It was not long before he found himself in the realm of heresy.

The clearest evidence of Serge's straying from the Marxist straight and narrow was his exasperation with Trotsky, the man he admired more than any in the world. His differences with the founder of the Red Army, known to his admirers as the Old Man, were made clear almost immediately after Serge settled in Belgium. In May 1936, just weeks after his arrival, the election of a Popular Front government in France led to a popular explosion, with workers occupying factories across the country. Trotsky immediately proclaimed that "the French Revolution has begun." Serge was not convinced that this was the case, writing to Trotsky to correct him: "Not at all. It's only the recovery of the French working class that's begun." Serge differed with Trotsky on a variety of issues, from the Spanish Civil War to the foundation of a new International to replace the Stalinist Third International, a possibility that Serge, to Trotsky's dismay, dismissed as futile.

Their relationship hit its nadir when Serge translated Trotsky's essay "Their Morals and Ours." Serge disapproved of the work, a vitriolic exploration of revolutionary ethics, and wrote an attack on it in 1940 in an essay that was never published. This critical essay is a central document in tracking Serge's shift away from the Bolshevism that he publicly espoused for twenty years. In it he expressed grave doubts about nothing less than the moral, political, and human underpinnings of the Russian Revolution. For Serge, Trotsky's pamphlet was an expression of "the Bolshevism of its great years," but also of its "decadence." Though Serge admits that "the modern world owes [Trotsky and the Bolsheviks of the October Revolution] a great deal [and] the future will owe them even more," he warns against the impulse to "blindly imitate them."

Serge insisted that Trotsky's "tone" was significant because it was "domineering," a tone that was common to Bolsheviks of the time and to Marx before them. A typical example of Trotsky's vicious tone was his comparison of Bolsheviks and social-democrats: "Compared to revolutionary Marxists, the social-democrats and centrists appear like morons, or a quack beside a physician: they do not think one problem through to the end, believe in the power of conjuration and cravenly avoid every difficulty, hoping for a miracle. Opportunists are peaceful shop-keepers in socialist ideas while Bolsheviks are its inveterate warriors." Serge perhaps never wrote anything truer than when he said of this tone that it "is something of great importance, for this tone is essentially one of intolerance." Trotsky's attitude, he boldly continued, "implies the claim to the monopoly of truth, or to speak more accurately, the sentiment of possessing the truth."

Serge's later disputes with his comrades in Mexico, the development of his ideas on society and social struggle in a way that radically revised and even in some ways jettisoned Marxism, was already present in germ in this essay, for example in this brave and splendid observation: "The truth is never fixed, it is constantly in the process of becoming and no absolute border sets it apart from error. The assurance of those Marxists who fail to see this is quickly transformed into smugness. The feeling of possessing the truth goes hand in hand with a certain contempt for man, of the other man ... This sentiment implies a denial of freedom, freedom being, on the intellectual level, the right of others to think differently, the right to be wrong. The germ of an entire totalitarian mentality can be found in this intolerance." For Serge, respect for the human person, and the acceptance of other opinions as legitimate, must be the guiding principles of a reborn democratic socialist movement.

In this he was in the direct line of many anti-Stalinist revolutionaries. But increasingly a new concern became essential to Serge. It was no longer enough to defend the revolution from its enemies within and without, which he called his "double duty." From the late 1930s on, a new phrase enters his lexicon, one that he would use and reuse as a leitmotiv in his final years. What was important for Serge was "the defense of the human person." The phrase sounds fairly unexceptionable, another expression of his discontent with the dictatorship in the land of the revolution, but nothing could be further from the truth. The "defense of the human person" was not an empty slogan that he threw around lightly. Those five words were an epitome of the philosophy that Serge adopted as a supplement to Marxism, which in his view needed to be totally revised.

II

Serge's final years, and the culminating heroism of his intellectual career, can only be understood within the context of his adoption of the philosophy known as personalism. The phrase *der Personalismus* was first used by Schleiermacher in his influential book *On Religion* in 1799, and in America it was introduced by Walt Whitman in 1868, who wrote an essay by that name on "the single solitary soul." The twentieth-century version of personalism was largely the work of Emmanuel Mounier, a French Catholic intellectual and the founder and editor of the review *Esprit*. Mounier was born in Grenoble in 1905 and studied philosophy at the university in his hometown. As described by the French historian Michel Winock in his fine study of *Esprit*, "the young Emmanuel burned with an uncommon faith in God." Mounier also burned with a hatred for what he appositely called "the established disorder." He and a group of young people who shared his ideas established *Esprit* in 1932. In their pre-war incarnation, *Esprit* and Mounier were opponents of both the bourgeoisie and Marxism, though finding some good in the latter and none in the former; but in the post-war years, as we will see, Mounier's relationship with Communism become entirely positive.

In the October 1936 issue of *Esprit*, Mounier published his "Manifesto in Service to Personalism," in which he summarized the essential points of his philosophy. It began with a definition: "We call Personalist every doctrine, every civilization, that affirms the primacy of the human person over material necessities and the collective apparatuses that sustain their development." The anti-materialism alone was a great affront to Marxism. And Mounier's personalism was not a contemplative doctrine, but a philosophy of action. He insisted that "we be judged by our acts." Mounier sought to refine the notions of action and act: "Not every action is an act. An action is only of value and effective if in the first instance it has taken the measure of the truth that gives it its meaning, and of the historical situation which gives it its scope and its conditions for realization." Personalism was politically optimistic, for "there is no doubt that we can already considerably renew the visage of most lives by freeing man from all the servitudes that weigh on his vocation as a man." Moreover, "personalism does not announce the constituting of a school, the opening of a chapel, or the invention of a closed system. It testifies to a convergence of wills and puts itself at their service without impinging upon their diversity, so as to assist them in their search for the means to effectively weigh on history."

There was no necessary contradiction, then, between personalism and Serge's existing ideas. When he discovered personalism, it was mainly a form of anti-bourgeois non-conformism, which suited Serge's temperament. Freshly released from the *univers concentrationnaire* of the Soviet Union, he could not help adhering to a doctrine that sought to define, as Mounier wrote, "all the forms of mutual consent capable of establishing a civilization devoted to the human person." Serge had learned the hard way that Communism was a doctrine sorely lacking a focus on the individual. It was all of humankind, instead, that was to be transformed. Personalism, by contrast, represented a refutation of such lethal abstraction. *Esprit* had supported Serge's cause while he was in Orenburg, and Serge frequently appeared in its pages. He maintained an important correspondence with Mounier up until his death.

That Serge was a personalist is not a matter of speculation: his "adherence" to the doctrine, as he phrased it, was something that he hid in plain sight. It is only because of our unfamiliarity with this vital school of modern thought that we miss the signs of his having adopted its philosophy. The most obvious and incontrovertible proof of Serge's personalism can be found in the least obscure of locations, his autobiography. In *Memoirs of a Revolutionary*, he remarks that "I do not think of myself as at all an individualist: rather as a 'personalist,' in that I view human personality as a supreme value, but integrated in society and in history." (That "integration" could become a problem, a threat of totalization.) In his book Serge recalled Mounier as a "genuine Christian of fine, honest intellect," and he had this to say about the *Esprit* group: "They sensed sharply that they were living at the end of an era; they loathed all lying, especially if it formed an excuse for murder, and they said so outright. In their simple teaching of 'reverence for the human person' I felt immediately at one with them."

Serge most explicitly avowed his personalism in several letters. In an unpublished letter in 1938 to Maurice Wullens, a longtime comrade, Serge defended Mounier and his journal against an attack by Wullens in his magazine *Les Humbles*, protesting that *Esprit* "carries out with honesty and tenacity an excellent work too little known by our comrades." He goes on to speak in the highest terms of Mounier and personalism: "His doctrine, postulating above all respect for the human person *a priori* deserves the respect of the worker's movement, whose militants are, except for the Stalinist totalitarians, 'personalists' without being aware of it." He praised *Esprit*, explaining that "the openness of its views, the sincere desire to see clearly, and its intellectual probity are truly remarkable."

Serge had more to say on this topic to Wullens. In an unpublished and undated letter from 1938 (which might have been a draft of the previous one, or vice versa), Serge declared to Wullens that "I am above all unreservedly with the personalist movement when it affirms above all else respect for the human person." Serge then makes an important admission, pre-dating his adoption of personalism by several years: "I defined my personalism long ago, before knowing the word, in a message you perhaps know, where I notably wrote this (February 1, 1933): 'Defense of man, respect for man. He must be given his rights, security, value. Without this there is no socialism; without this everything is false, a failure, polluted. Man, whatever he may be, if he is the worst of men, a 'class enemy,' the son or grandson of a great bourgeois, I don't care. We must never forget that a human being is a human being. This is forgotten every day right in front of, everywhere. It's the most revolting and anti-socialist thing there is." Those sentences have been called Serge's "profession of faith." Mounier himself could not have better expressed the humanistic essence of his doctrine.

Serge made matters even clearer in a letter to Mounier. On September 10, 1945, only a few months after the end of the war, Serge wrote to his friend: "The respect for man, for all men, and consequently of the democratic institutions that are to be renewed, purified, and recreated in a Europe [now] in a state of gestation, is for me an absolute; and that this respect be at the very base of socialism as of any forward-looking movement. In this sense, I definitively maintain my implicit and clear adherence to personalism and I feel, in so doing, that I am in the great socialist tradition." Serge's correspondence with Mounier had been interrupted by the war, and his final note to Mounier before its interruption was written while he was en route to Mexico in 1941. He again referred to the philosophy that he shared with Mounier: "My dear friend, I remain a faithful friend of *Esprit* and will strive to remain in contact with you. I will be happy to be of use to you (without currently being fully in agreement with you [a reference, no doubt, to Mounier's suspected support for the Revolution Nationale in Vichy France]. But I believe that our agreement on personalism is much deeper than any circumstantial disagreements."

Four years later, however, the circumstantial disagreements would become fundamental disagreements. When they were able to pick up their correspondence at war's end, Mounier provided Serge with his view of the post-war situation, and though his hopes chimed with those of Serge, his analysis was radically different. Despairing of the dream of a renewed France, Mounier asserted that, owing to the strength of the right and to the weakness of a Socialist Party that was lacking in "men, energy, and historical imagination" and which had an "increasingly slim working-class base ..., it is necessary to speak a truth will be hard for you to hear: apart from the Communists there is nothing." Like so many left-wing intellectuals in France, most famously the circle around Jean-Paul Sartre at *Les Temps modernes,* Mounier and *Esprit* had made a choice that Serge abhorred. Mounier explained to Serge in a letter that "outside of a small Trotskyist minority there is only one way to explain the situation: the workers are Communist. As a result, the problem is a tragic one. One must both bear witness for everything that is dear to us, while not setting ourselves apart from the only remaining revolutionary force in France."

Serge's disagreement with Mounier's stance could not have been stronger, and he expressed it from the personalist standpoint that he felt Mounier had abandoned: "Our era of grief is also that of the decline of all values, since the primordial values, human life and the truth, hardly count anymore." Responding to Mounier's observation that there is nothing outside the Communists, Serge castigated his friend that he and those like him had "committed an enormous error in seeking to delude themselves about the latest totalitarian peril, which is immense. It would have been necessary, it is necessary, to remain firm by delineating the differences between even disguised totalitarianism and freedom, maintaining the right to speak the truth on the most inhuman regime in the world."

Serge was moved to write angrily to Mounier in January 1946 after reading his article in the November, 1945 issue of *Esprit*, in which Mounier made an unambiguous case for support of the Soviet Union and the Communists, writing that "without the vast infusion of humanity that could come from the East, the West will continue to die its little death. Without the decisive lessons the USSR offers us, the European revolution will be bogged down in the social democratic swamp." Serge was enraged. Serge did not mince words: "I think you are wrong, just as my executed friends and I were wrong for more than a decade, and for the same reasons: a profound confidence in man. The civilized individuals that we are refuse to believe the worst. You demand 'more precise knowledge... of the contemporary reality of the Soviet Union.' You certainly cannot be expecting it from official sources. Other information slips through, but they form a picture so horrifying that whoever would publish them in France (where I believe this would be practically impossible) would immediately be accused by the PCF [French Communist Party] and men of good will of infamy à la Goebbels." Serge then cites numbers taken from *The New Leader*, which was increasingly his favorite American publication. (*The New Leader*, which lasted in print until 2006 and for four more years online, was founded as a socialist weekly in 1924, and between 1936 and 1960, when it was edited by the remarkable Sol Levitas, it was an uncompromising liberal anti-Communist journal that went to great pains to report accurately on conditions in the Communist world.) Serge informed Mounier that there were five million deportees in concentration camps in Siberia, and that one and a half million of them were sent there between 1937 and 1940.

As far as Serge was concerned, Mounier would never be able to get at the truth with his current attitude.

Unless totalitarianism is denounced, honest information is impossible. And if we renounce this, we have no choice but to say that this totalitarianism has become strong enough to silence conscience and impose a general complicity with its official lies. My conviction, based on too much experience, is that no compromise is possible with this totalitarianism without abandoning Christian, humanist, and socialist values and without inevitably disastrous consequences.

> If there were a real hope for a useful meeting between Russia and America, I would be with you — despite what I am saying here. But I don't see any sign of such a hope. If totalitarianism sustains itself, which is possible, there will be no democratic renewal (by which I mean one ensuring the rights of man and truth) in the West; a permanent state of crisis exploited by the Communist Parties and, in the end, a Third World War. ... If, as is also possible, the USSR changes its appearance and once again becomes even an imperfect socialist democracy, all hopes are permitted for it and for Europe, and the nightmare of a Third World War is avoided. But I see no third possibility, if not stalling for time. In a word, your

> position seems to me utopian. I think that at bottom it is that of the best minds of France, and I understand the psychological motivation for it. And yet, as concerns you it disappoints me, because your starting point is the healthiest of doctrines, the one most capable of rallying all those who are honest, the one least compatible with the camouflaging of reality.

Serge's disappointment with *Esprit* and Mounier would only grow, and he bluntly summed up his objections in a letter to Mounier in March 1946, about the most recent issues of the journal: "I must say to you, with all the rigor that it seems to me that we, as men of good will, owe each other, how disappointed and distressed I am to see the review take the wrong road, and so badly deviate from the will to defend man and truth as to enter into contradiction with itself and to engender its own negation. *Esprit* leaves the clear impression of being a pro-totalitarian, pro-communist publication that wants to ignore the crushing of man and the annihilation of the truth by an essentially inhuman regime." The correspondence with Mounier ended in July 1947, and in the same disappointed and agitated spirit: "I remain in profound disagreement with *Esprit* concerning the very singular pro-Stalinism of the journal, which I consider the gravest of intellectual errors — and a moral failure. When will the journal decide to finally to take account of the colossal and irrefutable documentation published on the concentration camps in the USSR and on their ten or fifteen million pariahs?"

III

It was not only in his writings to Mounier that Serge expressed a fervent anti-Communism. His anti-Communism has been denied by many of those who have helped raise Serge to prominence. (Sontag was an exception.) It is a commonplace in writings about Serge to say that he never became a Cold War anti-communist; he is presented instead as holding a firm revolutionary anti-Stalinism, combined with the hope of a revival of the Soviet enterprise, whose Leninist purity had been perverted by Stalin. But such a view is false. As we have seen, even before the semi-official declaration of the Cold War by Churchill in Fulton, Missouri in 1947, Serge was calling for the banning of Communists — or "totalitarians," as he called them – from any new socialist movements that would spring up in the post-war world. Serge was advocating for blacklisting Communists from the left, while already placing them outside the pale of acceptable political life.

The New Leader in New York published many articles by Serge in the final years of his life. Almost every article that he submitted to the magazine included a personal note to Levitas in which he disclosed behind-the-scenes information about European politics. These are among the most anti-Communist writings in Serge's oeuvre. His involvement with *The New Leader* very much displeased his most consistent American supporter, Dwight Macdonald, who provided Serge with a forum in his own magazine, *politics*. But as Serge's politics began to take on an increasingly intense anti-Stalinist and then anti-Communist tinge, Macdonald felt the need to pull his friend's coattails. In a letter dated February 27, 1945, Macdonald wrote that "our political views seem to be diverging rapidly." He gave Serge his unvarnished opinion of both *The New Leader* and Serge's new political line: "*The New*

Leader has no political ideas or principles except anti-Stalinism. The only reason I can see for someone like yourself, with your past record and your fine moral and intellectual sensitivity to the real needs and interests of the masses, to accept such a political milieu is that anti-Stalinism is becoming your own basic political principle."

The extent to which Serge had swung to a deep anti-Communism was revealed in a letter written to Macdonald in Mexico on April 21, 1945. In that month's issue of *politics*, Macdonald had dismissed what he considered the error of "regardin[ing] Stalinism as an all-powerful Principle of Evil that operates independently of concrete historical circumstances. I cannot believe that any man-made organization can be so perfectly effective, whether for good or for evil." Serge responded to this with barely contained anger, similar to his tone toward Mounier in the same period. "Comm-totalitarianism," he thundered, "is, in fact, a principle destructive of human values that are essential for us, a principle, to be sure, that is not 'all powerful,' but at this time extremely powerful because it is acting in favorable historic circumstances." Those words are underlined in original.

Against Macdonald, Serge believed that totalitarianism — which, in a sign of his adoption of Cold War rhetoric, and long before it became philosophically and politically uncontroversial to lump them together, included both fascism and communism — had in fact "achieved a degree of perfection and effectiveness (have been 'perfectly effective' [in English in the original]) sufficiently to, in Russia, exterminate entire generations of elite men, in Central Europe to exterminate millions of Jews. The GPU and Majdenek demonstrate the perfect efficacy of the man-destroying totalitarian organization." Positing an equivalence between Communism and

Nazism, Serge wrote Macdonald that it is a mistake "to forget that the Communist Parties are to the same extent as the GPU [the Soviet secret police] a part of totalitarian machinery, and that for the past while the camp at Majdenek has been used by the GPU." It is worth noting that similar sentiments were expressed in 1933 by Simone Weil in her article "Are We Headed to Proletarian Revolution?" a scathing attack on Stalinist totalitarianism. Like Serge a decade later, Weil paired Hitler and Stalin. Coincidentally, Weil's article appeared in Serge's preferred French outlet, *La Révolution prolétarienne*, in an issue that also included selections from Serge's correspondence of 1929 recounting his own persecution by the Stalinist regime. Weil, who was also attracted to personalism and wrote essays about it, described the goal of socialism in terms that Serge could fully accept: "We should assign the highest value to the individual, not the collective... In the subordination of society to the individual lies the definition of democracy, and that of socialism as well."

Unlike many on the anti-Stalinist left, Serge dismissed the possibility that any alternative communism to the Stalinized Communist Parties was possible. He accused Macdonald of "wishful thinking." The hope for non-Stalinist communism, he believed, defied "all observed facts of over twenty years." Serge, in this letter to Macdonald, then makes an important observation. The opposition to Stalin in the late 1920s had led only "to political suicide and millions of brave Russians to physical extermination," proving that any attempt to reform Communist parties was futile and would be "inexorably and easily destroyed." And the mass destruction of the reformers took place "whether it was a time of social peace or in time of civil war." His life as an opposition communist, in sum, had been a tragic error. In the end, showing "the least complacency towards communism is the first step to suicide; it can only be resisted by rejecting it out of hand, completely and en bloc, its influence, its maneuvers, its masks and its faces." Anti-communism cannot be more total than this. He had moved from heresy to apostasy.

In Mexico, where he arrived after a roundabout journey (in which Varian Fry played a part) in 1941, Serge became a member of a circle of anti-Stalinist leftists made up of exiles largely from Spain, France, Austria, and Germany. His friends and comrades believed that, as was the case after World War I, World War II would result in socialist revolution. Serge begged to differ: in his last years he denied this possibility, maintaining that the victory of fascism in Germany and Italy, and the war itself, had completely demoralized the workers. The bulk of them, rather than choosing the revolutionary road, continued to support social democracy. But then, in the 1940s, Serge made his most interesting turn.

Owing to his enthusiasm for personalism, personal freedom and "respect for the human person" became the alpha and omega of his belief system. His insistence on personal freedom and personal dignity intensified his hatred of Stalinism and, more broadly, of Communists. These concerns inevitably led him to view any movement that arose in the post-war world in a way that contradicted the precepts that guided the revolutionary left of which he was a part. In doing so, he abandoned the idea of revolution. The young man who left the reformist socialism of the Belgian Worker's Party because it was no longer a vehicle of radical change, now, in the last years of his life, made the bold move of repudiating political purity and ideological righteousness in order to ensure a more just, more humane, and more democratic world, and, more specifically, a unified Europe.

Serge's insistence on respect for freedom of opinion led him to exclude Communism and Communists from the socialist movement, as they were incompatible with the democratic values that he had come to prize. He even quoted Thomas Jefferson in defense of these values. In 1945, in response to a questionnaire from Britain's Independent Labour Party on the possibility of a new international socialist grouping, Serge wrote that he sought the unity of all socialists, including in this virtually every tendency save one: "No socialist international can, [without] betraying its mission and dishonoring itself, accept within it totalitarian communists led by secret bureaus provided with secret funds and subject to a discipline that annihilates the critical spirt." This same exclusion should apply to international labor organizations, since Soviet labor unions are nothing but organs of the totalitarian state. "The notion of socialism is henceforth inseparable from the respect for the human person, from the spirit of freedom, and from truly democratic institutions."

The distance that Serge had traveled, his disgust with the standard leftist nostrums, can be seen in an incident described in his notebooks. At a meeting in September, 1944 of the Commission of Independent Socialists, a programmatic document was presented that Serge described as "a sort of Communist Manifesto, very rudimentary, recycling all the old phrases of the genre." He proceeds to indict the document, which he listened to, he said, "with interest and suppressed hostility." The basis for his opposition to the document was that "every term, every idea must be revised in the face of new realities and launched in the middle of a hurricane," which the document's left-traditionalist authors failed to do.

All of Marxist thought and activity needed to be rethought. Serge's attack went to the very roots of socialism, asserting that "it is false to write that in a bourgeois democracy the working class has only its chains to lose, [for] it enjoys—in Europe enjoyed—real well-being and real freedoms." Not content with this heresy of worker satisfaction under capitalism, Serge made the further point that the notion of the state as an instrument of the ruling class, so dear and essential to Marxists, no longer obtained. "The state is no longer the 'armed band of one class for the domination of another,' as Engels said. Or rather, it is. But only in one country: the USSR. The state has a positive role now, in fields like education and communications." Serge described his comrades mercilessly: "idealists hemmed in by the sclerosis of doctrines and circumstances, and dominated by their convictions and their emotional attachments; in short, by fanaticism. Under such conditions the person who disturbs the inner security of the others is a hateful heretic."

In an essay from January 1945, called "The Time of Intellectual Courage," Serge repeats many of these arguments, and continues his relentless critique of Marxist doctrine.

Returning to the nature of the state, Serge asserts that "the anarchist thesis of the destruction of the state and the Marxist thesis of the withering of the state through the natural functioning of a socialist democracy ... have shown themselves to be equally unreal." The world of 1945 demanded intellectual courage, the ability to revise ideas in keeping with new realities. Despite his disappointment and his pessimism, the essay ends on a note of hope: "All the elements of an action program and an ideology look to be within our grasp at a time when history on the march demands that we have the courage to become conscious of new facts and to recognize that the syntheses and doctrines of the last century no longer suffice. And nothing would be more dangerous for us today than to follow the path of intellectual routine." The logical end of this was expressed in July 1945: "The ideas of the Revolution are dead. The hammer and sickle have become emblems of despotism and murder."

This hero of modern honesty died of a heart attack on November 15, 1947, and was buried in a pauper's grave in the Spanish Republican section of a cemetery in Mexico City. Yet controversy followed Serge into the grave. On January 31, 1948, the Gaullist newspaper *Le Rassemblement* published a letter that Serge wrote to André Malraux after the victory of the Gaullists in France's municipal elections in October 1947. The Gaullist wave had crushed the Communists, who in the immediate aftermath of the war had been the largest party in the country. The Gaullists of the Rassemblement Populaire Français (RPF), founded only in April 1947, in which the formerly Communist-leaning Malraux was a prominent figure, won thirty-eight percent of the vote against the Communists' thirty percent, displacing the Communist mayors of Marseille and Nantes and the Socialist mayors in Paris and Bordeaux. The RPF victory was immense, sweeping also Lille, Strasbourg, and Rennes.

1947 had been a tumultuous year in France, with massive strikes occurring in major industries. When Serge's letter was posthumously published in January of the following year, emotions were still running high. Serge's apparent celebration of de Gaulle's victory could only be taken as it was intended: as a slap in the face of the Communists. But it was much more. In supporting the conservative de Gaulle, the quintessential man of the left was renouncing the left.

The letter did not cause much of a stir until it was republished in April 1948 in one of Serge's main outlets, the revolutionary syndicalist magazine *La Révolution prolétarienne*. "I would like to tell you," Serge wrote to Malraux, "that I find both brave and probably reasonable the political position that you have adopted. If I were myself in France, I would be among the socialists partisan of collaboration with the movement in which you participate. I consider the electoral victory of your movement a great step toward the salvation of France, which I predicted but whose size surprised me... True, more long-term salvation will depend on how you and many others will be able to accomplish what I call the double duty: that of combating the enemy of a European rebirth and that of mastering the threats we bear within ourselves."

If the Gaullists celebrated the letter, it caused unsurprising shock and dismay on the left, which continues to this day. In a note accompanying its publication of the letter, the editors of *La Révolution prolétarienne* wrote of their "surprise," since "in the many letters that he sent from Mexico to revolutionary friends in France, Victor Serge never spoke, to our knowledge at least, of the sympathy towards the RPF we so sadly find in the letter to M. Malraux." Along with this expression of shock, the editors of *La Révolution prolétarienne* added that Serge was wrong in saying there were many more socialists like him who felt as he did, since "that variety of socialist has not yet asserted itself publicly." Significantly, *La Révolution prolétarienne* did not dismiss the authenticity of the letter. They were disappointed by it and in disagreement with its contents, but they made no attempt to explain the source of Serge's alleged error or to deny the letter's genuineness.

The matter did not rest there. In the following month, Serge's son Vladimir Kubalchich, who was twenty-eight years old and beginning a successful career as a painter, joined the fray. Expressing his "indignation" at the magazine's interpretation of the letter, Vlady (as he became universally known) insisted that it was intended as a means of "reestablishing courteous relations," justified by the active part that Malraux had played in the liberation of Serge in 1936. The new courtesy was necessary because of a stormy conversation between Serge and Malraux in Marseille after the French defeat in 1940, during which Serge had bitterly attacked Malraux for his pro-Stalinist activities, in one version of the story throwing his coffee at the writer. Vlady insisted that his father's "attitude towards Gaullism was never one of sympathy, and even less of identification." He admitted that "in observing the events from afar [Serge] might have been led to rejoice at the development of an opposition to Stalinism, but that never signified approval." But this was his conclusion: "I assure you there was no unfortunate change nor any pro-Gaullist encouragement on the part of Victor Serge. If that had been the case, we would all be there to condemn him. But doing so would mean misunderstanding the profoundly revolutionary spirit of a man who had never ceased to give proof of it." Several months later, on June 3, 1948, the independent left-wing daily *Combat* reported that Kibalchich had called the letter "a falsification, the subject of a lawsuit." If a lawsuit was brought, there is no evidence of it. (An edited version of Serge's letter appeared in *The New York Times* on February 14, 1948, in an article by C.L. Sulzberger, datelined Paris and bearing the headline "Europe's Anti-red Trend Inspiring Strange Tie-Ups." Sulzberger reported that "the gradual development of anti-Communist fronts in Europe is making for some curious ideological combinations and strange political bedfellows.")

Serge correctly saw de Gaulle for what he was: the primary

countervailing force barring the road to the Communists' accession to power. Only de Gaulle had the prestige and the record to block the Communists, who presented themselves as the *parti des fusillés:* the party of the executed, the party of the armed Resistance whose members were murdered in the thousands by the Nazis. The Communists in power meant the implantation of Stalinism in Paris, which meant the fall of Europe. Serge in his final days was an advocate of a united Europe, which he discussed in the final interview that he gave, to the newspaper Combat. Europe, he said, had to be protected against "the new Russian imperialism." Preventing this was Victor Serge's final battle.

MATTHEW ZIPF

Cleopatra's Nose, Renata's Braid

1. There was a myth in college that Renata Adler had come over to America in a suitcase, and that's how she got her tremor. Students gossiped about her at Bryn Mawr in the 1950s, and so did writers in Manhattan, later on, when she started working for *The New Yorker*. One man apparently thought that she was an alcoholic, just as some people, meeting her now, have suspected that she has Parkinson's. But hers is an essential tremor — a familial trait shared with an older brother — and it has dictated small facts of her life since youth. She does not annotate her books. She apologizes for her handwriting. Her system of note-taking is to type emails to herself (she has about seventeen thousand at last count).

The problem has added, at any rate, to her shyness. Growing up, there were times that she could not so much as write down her name. When her father sent her to secretarial school, the teachers singled her out and explained, *We never say this to anyone, but you really can't do this*. She was quietly and tactfully thrown out. She still types with her two middle fingers. But for all her apologies, her handwriting is beautiful. It comes in two scripts: even rows of printed capital letters, or an elegant, slanting cursive, the kind that depends on detailed childhood training.

2. I asked her once about her hair, which runs in a long braid, almost to her waist. That braid has become somewhat famous, sung by those who meet her, and "immortalized," as one writer said, in a Richard Avedon photograph. I had seen the Avedon picture and several others of her, and noticed that in practically every single one the braid falls to her right. Once or twice, it runs down her back. But never to the left. That, too, she told me, was a product of the tremor. She can weave her braid from just one side.

Everyone has something to say about the braid.

There is awe: "the gravity of her long thick braid over her shoulder representing a modern-day Athena."

There is hostility: "a dramatic grey rope that falls just shy of her waist and almost cries out to be stroked — or perhaps yanked."

There is the search for novelty: an "elegant snowy braid," for one writer, or "spartan," for *Vogue*. A "nimbus of blond hair," a "bellringer's braid," a braid "thick as a horse tail." Or just that "famous gray braid down her back."

After the Avedon portrait, people began to measure her against the still picture. Guy Trebay, a style reporter, delighted to find Adler's braid "looking just as it did in the famous Avedon photo." And it still looks that way, only grayer now. The braid endures as a kind of synecdoche for Adler herself, eclipsing all other physical traits: her short stature, her brown eyes, her fastidious style. Friends and critics circle the braid, return to it, freight it with their opinion of the wearer. It is her epithet: "Long-braided Renata," one might have written in an epic, trying for dactyls.

3. In twentieth-century France, there was an interesting but somewhat cracked writer named Marcel Schwob, who argued that a good biography would "describe a man in all his anomalies." Schwob disliked the standard accounts of great men that spoke only of their prominent deeds and philosophical thoughts. What mattered most, in his view, were the quirks and the oddities of a person's character. If the genre of biography could study those, it would become stranger and more beautiful.

Schwob latched onto a great insight: only the small things in our lives are distinctive enough to identify and preserve us. He provided a thought experiment. Compare two Greek philosophers: "Thales might have said *know thyself* as well as Socrates," Schwob wrote, "but he would never have scratched his leg in precisely the same manner before drinking the hemlock draught." If you wanted to know who Socrates was, you needed that scratch, and not just the public maxim, which anyone could have taken from the Delphic Oracle.

Most biographies have only the occasional mention of a revealing quirk. James Boswell, the most famous example, noted the orange peels that Samuel Johnson mysteriously stored in his pockets. But that is a rare gem, and Schwob wanted the full trove. He found his model, finally, in the late seventeenth-century writer John Aubrey, who kept epigrammatic notes on contemporaries such as Hobbes and Shakespeare. Aubrey's *Brief Lives* brim with odd details. Some passages consist almost entirely of sparkling, disconnected facts, which we might now call gossip or trifles. One learns from Aubrey, for example, that

Milton "pronounced the letter R very hard," and that Erasmus "loved not fish, though born in a fish-town." Marcel Schwob loved all those details. Artistic biography meant finding not the "important" facts, the ones that changed history, but the traits that separate us and mark out our character. The leg-scratch, the hard Rs, the dislike of fish. "Each subject finds, under his pen," Schwob wrote of Aubrey, "some unique trait distinguishing that man forever among all men."

4. In the Danbury High School yearbook from 1955, you can find a "senior class prophecy" that tells the future for pairs of graduating students. The prophecy said that in fifteen years one graduate would move to Paris, where she would design hairstyles for Renata Adler. The fame of Adler's hair started that young: in high school, among her classmates. The tremor was there, too. Adler's boyfriend from a nearby technical school helped her by teaching her how to shoot, as a primitive therapy. He was the kind of boy who went hunting and trapped muskrats in the Connecticut countryside. Adler got good at shooting with him. "It was the only thing I could do, as far as I knew, without a tremor," she said. She took off days from school and went up to the pond on her family's property, where she had set up a range. One day she stuck a dime on the target and aced it. When she took it off, lead was still embedded in the coin. She placed the dime in her jewelry box, and when her son came along, decades later, she showed it to him with pride.

5. Samuel Johnson would not have agreed with Marcel Schwob. In his moralistic fashion, Johnson disliked all isolated trivia. He complained about a certain biographer, Tickell, who included information of no use to readers. "I know not well," Johnson wrote, "what advantage posterity can receive from the only

circumstance by which Tickell has distinguished Addison from the rest of mankind, 'the irregularity of his pulse.'"

Minor quirks — the particularities that Schwob delighted in — irritated Johnson. Schwob hoped to free biographical facts from the pressure of a larger point; Johnson wanted to place them in the service of usable truths. He gave an example to contrast Tickell's mistake: "Sallust has not forgot, in his account of Catiline, to remark that 'his walk was now quick, and again slow,' as an indication of a mind revolving something with violent commotion." An oddity could be mentioned, but only if it carried a lesson, the way that Catiline's alternating walk said something about his style of thought. Such private details and "invisible circumstances," Johnson wrote, should be well selected to "enlarge our science, or increase our virtue," and not just for the amusement of learning which idiosyncrasies belong to a certain man.

6. In her early days as a journalist, Adler pinned her hair up in a crown, or sometimes in a chignon — a complex formal arrangement that made her hair look, from certain angles, as if it had disappeared behind her head. An editor, after seeing Adler's hair thus wound up, wrote that she looked like a Modigliani painting. Some writers found Adler extremely beautiful. Jane Kramer told the *New York Times* that she was "very singular, very, very sophisticated." Others felt differently, perhaps with varying degrees of objectivity. Gay Talese described her as "determinedly dowdy." For Mary McCarthy, it was up to the viewer. She described Adler, who was dating her son, as "a thin, rather Biblical-looking Jewish girl . . . who is either quite homely or a beauty, according to taste."

Once she was more established, Adler replaced her chignon with the braid. She made the change at Avedon's prompting, after they had met in the '60s and become friends. Around the first time Avedon took her photograph, he said to her: "Why don't you wear your hair in one braid? And stop wearing lipstick." Adler followed his instructions. She took out the hairpins that were holding up the elaborate crown — the pins were sharp and uncomfortable anyway — and she put her hair in a braid. In time, she stopped wearing lipstick.

When an exhibition of Avedon's photographs opened at the Metropolitan Museum in 1978, Janet Malcolm, a friend of Adler's, reviewed the show. She wrote in *The New Yorker*: "The portrait of Renata Adler was taken in the French West Indies, and its sun-struck aspect turns one's mind to the novels of Conrad, suggests exquisite Conradian moral dilemmas for the boyishly slender young woman with tragic eyes and proud mouth and long castaway braid."

That last adjective, "castaway," begins to suggest the braid's significance. It is the detail that sketches a character: it tells of loneliness and self-enclosure and complexity and strength. For although Adler toured the White House with Brooke Astor, corresponded with J. D. Salinger, and studied with Claude Lévi-Strauss — in other words, *knew everyone* — she was still, throughout her life, in her own terms, a "wallflower." That is: shipwrecked, stranded, castaway.

7. In her student days, Adler wrote a paper on the question: "What is a historical fact?" She liked the idea that little things, like the colors that Cleopatra wore, could change the course of history — that such things were as much historical facts as the shape of a battlefield. It appealed to her sense of absurdity, randomness, and fate.

The source of her thinking must have been Pascal. The French philosopher had speculated, in a famous passage, that "if Cleopatra's nose had been shorter, the whole face of the world would have changed." He was proposing, in a fragmentary way, a theory of history. Small facts could alter everything — could stop invasions, combine kingdoms, forge a new religion. There was plenty of proof. "Cromwell was about to ravage all of Christendom," Pascal wrote, "but for a little grain of sand which lodged in his bladder." Schwob regretted that Pascal, like Johnson, seemed to demean facts in the search for a larger purpose. "All these facts are valued only when they modify events," Schwob wrote, almost indignantly, on behalf of his beloved quirks. He believed that Cleopatra's nose had a beauty and interest of its own, apart from any historical significance. No one had to justify it.

Most facts do not change history. A nose is just a nose, unless it belongs to Cleopatra. The average kidney stone is more like Montaigne's than Cromwell's — a personal trouble rather than a historical turning-point. But then, who can isolate any part of our fate? Each fact modifies at least some minor event, known or unknown. Montaigne was moved to philosophize upon his kidney stone, writing a set of reflections for which he is still remembered. The facts that Aubrey recorded might turn out to be of some moment, too. Milton's hard Rs could reasonably have changed his sense of the poetic line. As for Erasmus, it was in part his hatred of fish, and the church's enforcement of "fish days," that led him to question the religious customs of men and write his masterful satires.

8. After graduation, another rumor went around among Adler's Bryn Mawr classmates. Two girls told the story of how she had once, out on the quad, lit her braid on fire. As it happens, Adler says she did not start wearing her hair in a braid until over a decade after graduation. But one can still marvel at

the imagined incident — the startling intensity of the scene — and the character that must have, in some way, given rise to it.

Certainly it now seems as if Adler had always worn her hair in one style. Arthur Lubow called it "her trademark braid"; Christopher Bollen described "the signature white braid cast over her shoulder." The terms suggest a commercial brand — "trademark," "signature"— and bring to mind Susan Sontag's streak of undyed hair. That, too, seemed timeless, and was part of her celebrity and fame.

The braid has lasted some fifty years, from Avedon's suggestion to now. As a matter of physical memory, it pays tribute to their close friendship. "Avedon was," Adler wrote, "for many years and in many ways, my colleague, partner, near-twin, and close, beloved friend."

9. For a while, Adler used a rubber band to hold the braid in place. But a band tears at the roots, which is especially harmful when hair starts thinning with age. Nothing holds the braid in place now. Just friction, inertia, and renewed weaving.

Braids solve some specific problems. They prevent tangles and snarls, and they keep the hair out of your face. But a long braid can start a surprising amount of controversy. In a piece in *The New York Times*, a middle-aged writer loudly defended her choice to keep up long hair past youth. "I am rebelling, variously," she wrote, "against Procter & Gamble, my mother, Condé Nast and, undoubtedly, corporate America in general." People will judge you, certainly, for your hair. Ulysses S. Grant took a dislike to an American diplomat simply because he parted his hair in the middle. And for that, Henry Adams did not think Grant a fool: "Very shrewd men have formed very sound judgments on less material than hair — on clothes, for example, according to Mr. Carlyle, or on a pen, according to

Cardinal de Retz — and nine men in ten could hardly give as good a reason as hair for their likes or dislikes."

Adler did not use her braid to rebel against anything, nor to make a stand; it was not something on which she expected judgment. Though she once wrote that, in certain periods, even small decisions become political, she did not intend any statement with her braid. She was not joining the longhairs. "The way I wear my hair is associated with a style of life that has nothing to do with my politics at all," she told an interviewer. "It just happened to be the way it came out."

You can hear passivity in her impersonal speech: It just happened to be the way it came out.

Does that make the braid more revealing, or less?

10. For all that Schwob admired Aubrey, he did not think, in the end, that his *Brief Lives* achieved the highest potential of art. Biography had a double charge: it must attend to individual facts while still assigning its subject a place in the wider field. A portrait could not just be a series of unrelated particulars. Aubrey, unlike painters such as Holbein, never learned "how to fix an individual forever in our minds by giving us his special traits against a background of resemblances to the average or the ideal." Schwob tried to clarify his point further. The trouble with Aubrey was just this: "He put life in the eye, the nose, the leg or the pout of his models; he could not animate the face."

In the *Times* article about beauty in middle age, Adler appeared in the comments section as an example of elegant long hair. "I will never forget seeing Richard Avedon's portrait of Renata Adler, a middle-aged woman with her long gray braid," a commenter wrote. "Talk about beauty!"

An English model went into still greater raptures. Avedon was staying at her parents' house in Barbados in the early 1980s, and the model remembered: "Renata Adler was with him, and I'll never forget how perfectly she backstroked out to sea — it was just so classy."

The style of her hair, the tremor in her right hand, the way she swam out to sea. From such items alone, only a dubious portrait is formed.

11. In *Speedboat*, her first novel, Adler told a story that echoed the rumors that had spread among Bryn Mawr graduates. The scene involved Christmas celebrations at a progressive school similar to the one that she had attended as a child. "In one year's holy pageant," she wrote, "a girl's hair caught fire, from a candle held reverently by the boy behind. A father leaped to the balcony and put the fire out." I am unsure what to make of this motif: the burning of hair.

The image seemed to follow her. When *New York Review of Books* republished Adler's novels and nonfiction a decade ago, the media started writing about her again. *The Atlantic* put out a piece under the self-parodic headline "Renata Adler: Troll or Treasure?" and included an illustration showing Adler with a caricatural, swirled, almost Francis Bacon–style face. Against a bright orange background, her hair lights up in flames. The writer of the accompanying piece revisited Adler's great fights: her criticism of Pauline Kael, and her embattled memoir, Gone, about her years at *The New Yorker*. "In due course," the *Atlantic* piece read, "nearly a dozen unfriendly articles about Gone appeared in *The New York Times*, and so another flame cycle was initiated: Adler versus *The Times*." The rumors, the burning, the flames.

When I met her, I saw for myself. I noted how the strands combine, how the braid tightens and turns darker, a deep blonde. The hair that looked white, when loose, was shown to have color.

A year later, when we met again, she had recently come out of the hospital, and she warned me that her hair had spun out into "the most amazing nests." But the braid looked perfect, and safe, and permanent, when I picked her up from the airport.

12. In the 1980s, a writer for *New York* magazine confessed, after seeing Adler at a book party, "I love Renata Adler's mind. I love her gaze. I love her posture. I love the honest bobby pins and the forthright Bryn Mawr braid that hangs on one side and is never held together by a rubber band, but stays mysteriously. It abides."

Adler does not remember wearing a braid at Bryn Mawr, but it does abide. It abides in the glossy magazine photos, in the testimony of the writers whom she encountered, and finally, definitively, in the famous Avedon photograph, the one that hung in the Metropolitan Museum of Art and which is printed large, five-and-a-half by seven inches, on every copy of her last book. The picture is steady. It has nothing to do with "flame cycles" or burning or destruction at all. We see her wide dark eyes, her hand ever so slightly in motion, and then the braid.

The image did for Adler what Schwob had hoped for biography. Avedon found what was unique about her, and he set that uniqueness within a full canvas.

"The power of portraits by the great photographer," Adler wrote of her friend, "comes, in the end, from this: the ability to apply one's talent and will to saying, showing, This is who, for at least a moment, this person was. The power to have, in many cases, what becomes enormously important: the last word."

ADRIAN NATHAN WEST

Vladimir Jankélévitch: A Reader's Diary

There are writers you do not so much read as live alongside: writers of a depth, a density, a multiplicity of suggestions that resist the sort of encapsulation by which their names wither into the occasion for empty allusions and knowing nods. For nearly twenty years now, the French philosopher Vladimir Jankélévitch has been such a writer for me. I know of few accounts more moving of the tragedy of the human condition than his *The Irreversible and Nostalgia*. His *Pure and Impure* has aided me in keeping my distance from many petty fanaticisms fashionable at present. He reminds me that "philosophy is not the construction of a system, but the resolution to look naively in and around oneself," that the first sincere impulse toward knowledge is the patient articulation of one's ignorance.

Born in 1903 in France, the son of Jews from Odesa, he studied in Paris with Henri Bergson, who was the subject of his first book in 1931, and whose ideas would remain central to his philosophical and musicological writings over the following half a century. He fought in the French Resistance in Toulouse, writing tracts encouraging Russian collaborators with the Wehrmacht to abandon their posts and giving the underground lectures in moral philosophy that would form the basis for his three-volume *Treatise on the Virtues*. Though he had written his dissertation on Schelling, and had even declared in his twenties to a friend that "only the Germans think deeply," after the end of the Second World War he made an acrimonious public break with German culture (with exceptions for Nietzsche, Schopenhauer, Liszt, and a few others) that extended even to Jewish thinkers writing in German.

This intransigence, and more specifically his contempt for Heidegger and his relative indifference to Marx, placed Jankélévitch outside the major currents of French thought, though thinkers from Levinas to Derrida acknowledged a debt to him. (He also cared little for Freud, ironically, as his father had translated him into French.) Hence he was little known and little read even as friends and peers — Sartre, Foucault, Derrida — became minor or even major celebrities. It is hard to say how deeply this affected him. Biography is an English and American genre, and sadly, a recent life of Jankélévitch, François Schwab's *Vladimir Jankélévitch: Le charme irresistible du je-ne-sais-quoi* (Vladimir Jankélévitch: The Irresistible Charm of the I-Don't-Know-What), is uninformative on this and many other matters. He did say that he saw himself more as a teacher than as a writer, and remarked, who knows whether with bitterness or ironic forbearance, "This era and I are not interested in each other. I'm working for the twenty-first century." He died in 1985.

In the present diary, I have not wished to arrange into any schema the thoughts of this philosopher who affirmed that his only system was to have no system, for whom philosophy was a living thing rather than a specimen to be preserved in the formol of empty deliberation. I would only like to share, as though from one friend to another, a sampling of what I have learned — what I am still trying to learn — from him, for the benefit of those who cannot read his many works not yet translated into English, or for others who have yet to make his acquaintance.

Time

Time is the medium and ultimate boundary of human freedom. In *The Irreversible and Nostalgia,* Jankélévitch describes movement as the elementary form of freedom, and locates the basic tragedy of human life in our inability to travel back and forth in time as we can in space. The irreversibility of time is the root of nostalgia, of guilt, and of regret; its unceasing transformation of present into future is the ground of hope; and the inevitable conclusion of this future in death is the origin of anguish and despair. Yet so long as death has not yet come, it is the endless openness of time, the endless regress of its horizon, that permits an endless rejuvenation of hope, and hope is, and must be, populated by yearnings shaped by the past.

These considerations seem elementary, and my attempts to share my enthusiasm for Jankélévitch have more than once foundered before the shrugs of people to whom this all appears obvious. I can only respond that its obviousness is not an indictment of its truth, and that to ignore the obvious, perhaps even because it is obvious, because it lacks the airy beguilements of the contemporary and the urbane, is unserious; it suggests that we are justified in living as though the most superficial values pertained, or that by some strange alchemy our frivolous engagements might ripen into significance, or that we have not yet reached the moment when we must look at our life as a whole, and shall do so later, when this or that more pressing business is dispatched. Jankélévitch frequently cites "The Death of Ivan Ilyich" to illustrate the error of this way of thinking. Too much time devoted to subsidiary lives (it is noteworthy that in Tolstoy's tale life is divided into "family life," "married life," "official life," and so on) impairs an awareness of life taken as a whole.

The Adventure, Boredom, The Serious

Of the many ways conceivable of distinguishing the philosophical from the sophistical, the most urgent takes as its point of departure what we already know in our hearts. The heart's knowledge is like the appeal to the stone in Boswell's *Life of Johnson*:

> After we came out of the church, we stood talking for some time together of Bishop Berkeley's ingenious sophistry to prove the non-existence of matter, and that every thing in the universe is merely ideal. I observed, that though we are satisfied his doctrine is not true, it is impossible to refute it. I never shall forget the alacrity with which Johnson answered, striking his foot with mighty force against a large stone, till he rebounded from it, "I refute it *thus*."

Johnson wasn't so stupid as not to grasp Bishop Berkeley's idealism; he simply knew that it was inconsequential outside the realm of idle speculation. We cannot live, he means to say, with the idea of the immateriality of objects; we must live with the intuition that the things we know are real. No knowledge of the limitations of the human eye can disabuse me of the certainty that I see things the way things are; and no matter how persuasively Thomas Metzinger and others argue against the existence of the self, they cannot begin to offer me a way of living that dispenses with it as though you and I do not exist. Being inevitable, the acceptance of these pragmatic certainties, however unstable their foundations, has the character of a duty one can only shirk from insincerity or irresoluteness.

Freedom is another such elemental fact that persists irrespective of its confirmation. Let us say that I am a determinist; let us admit that science persuasively argues that we may reduce behavior to its biological and physical determinants. This is fine for my abstract view of human life, but you and I will never grasp it in the innate manner in which we grasp freedom. The truth of determinism is like the existence of dark matter or the unsettling properties of quantum objects: all are incidental to the kind of being we are doomed to be. Freedom reveals itself in the moment when something must be done; its privileged instance is the recognition that only I can decide whether and how I must act. This, and the fact that the burden of responsibility is coeval with consciousness or conscience (the same word is used for both in French, and in Jankélévitch's thought they are rarely separable) is what makes morality the *a priori* of all problems, the "chronologically first question."

There are three privileged responses to freedom in Jankélévitch's thought: adventure, boredom, and seriousness.

These correspond to the passion for the future, to the contempt for the present, and to the recognition that all that is and will be must elapse. Each of these maintains a more or less sincere relationship to death. The adventure is the passionate expectation of the future; it is by its nature a beginning, which in its continuity will be serious or boring. Erving Goffman's "anticipated fateful activity" is a nice approximation of what Jankélévitch means by adventure, and Goffman, like Jankélévitch, recognizes the centrality of the sense of risk, which, when taken in its greatest extension, is always the risk of death ("death is at the end of all avenues prolonged indefinitely, no matter where they may lead"). Adventure is the freest possible response to the semi-openness of life: to the brief but indefinite concession to live and to the perpetually postponed imminence of death.

Adventure, in advancing toward the future, has in a sense sidestepped the present; it is by definition *underway*. Boredom, meanwhile, remains mired in the moment prior to the decision. Boredom is scarce in vitality: it is the privilege of those who need not concern themselves with the basic tasks of life. Boredom is exemption from the stream of life, the relegation to observer status of one who feels he should be a participant, but cannot participate, or knows not how, or despairs of his capacity to do so. The hostage, the soldier, the base jumper are not bored; the bored person is rather one for whom the surrounding world falls short. It is the fruit of a civilized, convoluted consciousness that does not so much struggle to satisfy its needs as it satisfies them and finds no satisfaction in this satisfaction. Boredom is acquainted with the adventure, but has lost the taste for it; its longing for experience, too enfeebled to seek out new thrills, remains as the "froth" of self-consciousness upon a bodily sensation of unease.

Boredom that persists into general malaise is a consequence of selfishness. What it lacks is "the tender solicitude of the second person, which alone is capable of filling an entire existence." What Jankélévitch means here is love, a concept central to his work but one not adequately defined. He calls love a duty, fidelity, the essence of all virtue, the realization of the good, the endless and unconditional obligation to the other, but these seem like attributes or signs of love rather than its sensuous core. Love is not love of self, the love of abstract principles, or love of being in love; it is ecstatic, but falters when it revels in ecstasy at the expense of the beloved. Given Jankélévitch's assertion that consciousness is always involved, it strikes me that what he means by love is the sincere recognition of others' presence and the zealous embrace of living alongside them — the channeling of the élan vital into shared rather than "proprietary" happiness.

The adventure turns intervals into instants, boredom turns instants into intervals. The person of adventure, in frenzied pursuit of he knows not what — because without the element of enchanted ignorance, his pleasure would be the serene one of seriousness or the cloyed hedonism of the bored — gives life no time to open up and take on texture, complexity, resonance. The adventurer moves through life rather than gathering it, whereas the bored person has gathered erroneously, asking time to yield freely to him what can only occur when he lives generously in time. Of him, Jankélévitch writes, "How many years so short are made of hours so long?" The bored person is like the connoisseur of wine, who believes that his attunement to ever finer distinctions is the prelude to recognizing higher sorts of pleasure, when in fact he is teaching himself to enjoy less and less, making the objects of his fancy so rare that it may be finally said that he does not like wine at all. It goes without saying that such a person has entirely missed the point of drinking.

What makes adventure and boredom unserious is their failure to reckon with the possibility of death. Jankélévitch is careful to differentiate between the possibility of death and death itself. Death is nothing; death eludes thought; death, in Wittgenstein's phrase, "is not an event of life" — but the possibility of death is an ever-present reminder that desire, the remit of our freedoms, is bound by time in ways that we cannot understand. Adventure and boredom are unserious in averting their eyes from this boundedness. Adventure mistakes the brief pleasure of insouciance as evidence that we can live without care, and too often, when the taste or the aptitude for adventure are past, the instances in which we might have employed our freedom in the service of care are past as well. Boredom delays beginning in the delusion that the impulse to begin is growing within us, when with every calling — apart from the most frivolous and barren of pleasures — appetite comes with eating.

Seriousness is wedded to sincerity; it demands an earnest inquiry into what matters, and the courage to pursue it with a steadfastness that avoids the siren song of adventure and the cavalier aloofness of boredom. Seriousness is the reasoned approach to duration. It does not shout *carpe diem* in the thought that death may come at any time, because it may well not come quickly and we will be stuck with the consequences of our actions; and it does not tell itself there will always be time, because a time will come when there is none. "The serious is an allusion to passion and a call to order" that seeks the just measure in the pursuit of enduring joy.

Virtue

Desire places limits on freedom, but it is in responsibility that freedom is realized. Hence the freest gesture is the response to the call of conscience. Conscience is of a piece with consciousness: the stimulus that rouses the mind from its stupor, sharpening the edges of awareness, is at the same time a state of distress, the intimation that something unresolved is at play that we have a role in rectifying. The tragedy of the human condition is that the wrongs that call conscience and consciousness into being can never be fully righted, because they exist in time, which cannot be reversed. And so conscience and consciousness strive together for an impossible but also impossible-to-ignore reconciliation.

Fundamental to Jankélévitch's ethics is the belief that "all consciousness is more or less adhesive," that all consciousness tends inescapably toward virtue or dissipation. Virtue is fidelity to the moral orientation that suffuses consciousness in the moment of becoming conscious; dissipation, or neglect of this orientation, cannot quell the ache of consciousness or conscience, both of which attach preferentially to the sense of something not right. The person who tries to drown out his scruples in nihilism or forget them by exalting the sensuous over the moral is like a cat trying to run away from its burning tail. "Not only does the a priori of moral valuation anticipate and impregnate all paths of consciousness, but also seemingly, through the effect of an ironic ruse, the rejection of all valuation accentuates its impassioned character: as if, in clandestinity, axiology [the belief in an ordered scale of values] had recovered its strength and acquired a new vitality: repressed, harried, persecuted, it becomes only more fanatical and intransigent."

Jankélévitch's rejection of hedonism puts one in mind of the contrasting meanness and extravagance of certain heroes in Dostoevsky, whose conscience stalks them even in their fits of vice, and who preach morality and religion over banquets of suckling pig and cognac. They are prey to the "anarchic and even contradictory system" of pleasures — but at the same time good deeds exert a depraved temptation upon them, and they mistake this temptation for virtue. What they lack, first of all, is sincerity: the understanding that what they call good in a drunken fit of penitence is merely an "aesthetic intermittency... a luxury article, a supplementary and gratuitous ornament of our nature" coveted by the morally enervated consciousness. They cannot admit that they are not yet ready for "the infinite movement through successive exponents that constitutes moral life."

Good deeds bear the same relation to virtue as the lone note to a musical composition. No inherent property of good deeds forces virtue into being. The passerby who, he knows not why, flings a dollar at a beggar's feet is not virtuous, nor is the abuser who, in a fit of remorse, hysterically showers his victim with gifts. The bad person's good deeds are "spasmodic," representing a temporary concession to others' ideas of virtue or the flareup of a truncated conscience that tries but fails to overtake the whole person. "Virtue (if it exists) must be chronic," Jankélévitch writes. It reveals its presence in "the occasion": the test we face to show that our idea of goodness is substantial.

Pure and Impure

Jankélévitch contrasts the "relativism of effort" with the "absolutism of perfection." The latter, a property of Kantian maxims officiously fulfilled, of the realization of all utopias from Plato's republic to the workers' paradise of socialism, is instantly repugnant to whomever loves the human. What will there be to do when heaven has come to earth? What will the point of doing be when our acts are no longer consequent, because there is no more evil to banish nor good to bring about? A moral life demands friction, the possibility of failure, whereas the ossification of virtue into reflex divests it of moral content, yielding a world of good deeds populated by morally vacuous individuals. Virtue cannot be static: it requires the tension of temptation. For this reason, "the moral is, in essence, the rejection of selfish pleasure."

The je-ne-sais-quoi and the presque-rien

Rarely does Jankélévitch proceed by telling us what things are. His method is reductive — he glimpses his object, a *je-ne-sais-quoi*, an I-don't-know-what, as yet unidentifiable, and peels away the predicates that opinion spuriously attributes to it, until what is left is the pure but elusive intuition of the *presque-rien*, the almost nothing. Emblematic here, once again, is death, the object of "a crepuscular thought," a "pseudo-thought," the center of ruminations that progress not forward but only deeper into themselves. We can say of death only that it is there — but death is nothing, and it is not. An almost-nothing, an "opaque destiny," it exerts a refractory effect not on our understanding of life but on the feeling of being alive. Let us add to the list of the *je-ne-sais-quois* time, the self, consciousness, love, being, and all else that the eye fixes upon in a philosophical mood. To say what they are requires saying what they are not, and when all that they are not has been said, what remains — the *presque rien* — is as elusive as mercury. The *je-ne-sais-quoi* "is a manner of naming the impossibility of going to the end of things, of digging into their limit," and a reminder that philosophy is a vocation rather than that laborious enumeration of primitive notions, inference rules, hypothetical cases, and ideal solutions by which the Anglo-American analytic tradition seeks less to philosophize than to render philosophy obsolete. Indeed, if Jankélévitch is right that what is moral cannot be the act itself but the only nature of the consciousness of the act, then the gargantuan ethical cheat-sheet to which utilitarian ethics aspires would mean not the perfection of morals, but their disappearance into rote obedience. The same is true of epistemology: the texture of existence, its bittersweetness, is indistinguishable from the heuristic value of error and uncertainty, and to replace these with facts, axioms, and laws is to divest human consciousness of the very things that make it human.

The organ-obstacle

The organ-obstacle is an impediment to a desired state and a catalyst that makes possible its attainment. Fear is the organ-obstacle to courage: courage must overcome fear, but without fear what might otherwise be courage would be mere rashness. It is transcending frugality that elevates generosity above extravagance, transcending selfishness that makes altruism altruistic. The body is the organ-obstacle of the soul; words are the organ-obstacle of thought. In the broadest sense, freedom, bound to irrevocable choices, is the organ obstacle to freedom.

"The resistance of matter is the instrument-impediment of form that the artist's hand pulls from the rebelliousness of marble: you cannot sculpt a cloud! Poetry and music, in turn, invent a thousand arduous problems, impose the gratuitous rules of the sonnet and the often arbitrary prohibitions of fugue and counterpoint, enclose themselves in a strict play in order to find their reason for being... to feel free, the artist must find quandaries in his anagrams and calligrams."

Austerity and Moral Life

Jankélévitch denounces the "pseudo-austerity" of moral purism which, driven by a hatred for pleasure, offers its exponent "an aesthetic compensation for ethical disorder." Pseudo-austerity is a degeneracy that imputes moral value to self-castigation. This malady is especially prevalent now, when so many have learned to prefer to sacrifice on behalf of ethical causes the fabrication of virtual moral avatars that will earn them the accolades of others, in the pretense that, if the gospel of self-abasement spreads, the moral order of the universe will be restored. We call this virtue-signaling. Such behavior "attests to the will to power of a spirit in delirium on the lookout for alibis for its basic indigence"; in plainer terms, it is a way of feeling righteous while doing nothing. In this stylization of his own existence, the would-be moral agent "disappears beneath the pathetic characters he finds it opportune to embody, is blurred behind the statue he deems it opportune to sculpt." Sham mortification, melancholy for public consumption, trauma and despair twice-removed from tragedy – they all masquerade as the prelude to ethical action while burning through the moral impulses that might drive it. The pseudo-austere subject scrutinizes his conscience not for the good of what he does but for the good he tells himself and others he wishes to do, in the illusion that his zeal is a prelude to action when in truth it is a byproduct of his reluctance to act.

Forgiveness

Forgiveness is not forgetting. It is not exculpation through attenuating factors — for if there is no naked, undiluted fault, then there is nothing to forgive. It is not the oblivion into which the offense vanishes into over time, because time cannot affect the moral gravity of wrongs. It is not the expression of an imperturbable magnanimity: rancor being the organ-obstacle of forgiving, the person who does not feel the pain of the offense has never truly been harmed and is thus in no position to forgive. Forgiveness is not a dogma or intellectual disposition that accepts the place of evil in the world: neither theodicy nor determinism has a second person; both concern the "anonymous universality" of third persons, which are creations of the mind with no necessary relation to persons of flesh and blood. Nor can we excuse a person without debasing him morally: forgiveness is the mode of acquittal proper to relations among equals, but we reserve excuses for children, drunks, the senile, the mentally unwell. The mutual recognition of dignity that invigorates equality collapses when I treat myself as master of my decisions and the other as a plaything of destiny. "It is possible that a forgiveness free from any ulterior motive has never been granted here below," but this is no rationale for surrendering before the "replacement products" of unwarranted grace or forgetting; forgiveness is a *presque-rien*, but this does not make it a *rien*.

Music

Jankélévitch's writings on music are nearly as numerous as his books of philosophy. In the Russian émigré community in the France of his childhood, he recalls, musical ability was more highly prized than good spelling. Visitors to his apartment invariably mention the two grand pianos and the teetering piles of musical scores; privileged guests were allowed to accompany him as he played his favorite composers. His taste was stuffy, with a pronounced favor for the romantic: the "anti-hedonism" of the twentieth-century avant-garde lacked the enchantment of evoking "affective reminiscence," which was, for him, one of music's primary functions.

With music, as with death, as with love, his aim is to clear away the discursive ornaments that delude us into thinking we have something to say about it. Being "both expression and constituent element," music lacks the gulf between thought and its objects of which language is the bridge, and for this reason, it has no communicable meaning. Music is rather a mode of organizing experience. It possesses a vital structure, with a tentative beginning, a moment of plenitude, and an end; but unlike lost and yearned-for days, we can revisit it again, and because hearing the second time is not the same as hearing the first, re-exposure to it is "not repetition, but the beginning of an order," an arrangement of the sentiments in some sense analogous to the self. To relisten to a favored piece again is like seeing the arrival of dawn that tells us death has not yet come for us. The passionate energies invested in music, lived in repetition, make of it "a protest against the irreversible."

Decadence

Jankélévitch examined decadence explicitly in a brief essay in 1950, but it is alluded to in other works, and his philosophy in its entirety may be described as the attempt to rescue the primary moral intuitions from the distortions that decadence effects upon them. Decadence is "the confusion of pure and simple consciousness with the consciousness of consciousness," and mistakes conscious involvement in the world with consciousness's involvement with itself. Decadence produces "two families of monsters: narcissistic monsters of introspection and monsters of excessiveness." Both of these abound at present, the one busy attuning itself to ever more microscopic violations of pseudo-moral tenets that serve only to browbeat others and exalt the faithful, the other renouncing mutual respect and decorum in the name of a supposed authenticity, as though a self constrained by care and consideration were somehow less valid than the one whose meanest impulses are allowed to run free. The decadent consciousness redoubles on itself infinitely: "In despair at its own ease, the decadent spirit will create imaginary difficulties and invent artificial obstacles in order to salvage by diktat that resistance which is the only thing capable of preserving life from boredom and stagnation; for want of real problems, the spirit takes refuge in charades, riddles, rebuses."

The nostalgia for a supposed golden age, almost always a veil for reactionary tendencies, is a symptom of decadence and not its antidote. Decadence is a loss of attunement in moral and aesthetic terms: in the moral realm, it prefers the virtual to the material; in the aesthetic, it opts for the copy over the original or for the *mise-en-abîme* of ironic parody. Decadence is "crumbling and bloated," seeking creative unity in vain. But this seeking itself remains a positive force that may announce the spring to decadence's autumn. In this way, decadence is in fact inherent to progress. What it requires, in the first place, is seriousness: a sense of the brevity of time and the gravity of what is at stake.

DANIEL HALPERN

Dust

So when I think of you
there is light.
There is a window
that disappears at night
and returns at sunrise.

There is the dust of us
on the slant of incoming rays
warming the rooms where we were,
the many rooms, the dust of us
blended, one sheath of light.

Afternoon Idyll

You were dreaming again, of holding her
in the failing light of some failing
stop over or another, some merely broken down
town with nothing operative but corruption.

The sun like a cavity filling with blood
on the western horizon
made the ocean Pacific, the late afternoon
dangerous in its willingness to reveal.

Were you dreaming? The warm beer stamped a ring
on the bamboo where you left it, a green dress,
moss green, just tossed
over the cane chair, a pale dress
of cloth, abandon, something — what? Your hand
finding for itself a little game with another.

While you were dreaming she walked out to the veranda
wearing your starched white shirt, rolled to the elbows,
the tails down to her knees.
Her feet left small damp marks on the plank flooring.

You watched as the light dyed her red —
was she dreaming? In the sink, the emptied shells
of crustaceans, three chopsticks and two paper plates.

In the clay pot on the railing, she notices
a slender vine-like plant tied with twine,
staked with a chopstick.

Immigrants

Aren't we all,
all of us?

Coming from a world
before time and dream,

a place without time
a place that does not exist

into a world that does,
of time and content. The clock starts

with a slap, breath,
an intake of

our air, the colors of this world
and first dreams of what's ahead.

Open your eyes. Breathe
in the spice of your new world.

The mountains here
are everything new to you,

the rivers to cross
whose currents pull

you to other shores,
beaches shining with an infinity

of reflecting grains,
borders, a geography of constellations,

stellar borders,
everything in a single grain,

just reflecting. I've seen you
in lines outside,

in the heat, in the cold,
looking to inhabit beyond

these lines. And soon, as the days
and years turn over, you'll again need

to begin the journey, the familiar journey,
the long emigration back

to the world
where time is not a dream

but an airless landscape, without scent,
at the border where the dream sleeps.

No documents of transition. Breathe.

Language

So the word for
Did you know her
You may be thinking
Are you thinking
Of someone else
The red oak survives
Life in the city
Feng is wind in Chinese
Sirocco wind
Over the Sahara
A wind off the dessert
Burdened
Memory now sand
A lost ring
Buried there
Bells In European towers
Sound and light shows
The three pyramids of Giza
We knew them in those years
A few decades
Restaurants and country fairs
The O of a lighted Ferris wheel
The swinging gondolas
Returning with the word for

Light in shadows
The mirage of water
Puddled in the road ahead
Liminal
Lagniappe
The yet to come

DAVID THOMSON

Why Did Humprhey Bogart Cross the Street?

This is a small thing, but it happened in a time when we were content to hang on the marvel of moving photography. In 1946, without undue fuss or fraud, the medium could record actual things and say, look, *this* happened. That's what we were up for then, the appearance of a changing now. Even if it was just being on a street in Los Angeles and waiting for the afternoon to subside.

A man comes out of one bookstore and looks across the street at another: was this the heyday of American civilization? The street is moderately busy, passersby et cetera, and there is subdued Max Steiner music in the air, alert or wary, call it background italic, as if in 1946 such readiness was as detectable as smoke in the city's crisp fragrance. In a dark suit and a fedora, the man walks across the street. He seems headed for this other bookstore. But as he comes to the far sidewalk he passes a fire hydrant, and then, without a need in the world, but as if he has an inner life we'll never know, he pats the top of the hydrant and moves on. If you want a glimpse of how good we were then, and what it meant to us — the movie thing — you could find worse than this.

I forgot to tell you: there is a roll of thunder as the scene unwinds. It could be from out by Pasadena, but getting closer. No, this is not a disaster film about weather, or an earthquake splitting the street. But in a film called *The Big Sleep* you may wonder in the back of your mind whether some sleeper is stirring. It's in that back of his mind that a man could think about thunder as he taps a hydrant on its head. Like touching wood for water.

Or maybe the director Howard Hawks thought, Well, if this fellow is going to cross the street, we need a little extra to fill the time. Get me a dash of thunder, will you? Like putting mustard on a hotdog. But then perhaps the man in the fedora queried the director: Tell me, why am I crossing this street? And Hawks could have answered, Well, we need enough visual to make room for the thunder — and I like to watch you walk.

We are attending to *The Big Sleep*, from the Raymond Chandler novel. This actor is Humphrey Bogart and he is playing Philip Marlowe, the private eye. Marlowe is on a case, so you'd assume that this street scene has to be significant — don't we know that movies are loaded with all the big things about to happen? Isn't it the rule on screen that every last thing is vital? The details are clues, and that's how we are always the private eye. The process of a story is us finding something out, and over fifty years or so that became claustrophobic — as if every damn detail was weighing on us. The visual is so single-minded as a construct. It can't breathe without insisting on focus and action. No one on a film set ever called out, "Inaction!" And yet there were listless streets in Los Angeles, or anywhere, where not much was happening. Certainly not enough for a movie. Think of it as life.

And that's a loveliness, like Mrs Dalloway saying to herself, "What a lark! What a plunge!" as she sets out walking on that summer morning in London to buy the flowers herself. That is a lyrical if unimportant moment, so exciting yet so ordinary, and it's the kind of thing that is hard to get on film. Oh, the grind of all that relentless purpose! Making sure everything is underlined. When another wonder in photography is how it can be open to the light, to chance, to just the persistence of vision. Open like a window on a good morning.

If you watched *The Big Sleep* over the years, you saw that the scene coming up at the Acme bookstore is blissfully unnecessary. That is curious, since it is among the most delectable scenes ever managed, even in the work of Howard Hawks, who loved to be casual yet provocative at the same time.

It's a good thing this is a classic, because it would never get made now: two bookstores on one block, and flirtation for its own sake? What happens is that Marlowe goes into the Acme bookstore (it is empty except for a young woman who works there – she has "the look of an intelligent Jewess" in Chandler's novel). He talks to her; he impresses her to take off her spectacles and let down her hair (not in the novel). She knows her books and teaches Marlowe that the bookstore across the street is a sham. Not that that matters; we already knew that its owner was a crook. But this woman (she has no name or story, apart from her pliancy and letting her hair down) is persuaded to put up the "Closed" sign, find a bottle, and let the thunderstorm that was coming pass away. We have to imagine what happens next (that's where the Code was terrific), but this may be disconcerting now because the film takes it for granted that she is smitten and just a lark and a plunge in male fantasy. Most of this is Hawks, not Chandler.

I don't mean to forgive the scene. I can't rule out the possibility that it exists because Hawks had found this young actress, Dorothy Malone, and wanted to have something for her to do, some flowers they could sniff together. But I'm not shocked by it. I'm looking at it to reinhabit the miracle of movie things that hardly need to happen, and the radiance of the nest-like places where they occur. You see, it's not just that the medium is in a cul-de-sac now, where it cannot condone the male gaze of Howard Hawks or the fantasizing that he lived for. I'm also thinking about the loss of such small scenes and what I'll call movie day-dreaming. Was there ever a nicer bookstore in a movie? Just watch how Malone moves. And feel the onset of evening.

That may make the bookstore seem unduly cozy. But it is part of *The Big Sleep* and movies of that era that the sets were not just plausible; they were done with affection and emotional ownership. Marlowe's office is a bare waiting room, but Hawks treats it kindly, so when Bogart and Bacall run their delirious telephone routine, the mundane is complicit in the marvelous. She has an itch above her knee so he tells her to scratch it. Is it absurd to see an empire at its pinnacle in that tremor? Just see how the ordinariness of these rooms sustains rapture. Maybe this was as much stage as screen, but Hawks guessed that we liked to imagine ourselves in these plain interiors. That's how Bogart might become iconic even if his Marlowe has only one suit. (In the book, he's a bit of a dandy — unthinkable for the movie.)

Bogart is known still (I hope) as an illustrious tough guy — sardonic, abrasive, a needler, and rough when he had to be, while still willing to be romantic occasionally. And so anxious to be liked: don't forget how in his two Hawks pictures in 1944–1946 he was talking to this woman who did the fondest thing for him — she answered him back, so he learned he didn't have to be Warner Bros hardboiled all the time. That happened, let's say, by chance, and it wasn't that Hawks hadn't had his eye on Lauren Bacall first. But Hawks always rejoiced in the principle of impressive guys being taken down. What most preoccupied him on *The Big Sleep* (and *To Have and Have Not*, the film that preceded it, the one where the nineteen-year-old Betty Perske slid into being Lauren Bacall) was the way Bogart walked.

If you think that's fanciful, look at the film again and count how often Bogart has to walk across a space, a room or a street, and sink into Hawks's rapture over this fundamental action. There's a great deal of daft mystery in *The Big Sleep*, if you take it seriously or draw timelines to puzzle it out. But while you're trying to follow the mystery, slip into the enchantment of this un-tall man, very plainly dressed, strolling into mythology. In the same way, in the first pages of *Mrs. Dalloway*, you feel for Clarissa walking in the June morning, counting off the chimes of Big Ben on her way to the florist. "I love walking in London," she says. "Really, it's better than walking in the country."

I'm not saying Hawks had a crush on Bogart (or more than Mrs. Woolf adored Mrs. D). But in the age of movies directors loved everyone who moved, and gladly endured a certain amount of story or drama to get into simply photographing the way a Bogart walks and talks and listens, or flat-out exists. He was an actor, of course, so long as no one caught him at it, but he walked with soul, in the way you might touch the top of a hydrant as you crossed a street. You can list Marlowe's Chandleresque credentials, his career record, his sworn testament, and so on, but *The Big Sleep* is that hydrant, it is him turning up his hat brim and lisping about the *Ben-Hur* edition with the erratum slip, and his telephone manner, and the way he catches Carmen Sternwood (Martha Vickers) as she tries to sit down in his lap while he's still standing, and so many other moments that would have been cut if you were monopolized by plot and solving the mystery.

Then there's the patience with which Hawks was watching him and finding little things for him to do. Plus the way the director did movie after movie without being picturesque, stylish, or what was called cinematic. He had never thought of rivaling Hitchcock, whose incessant unique angles on everything trembled with his fear of life and looking. That's where the claustrophobia can take you. But Hawks looked at the world and living rooms like a horseback rider in Wyoming.

He liked life and day-dreaming and the way movie married the two and left room for pretty women in cameo parts. That is his shady elegance, and the airiness of those years when the world was desperate, circa 1945, but so much calmer than it can be now. Mrs. Woolf killed herself — we know that story — and *Mrs. Dalloway* culminates in a suicide, but you don't forget its feeling for the epiphany of London and the florist shop aromas in June. That novel talks to itself about writing a book like *Mrs. Dalloway*; it is enthralled by the balance of composition and dismay. It's like Bogart asking Hawks, What's this scene about, Howard? and Hawks telling him, Well, this is the Sternwood house and you just follow the butler down the hallway, looking at stuff on the wall, and then after seven or eight paces there's Martha Vickers coming down the stairs to meet you. She'll goose you.

What's she going to do?

I don't know yet.

So it feels like a rehearsal. For all we know, Bogart had not the least idea what he was meant to be doing, or why he was wearing out his shoes on the picture. But look at it now, and you can't miss the pilgrimage.

Books and professors tell you that *The Big Sleep* is a film noir, a whodunit, a tough guy picture. There are traces of that genre to be sure, but don't settle for the dead end. *The Big Sleep* is a chamber work, a screwball comedy so relaxed or evasive that we don't need to get ready to laugh — it just happens. For all the terse fisticuffs, the offhand shootings, and the corpses left behind, it is a tranquil movie about optimistic motion, standing still and doing as little as you can get away with while giving everyone the eye. No one — least of all Hawks or Bogart — would have dared think this, let alone say it, but the picture is into momentary beauty. The wittiest summary of that aspiration is the credits shot, the silhouettes of a him and a her, both smoking then putting their cigarettes side by side in an ashtray — that is the bed scene in the movie. Hawks delivered it at the start so he could concentrate on talk.

"Beauty" gets to the heart of the matter. That's a concept we take for granted now, like oatmeal and other banal staples: it is the hope that helps us negotiate Hiroshima, Syria, and Ukraine; it's the luster and the sheen that lets us get along with cancer, poverty, and the ads on TV. "Beauty" is the code that humanism has been using to contest our ugly social nature. But I'm putting the word in quotes because it would have made Hawks or Bogart wince. To do pictures in their heyday was to come through on schedule and on budget; to have something that grew lines outside the theater; to put away some money and permit the various superiorities that came from making pictures.

Perish the thought that anyone would look at your movie and say it was beautiful. That cut against the grain of pictures being for everyone. It smelled of Soviet expressionism in the 1920s or French malaise in the 1930s. Something that alarmed Hollywood about Orson Welles and *Citizen Kane* was how it wanted to bludgeon us with show-off — or as critics learned to say, cinematically. That drop-dead emotional mouth uttering "Rosebud" was the warning shot, something out of nowhere meant to send us into nervous raptures and draw attention to itself. Whereas the keynote of movies, their astonishing habit, was to stay casual. Hawks was not alone in this. His avoidance of expressionism can be seen and felt in the work of Ernst Lubitsch, Preston Sturges, Frank Capra, Mitchell Leisen, Michael Curtiz, and most of the directors trying to keep in work.

If they were lucky they did not pause to think this through, but there was no need to press beauty on the screen or on audiences, because photography was already there. That was the amazing thing, the knockout; it was the way of confusing life and the lifelike that is the riddle and enchantment of the medium — and it was the quiet bomb that keeps going off. Ginger Rogers was surely pretty. But no one reckoned Fred Astaire was good-looking, or more so than Stan Musial. He had a tough time getting into pictures. But then the truth sank in, that Fred might work out a dance routine in which he and Ginger went all the way across the room in one unbroken shot. No need to cut to close ups of twinkling feet and all that nonsense. The thing about Fred and Ginger was the blithe spirit of this homely man saying, we can manage this room, just like that, so long as no one thinks to cut or asks how beautiful it is. The joy of their films is not because the dancing is hard — it's in seeing an ease in which everyone dances as a matter of course, like blessed walking. It's the non-dancing stuff that is difficult to take.

A theory of beauty existed in these casual lifelike miracles being put up on a big screen, so that all we had to do was wallow in the warm water of it. Yet it was trickier than that, for it played on our desire to be smart. It's only a movie, we told ourselves in philosophical delight. Here was a paradox that humanism had not faced before: for while it could be Philip Marlowe out in LA at some five o'clock in the afternoon, on a street resembling the real thing, it was also Bogart, a chronic actor, on a stretch of city that had been designed and fabricated and would likely be folded up once the shot was done, or tactfully repurposed as an avenue in a college musical. It's the threat buried in that disconnect now (the chance that our dream has been betrayed) that encourages gun-ownership and other panicky behaviors. The guns are held on to so tightly to cling to the idea of "the frontier."

We had been looking at a romance, and we might go mad from the reverie. Yet *The Big Sleep* was offered as a run-of-the-mill product, and not a great work from a genius. Long before Marshall McLuhan had thought of it, the medium had kidnapped most messages. Movies were such a rapture that no one needed to waste time saying they were beautiful, or getting to be art. Though it might have been useful if someone had thought to ask, Well, sure, I love these pictures too, but should we start wondering what is happening to reality? What are all these women doing — taxi-drivers, hat-check girls, pretty psychopaths, and graduates in bookstores — and what are we meant to make of them?

In every historical reckoning, this denial of beauty or the allegedly higher reaches of art was crucial. The movies and Hollywood itself were constructs designed to smother notions of creative elitism. There was only one elite and that was the money. Wasn't the medium for everyone, as no medium had been before? This was the inflationary boost served up for frightened people trying to get through the Depression, commonplace failure, and the disappointment at how the United States had turned out so far from its ideals. From 1776 on, we were suckers in the frenzy of advertising. The pursuit of happiness? Give us life, liberty... or Liberty Mutual.

In Hollywood, the abiding promo saw happy endings and lovely pictures as the rights of man. An end was nigh. As audiences began to stay home, film studies moved into academia, and movies turned self-conscious and sour about themselves. I put it that way because of our obstacle: it becomes more apparent every day that America will destroy itself rather than yield to measured, critical introspection. So it's easy to argue that *The Big Sleep* is as antique and as woeful as love songs, handwriting, pitchers who have to hit, and movies that practice flirt and then dissolve so that we can imagine what Marlowe and that clerk did while it was raining outside. For Chandler, "the big sleep" had meant death; for Hawks, it welcomed dreaming.

It's a leap forward, from books on Howard Hawks to the *New York Times* wondering whether the movies must really be dead if it takes Tom Cruise and *Top Gun Maverick* to remind the business of glory days. As if Cruise had any idea in his sixty-year-old triumphalism how Bogart had hesitated in *The Big Sleep*, considered some drollery, and let it pass by because it would be vulgar to draw attention to it. Long before the technical effects were available, Cruise was a photo-shopped actor, clinging to his grin — just don't remind him how he did *Magnolia* once upon a time.

The movies had been dying for so long. Like flowers, ripeness is only today and tomorrow. Audience numbers began to decline in that age of film academia, no matter that Hollywood had briefly fallen into the hands of young rebels who were making some films that approximated the turmoil of the country, and deplored it. That fierceness couldn't last — it struck at the virtue of money; and then George Lucas ordained a technological splendor that restored large young audiences and assured them that it was not just possible, but obligatory, to remain young forever, or for as long as that scheme lasted.

What happened to the movies was that the medium abandoned that delicate and adult task of looking like life, and passed into a realm where, because anything was possible, photography itself was given up.

That sounds odd, maybe, because we still live according to the homily that movies have been photographed. It is true that images are recorded, and then heavily doctored. But the digitization of appearance and the flood of computer-generated images mean that few filmmaking ventures respect the reality of that humdrum Los Angeles street. Everything can be handled, from stick-figure armies ready to be wiped out, to an actress, Vanessa Kirby, seeming at full-term pregnancy and having a baby in *Pieces of a Woman*. One may be more sentimentally inclined to the latter than the former. Kirby certainly seems more compelling or touching than Benedict Cumberbatch blundering around like a blind man in an obstacle course in *Doctor Strange in the Multiverse of Madness* (some titles can't help being warnings). But you need to understand the condition whereby many filmmakers (and audiences) now are drawn to their power to surpass appearance. Now actors have to play scenes with spectacles they cannot see: Cumberbatch may stare through vistas of sublime destruction, while Bogart actually crossed the actual street or actually caught the reckless Martha Vickers in that *Big Sleep* opening. We are at a point where the people in movies have the status and the flexibility of characters in animation. So many of them are only diagrams of humanity.

Live action and animation involve different degrees of experience, and a different contract with the audience. Chloe Zhao has every right to be a success, and she had a new opportunity after *Nomadland*, a hit in so many ways, and seemingly pledged to ordinary stuff happening, but still too pious or noble for my pleasure. One understands the creative pressure to make a picture about people who have given up on the world — so many special-effects extravaganzas ride on that dynamic — but it is hard for a mass medium to do that without seeming self-satisfied, fascistic, or religious, while securing its home on the high ground and keeping its own discreet firearms. *Nomadland* was picturesque and even sanctimonious in the director's gaze, where her earlier film, *The Rider*, had been factual, incidental and transfixingly commonplace.

It may seem archaic or forlorn now to favor the more humane approach, and one has to recognize that some young audiences at picture shows are more inclined to be wowed than moved. I am not knocking the wow: it has always been integral to moviegoing, where the urge to show people something they had never seen before was essential in the enterprise. Watching women talk back to men in Hawks pictures, and silencing them — once that was a wow. With several writers — from the lethally professional Jules Furthman to his drinking pal William Faulkner — Hawks pioneered smart small talk. It felt like a knack that could save the world. And he ran the lines serene in the knowledge that he would seldom be troubled by those policemen of significance named Oscar.

Still, it took only a few years for Chloe Zhao to go from that second film, *The Rider*, to *Eternals* made for Marvel Studios. The latter cost $200 million and a piece of that went to Zhao, as it should. But the picture was a disappointment, whereas *The Rider* — made with occasional actors on a South Dakota prairie, and maybe 1 per cent of the Marvel budget — was one of the best American films of this century. One reason for that was the film's faith in a world of life and death that goes on between people and horses. Do not forget for how long that transaction was one of the most reliable marriages in America.

It may feel contrived to locate a culture and a silver age in Bogart crossing a street in 1946. But twenty-four times a second in those days a photo-chemical reaction occurred with light and silver salts in the emulsion, and then some judicious pushing in the labs. It functioned for all of us who existed then, because we were still in love with the freshness of photography turning life into the lifelike with more enhancement than loss. We felt we might handle that risky in-between. I am not mining mere nostalgia, or saying that things were better then. Our race does not quite deserve "better" as a measuring stick. Let's just say it felt more ironic to be pretending then, while the gradual loss of amused fun is one of the saddest retreats our United States have taken. That is how computerized infinities have killed the notion of humdrum rooms.

The Acme bookstore scene is some kind of disgrace now — but it wasn't in 1946, even if it nurtured resentments that might close down its fun in sixty years. That's not my point, even if I own up to being a citizen of the disgrace. What's more significant is regret over how a cherished medium — in telling silly stories to all of us it was once the hope of the world — walked away from the nearly accidental radiance of small things happening in the light. It sounds farfetched now: how a few people put together a city of bookstores, with a street set, the rumble of thunder, and the unexceptional placing of a fire hydrant. But they found a harmony and a shabby spokesman for our wish to be more confident than we are.

As I was writing this essay, an issue of *Sight & Sound* arrived. It reprinted a 1971 interview in which Joseph McBride and Michael Wilmington talked to Howard Hawks. The magazine had enriched the interview with several photographs from its Hawks archive. One was a production still (not a frame from the film) of Angie Dickinson and Ricky Nelson on the Tucson location for Hawks's *Rio Bravo*, made in 1959. She is looking off frame to her right, and he is rather meekly following her gaze. He feels like an extra dressed up in cowboy gear but uneasy playing a gunslinger named "Colorado" who helps win the day in that screwball siege story.

They have a companion, or a question mark, between them. This is a horse with a white blaze on its head, looking at the camera but playing it very cool — I told you, the horse was pivotal in our culture — and edging the romantic pose closer to farce.

You see, she is dressed in tights and a leotard along with high heels, none of which seems appropriate for semi-desert Arizona at the close of the nineteenth century. But she is wearing this unlikely costume with calm assurance. She may guess she is a natural, an ideal, and hardly the least appealing person ever photographed. Dickinson was another of Hawks's discoveries, and in Rio Bravo (as "Feathers") she seems as subtly actual as Bacall (as "Slim") in *To Have and Have Not*. The photograph has an aura less of the West than of the "Western." It is ironic and Hawksian in teasing actuality, and how by 1959 it was hard to make authentic Westerns. That window had been eclipsed by the decades of pretend movies. We exhausted our brave dream. You can't kiss or kill anyone now without referring it to your movie repertoire.

But there might be heaven in a sly picture about a few straight-faced actors pretending to make such a story.

What am I doing here in the desert in tights and high heels, Howard?

You're giving that horse something to think about, and when you're ninety, if we're lucky, it'll be the same.

Bogey, why did you give that touch to the fire hydrant?

Did I do that? I don't know. I wasn't thinking.

CELESTE MARCUS

The Trance in the Studio

The vastness and nuance and intelligent, rough beauty of John Dubrow's paintings, the rhythmic turmoil which roils their cakes of paint, tempts one to conceive of them as natural wonders. How are such things made? These works sometimes put me in mind of the forces of nature that combine to create hurricanes and mountain ranges. In the deep geography of Dubrow's works there seems to be no mediation, no polish, no editorial mercy to bridge, for the viewer's sake, between what Dubrow was moved to make and what Dubrow meant by it. The painter's long toil — these works require years to complete — is rewarded with an extraordinary immediacy. He does not translate for our sake. We meet him entirely on his ground.

I thought all this before I had ever stood before a proper Dubrow painting. I had seen small oil sketches, the free power of which foreshadowed the force of the full-scale versions. Dubrow's paintings are enormous, not only in height and width but also in the sculptural thickness of their surfaces and in the demands that they make. A topography of calcified oil rises and falls from one edge of each surface to the other. Seen from the side, uneven protrusions testify to the force of the painter's impact. The surfaces are like the beaten ground of a paddock in which a wild horse has been penned. The man who made these paintings must have exerted prodigious energy to whip and slice and scratch all this paint so that it seethes the way it does. The edges of Dubrow's surfaces are never straight because the paint rises and cakes over them, the corners are rounded, there are no clean angles. Like any inch of the natural world, Dubrow's paintings are not neat. And yet they contain a beautiful order.

John Dubrow's studio is sheltered in a converted tobacco warehouse twenty minutes outside Manhattan along with some several dozen other artists of various kinds. The complex in which it sits, called Mana Contemporary, strikes the visitor as misleadingly unsuitable for the attainment of transcendent experience: it is made up of several slabs of brick in a gritty, graffitied stretch of Jersey City only a few yards away from the train tracks whose thunder protects against gentrification. The eponymous Mana, Moishe Mana of Moishe's Moving Business, is perhaps unaware of the condign allusion of his surname. Dubrow's work is itself like manna, by which I mean it is inexplicable, it seems to have fallen from heaven, and it contains enough to satisfy a variety of appetites. Above all, it must be experienced physically; the effect of its physicality is difficult to describe. The charismatic textures of these dense canvases are a challenge to descriptive language. So is the atmosphere of his studio, with its mixture of solidity and vertigo, of gravity and excitation. Describing it in words is like trying to paint the sensation of tumbling down a flight of stairs. This incongruity is frustrating, and that frustration is precisely what makes the painter's blood race and his paint hum and bellow. He is trying to describe in paint sensations that can only be felt in life. Something primary, something both sophisticated and atavistic, lives inside that studio. I will try to tell you what this means.

The path from the front doors of Mana Contemporary to the elevator winds past a number of John Chamberlain's gripping and enigmatic sculptural constructions made from welded scraps of colorful cars. John's studio is on the fourth floor. The elevator doors open in the middle of a hallway, on the left side of which a glass sheet covers the wall of a large dance studio in which a choreographer was presiding over a practice session. I turned right, walked down a few thin, high corridors lined with enormous iron sliding doors until I reached 411. On the other side of the massive iron door, another world. Paint, paint, paint. Speckles of it and streaks of it and mounds of it. Paint piled high on a table that had once served as a palette but has over the years calcified into a many-colored undulating mass. Paint encrusted on empty paint pails and paint brushes and paint tubes. Stains of paint on the ground, on the tables and the chairs. The smell of paint is thick even in the immense space of the studio. The room is huge. The white walls, way above human height, lose their paint stains as they stretch all the way to the industrial ceiling. Enormous windows, the kinds of windows artists pray for, gape on two stretches of the studio, suffusing the immense space in a big, gentle light. On the day that I visit it is pouring rain outside — the light is soft and strong, like the artist.

Where did he come from and how did he get this way? John Dubrow was born in Salem, Massachusetts in 1958, studied at Syracuse University, Camberwell College of Arts in London, and then the San Francisco Art Institute. Formative years spent in California, Israel, and New York — where he has lived for the past several decades — mark him as a man with many influences and admirations, a man from no place and every significant place. He has painted the landscapes and rooftops of Jerusalem and New York City, in equal parts a creature of the Bible and of Babel. Leaning up against the walls of his studio are portraits —in an especially lyrical picture, the poet Mark Strand peers from behind his folded arms — and landscapes of euphorically vital greens and blues. On some walls crowded cityscapes buzz across from near-abstract combinations of flesh tones. Everything is oil paint.

Paint is John Dubrow's air and water and food. His commitment to the substance is absolute, almost monastic. He has spent his whole life studying its capabilities and its effects. While I was working on this essay I dreamed that I had to wash pills down with oil paint — to squeeze a tube into my open mouth and toss back two small capsules. His fanaticism is contagious: for John, paint is medicine.

The paint which clings to the towering stretches of what John says are canvases — the paint wholly obscures the surface on which it was settled — impose themselves with great force. They are not violent, but they possess enormous power. Dubrow is very exacting in his observation and in his practice. (He is also slight and soft spoken.)

John rarely uses a paint brush. The paintings are too rough and large and a brush's texture is limited. As mentioned, he does not use an ordinary palette, but requires an entire table. Near the center of the studio a quarter of a large table is covered in half empty paint tins. The rest of it glistens with the colors which make up the painting with which he is currently wrestling. Often he uses an enormous palette knife to apply the stuff, but he also uses his hands, covered in blue surgical gloves. The masses of paint spread so roughly across the canvas with his knife form heavy planes. These colored planes establish the painting like bricks or sheets of cement. They are strong, weighty, and deeply intelligent.

Tension undergirds this intelligence. That tension is fueled by the force within John fighting for figuration and the force pulling him towards abstraction. The process of creating a painting, for John, is made up entirely of these two compulsions, these two antithetical conceptions of what the painting ought to be, which do battle over and through John as he works. The painting is a record of this agonistic tug of war between figuration and abstraction. He builds up one and then breaks it down in service to the other. "That's why they take me so long, I think." Every step forward has to be undone. The artwork is a record of new beginnings. Creation and destruction; creation is destruction.

For hours on that wet, tranquil afternoon we moved from canvas to canvas talking about art. When one asks John questions about his work, he answers in riddles, not because he is being coy but because he is trying to be precise about a process which is largely incommunicable in language.

CM: *What's the difference between pure abstraction and what you're doing? Is it color and texture?*

JD: *It's the difference between kinds of space and form and texture. In pure abstraction those things usually stay on the surface of the picture plane with an even frontality. For me, in my own work I'm trying to get things to jump around back and forth from deep to shallow, from solid to fractured — I want things to seem to be one thing but actually be something else. As far as texture goes, I never think about the buildup of my own surfaces. The thickness develops organically while I'm working, although I do notice them. Most contemporary painters who build up textures use it as a decorative or willfully emotional device.*

John is a scholar-painter: he has studied the history of his art, as the books scattered about testify. After many decades mired in the vernaculars of the art world, he invokes its language to defy its axioms. Translation is necessary for the uninitiated: when John talks about applying surface decoratively, he is gesturing towards the strides into flatness and abstraction which were sanctified in part by the ferocious hectoring of critics such as Clement Greenberg, who insisted that art history was Hegelian, that it traveled inexorably, with the force of a logic, out of figuration and into abstraction, and that painting should nevermore strive to communicate three-dimensionality. Modern painting, Greenberg decreed, had to distinguish itself, to justify its own existence, by confining itself to the two-dimensionality of the picture plane:

> Three-dimensionality is the province of sculpture. To achieve autonomy, painting has had above all to divest itself of everything it might share with sculpture, and it is in its effort to do this, and not so much — I repeat —

to exclude the representational or literary, that painting has made itself abstract.

This edict, issued repeatedly by Greenberg, who considered it his job to influence the art world rather than merely describe it, altered how artists — and the rest of us — conceive of art. Dubrow is still defining himself against the framework that the high church of modernism established. So, while purely abstract artists are not tangling with space and form and color all at the same time, John's post-abstract but incompletely representational pictures are persistently communicating space and establishing three dimensions.

JD: *The only thing I'm interested in is the volume of space, and building and breaking down form at the same time. For instance, this painting* [he gestured towards one of two canvases leaning against the wall in front of us] *is a painting of two figures falling in Paris.*

Eyes widened, I looked intently at the identified object and muttered *If you say so*. A near-square mass — 50"x58": John likes large surfaces — of swatches and scrapes of multicolored paint defied narrative explanation. In the bottom right-hand corner a cake had fallen, or was beaten, or was cut away, and a triangular gap of open space yawned between the edge of the canvas and the sheet of paint above it. It looks like the craggy cut of a cliff, so thickly layered was the paint. The painting was composed of colored swatches — some of them solid tones, some vibrating with multicolored flecks. The texture is uniformly uneven, sometimes like gravel, like stucco, like tesserae, like the mottled sides of buildings in beaten-up alleys. There is not a single stretch of smoothness. The dominant, heaviest colors are grayish purples — four of them arranged in slanted, flailing, and stretching masses from the lower left-hand side upwards to the middle of the rightmost edge. A deep blue anchors the left lower corner, grasping up to the upper left. A wide passage of distressed pink presides over the topmost edge. Flesh tones shimmer in fleeting scraps throughout, unsettled, disembodied. Crimson and cadmium scrapes dance in the upper left corner and the bottom right one. The whole thing teems with color in rhythmic, competing movements. This painting of two figures falling is not a painting of two figures falling — it is a painting of the feeling of a fall, the essence of a fall. An impossible thing to put into writing, and an impossible thing to put into paint. John conscripts his viewers into an exacting and mystifying exercise.

JD: *I was walking in Paris with my partner Kaye. We were holding hands walking down from Montmartre and she tripped. So when I came back I did a series of paintings of that experience.*

CM: *How does a painting usually start?*

He thought for a moment.

JD: *Kaye and I were in the subway last night going to Lincoln Center. We got caught in a human traffic jam underground, people going in every direction shoulder to shoulder. Not a visual experience, a psychological and physical one. Especially after Covid, that physical experience was like a revelation. I instantly had a flash: this is my next painting. Will it be? Maybe. If so I'll probably go up there to that spot and try to add visual pieces to the inspiration. At other times it's those same elements, physical and psychological, but predominantly visual which is more straightforward. I can follow the visual but sometimes it gets in the way too, as I usually need to break away from the visual to get to the real experience transformed into paint.*

CM: *The real experience? You mean the feeling of it?*

He nodded.

JD: *It's the feeling but it's also, well, for me it's very literal. You* *don't see two figures falling, but I see the figures clearly. What I'd like to do in all these paintings is have these opposites collide. I want to be building a form and breaking down a form at the same time. The building of volumetric space and the flattening of that space. So it's like everything is fighting with itself. I'm always describing something very literal, and then I'm breaking down the very literal. So at different points this painting — all these paintings — were very figurative.*

CM: *Why are you breaking it down?*

JD: *Because the intersection of these two things is what interests me. It's a Cezannist idea. It basically is the same project as Cezanne's. How do I build this and also have it fall apart and have it become an abstract patterning? I want both at once, in equal intensity.*

John is maniacal about studying the past masters. When I was at the studio a large volume about Giovanni Pisano was open and obviously in mid-study. One wouldn't recognize their styles in his work, but the spirit of the work, the seriousness, the rigor, the reaching for a breakthrough, is analogous. Any student of art who has had their breath taken away by Cezanne's simultaneity of structure and impression will recognize something in John's experiments and intuit the harmony that is his goal.

Greenberg, of course, would have bridled at the pronouncement that these two artists share a project. By Greenberg's lights, "Cezanne sacrificed verisimilitude, or correctness, in order to fit his drawing and design more explicitly to the rectangular shape of the canvas." Notice the distinction between Greenberg's understanding of Cezanne's project and Dubrow's conception of the same works, the same choices. Both men recognize that, for the purpose of achieving a desired end, Cezanne moved away from traditional representation. In Greenberg's mind, he did this because he wanted to create a painting fitted properly for a flat surface. Dubrow's analysis is precisely the opposite: Cezanne, in order to communicate space as it is felt, needed to repeat elements of the volumetric structures he was looking at but also to alter those structures such that the painting could communicate and even depict the vitality of the object. Communicating terrestrial vitality, for Greenberg, is straying from the ideals of modernism, since a flat surface cannot contain a living thing. But when John looks at a Cezanne, figuration and abstraction both contribute to representation, insofar as representation refers not only to the way the subject looks, but also to the way it feels — to the experience of the energy in the scene. It is a mark in favor of John's view that Cezanne's earliest paintings lack the movement that vivify his later ones. His earliest paintings were of darkly imagined scenes — a rape, a murder. Only later in life, when he became Cezanne, did he paint exclusively and fanatically from life.

CM: *Do you feel, like Cezanne, that you are trying to invent a new kind of painting?*

JD: *I feel that with every painting I'm constantly trying to push forward beyond what I know I can do. And so they take me several years. This one took me three and a half years because I'll be working on other paintings simultaneously and also going to see art that will help me break through to a new place in an old work. I went to Italy to see Pisano and when I came back I immediately returned to these figures and these figures became more organic like Pisano's figures. The movement, there's nothing static about those statues. And so when this happened here* [he gestured towards a part of the canvas] *then everything else was very clear to me.*

CM: *Can you show me where the figures are in these paintings?*

JD: *Well, there are four figures here. This* [he pointed to a passage] *is the actor Paul Lazar, this is Joanne Akalitis, this is the* *actress Wendy vanden Heuvel, and this is Annie B. Parson, who is a choreographer... And there's a table over there... And the catalyst was the moment when Joanne put her hand on Paul's shoulder so that was there from the very start.*

CM: *And would you expect your viewers to think of those four passages as figures?*

JD: *I don't care... People tell me they can't. They say "I have no idea what you're talking about." But for me, they're all... they're so specific in my mind. In this regard "people" are just a framing mechanism for determining where to put related masses of color on a canvas. But I'm imagining those specific people all the way through no matter how buried in paint they become.*

But that's how I look at Old Master paintings, too. It's always been this way for me, from the time I was twenty when I was obsessed with Titian. I never saw the narrative. The narrative is only important because you can tell by looking at the painting that the painter really cares about the narrative. But the intense attention is what matters, and however that informs the painting doesn't make a difference.

CM: *Do you want the viewer to be able to see the figures in the paintings? Because I look at this and I want to resist trying to find the figures. I feel that it is inhibiting me from giving myself over to your project.*

JD: *Well, I do feel like what I'm trying to do is to create a new construction. I don't want to give you exactly what you already see, I want to give you something else. I'm reconstructing the world and it's not going to look like the world as you or I commonly experience it. But one of the things about painting figures in this kind of context is... you know, I set up an abstract context and I can't just put figures into it. It wouldn't make sense. So basically I've had to learn how to reformulate and reimagine what a figure is.*

CM: *And you need both abstraction and figuration in order to make* *the painting feel like the experience?*

A swift nod.

JD: *Yes. I need it to feel exactly like the thing. Normally it has to lose the descriptive element in order to feel like the experience. The miracle of Cezanne, and the miracle that I'm looking for, is that there still is a picture box in Cezanne. By which I mean, there is the traditional conception of the canvas as a window through which you see a comprehensible scene, and there is a picture box here too, but I'm denying it simultaneously.*

The "picture box" conception of a painting engages with the canvas as if it is a stage, a proscenium in receding space, on which a scene is set, as in a play, with intelligible figures that are part of a legible narrative. Abstract painting, of course, is nothing like that. I looked around the studio. John's earliest works were certainly representational, painted in his own patchy and idiosyncratic (and beautiful) realism. As my gaze drifted from the walls closest to the door to the ones near the center of the studio, the images became increasingly unintelligible, increasingly abstract. I confess that the ones closest to me didn't look at all like picture boxes, and I strained to understand the distance traversed from door to easel. It seemed to me that over the years his pictorial enterprise has been entirely transformed. The new paintings, the ones that loomed directly over me, were making alien, singular demands of the viewer. They radiated a different energy. I needed to learn how to see them. Syncopating to their rhythm, acquiescing to their constraints and standards, required developing new muscles. How did the hand and mind that made the earlier pictures also make these recent works?

I thought for a while about how to formulate a question that might elicit a satisfying answer.

CM: *When you destroy it, when you break down the figures, do you know what you're doing?*

JD: *No. I have no idea what I'm looking for. I know only what I'm not looking for. I know that I'm looking for the painting to ultimately be a completely free-standing object that reminds me of what I am remembering — because there's no source material for most of these paintings except my memory. I might do drawings, but I'll rarely look at those drawings.*

John paused for several beats, apparently hesitant to continue. Finally his eyes flicked up to mine and he had the look of someone who was about to reveal something strange and unexpected.

JD: *The other thing that's going on is that eight or nine years ago I began going into a weird... not quite a trance state, but my eyes began blinking really rapidly while I was working. I made a recording of it and sent the video to neuroscientists at NYU and they came over. They tested me while I was painting, with blinking and then without blinking, and they told me that I was somehow going into an increased theta wave state while I am working. Theta waves are like a waking daydream state.*

This was startling. But John is not the only artist I know of who painted in a trance. The sculptor Chana Orloff became close friends with Chaim Soutine in the last decade of his short life. (He died in 1943, fifty years old.) She said of him: "He nurtured his idea for a painting for several months and then, when ready, started the work in a fury. He worked with passion, with fever, in a trance, sometimes to the music of some Bach fugue that he played on a phonograph. Once he finished the painting, he was weak, depressed, wiped out." Soutine himself used to say that, in order for a painting to begin, he needed to be seized irresistibly by a subject. He called this "the miracle." Between such trances, waiting for the miracle to intercede again, he would stew in sterile agitation.

Perhaps because Soutine called it "the miracle," or because John's studio felt overwhelmingly like a religious sanctuary, I interpreted the details about John's trance as confirmation that his paintings were made in a state of meta-rational or even mystical inspiration.

CM: *Do you pray?*

JD: *No. Well. Right, it's pretty close. So what happens is that all day long I'm going into that state to block out any rational thought. I used to be a different kind of painter, I used to be a figurative painter. And I'm always fighting that.*

CM: *Do you feel when you're inside the trance, or maybe when you come out of it because you're not conscious of what you're feeling while you're still in it, are you communing with something outside yourself? Or is it internal?*

JD: *It's inner-directed. The eye blinking is a way to not be able to look out. So I'm looking in at the image that I know is there in the painting.*

CM: *You said image just now. Is it an image or is it a feeling?*

JD: *It's a sense. I know a lot about painting. I've spent my life not only painting but looking at painting, so when I go to this painting I don't need to be aware of what I'm doing. All I need is to be present and I can fall back on it.*

I thought about what he said, about how the experience of painting demands that he retreat so deeply inside himself that his body moves to shut out any alien interference. At some point the change in his gaze abolishes the subject-object relationship. John's testimony paired strangely with what I knew about his obsession with traveling to see paintings. He makes pilgrimages to artworks around the world.

CM: *When you travel to go look at paintings, how can that help you as an artist who waits for the trance? Is it that you are going as deeply into their paintings as you try to go into yourself while you're painting?*

JD: *Yes, I go into the eye blinking state when I look at other paintings.*

I gasped. So the blinking had to be catalyzed by intense concentration, by some sort of raptness. I was reminded of Simone Weil's remark that "attention, taken to the utmost degree, is prayer."

CM: *What must it be like to have a sense of solidarity with great painters so deep that your own body treats their work as if it were a part of you? And does that feel inward or does that feel like going into them?*

JD: *It feels like Stendhal syndrome, like a kind of euphoria. It's this weird mixture of being able to look out but then bringing it inward. Everything is inward.*

Stendhal syndrome is a psychosomatic condition wherein exposure to extreme beauty induces physical symptoms, such as chest pains, fainting, and rapid blinking. The condition is named after Stendhal's report of his visit to the Franciscan church of Santa Croce in Florence, whose sixteen chapels contain an astonishing treasury of Renaissance painting. "I had palpitations of the heart..." Stendhal recalled. "Life was drained from me. I walked with fear of falling." There are more violent accounts. Six years ago a visitor at the Ufizzi Gallery died of a heart attack in the presence of Botticelli's Venus. I suppose he died happy.

CM: *It strikes me as a kind of mysticism...*

JD: *Friends often compare it to deep meditation... though of course meditation usually requires stillness, but here I am running around the studio. I think of it as an altered state.*

CM: *Can you simulate it?*
JD: *Yes. I can turn the blinking on whenever I want. I can turn it on and off. I'm lucky that I can turn it off.*
CM: *Does it ever overwhelm you?*
JD: *There are times when I've been here all day and then I'm walking to my car and it's still happening, and I have to stop myself. I can't let that happen while I'm driving.*
CM: *In those moments does it feel like intoxication?*
JD: *Yeah.*

I have seen a video of John painting. Well, painting isn't the right word exactly. In the clip he is using his hands, throwing them — and his whole body behind them — up against the canvas. A corporeal assault. It looks like intoxication. It doesn't look remotely meditative.
CM: *This area here* [I pointed to a passage in the Paris Falling painting] — *did you do that with your hands, too?*
JD: *No, it's mostly palette knives. Occasionally I use a brush. I also switched over from dominant hand to non-dominant hand just to have a second painter. You're using a whole different brain circuitry, so that has been a very important part of this whole shift into this kind of work.*

A second painter. What an extraordinary thought.
CM: *When did you start doing that?*
JD: *I've always been right-handed. After an injury fifteen years ago I had to use my left hand till the right hand healed. Then, six or seven years ago, tendonitis forced me to paint with both hands. After several months of that something shifted: I could comfortably switch from left to right and back, and I noticed that not only was I thinking about space differently but my color sensibility was also*

quite different. The mark-making was also different, but that was just a motor skill variation.

But I conceive of and treat color and space differently depending on the hand. My color left- handed has a wider range of tone and hue, also a warmer and slightly brighter palette, and a more arbitrary reaching for what seemed to be a more random or less controlled color. The eye blinking certainly helped facilitate that. I think I read somewhere that right hand/left brain is more rational. I followed that model, it seems.

I thought of the Portuguese poet Pessoa's heteronyms, the pseudonymous identities he invented, complete with names, biographies, and individual styles, in whose distinct voices he would write. Imagine them collaborating on a single project!

CM: *When you're in that state and then come out of it, do you ever feel like you've taken the painting away from where it needed to go?*

JD: *Well, the whole project is this tug between figuration and abstraction, and so I'm constantly losing my way.*

CM: *So you're really relying on your past. It's not just breaking down what you're putting on, it's breaking down all the years of study and work that you did before.*

JD: *Right.*

The painters who pushed Western art into modernity all started with a classical education. But most of them moved entirely away from that world. It was a ladder they climbed up and then left behind. Picasso was not fighting with his figuration in his cubism. And he went back into figuration out of cubism. But the two were never alive in him fighting one another in a single work — not the way they are in John's painting, anyway.

CM: *What would happen if you moved beyond that bedrock, if you didn't need it anymore? Could that happen?*

JD: *I think that's the interesting thing in my painting: are these* *opposites dependent on each other? Could I paint the same things without going back and forth the way I do. The poet David Yezzi was talking about the white painting over there* [John pointed across the studio to a far wall] *and he said that there are painters who would do that in a day or a week but you wouldn't have the spirit. It wouldn't make sense for me — it wouldn't feel the same, even if it looked the same, to make a painting that way. These canvases become a record of their own composition. Really that's what they are — they are a record.*

CM: *The idea that you mentioned earlier that seems central to the whole project is color making space. But then that has nothing to do with narrative. And yet you say that narrative is always central for you.*

I was thinking about the difference between conceiving of a painting as an instance of chromatic and spatial relations, and conceiving of it as a story.

JD: *It has to do with narrative because the memory is communicated through the color relations. Narrative isn't essential in painting, but color and form are. I think of all paintings — even purely figurative, utterly non-abstract paintings — in terms of color and spatial relations. When I go to Italy and I spend time with Duccio and Pisano... they seem to me like what I'm trying to do. Like I'm trying to get to what they're doing through action painting. It's the spirit of those paintings but with the method of action painting.*

The critic Harold Rosenberg christened the New York style of painting which emerged in the mid-twentieth century "action painting." Action painting was wholly new — which is to say, it was not to be found in Paris. Its practitioners, Pollock most consummately, conceived of painting not as representation but as an act in itself, wholly self-contained and self-sufficient, born of its own inner necessity. Rosenberg explained that "what was to go on the canvas was not a picture but an event." The act of creation was the record of creation, and of the discoveries made in the thick of it. What appeared on the canvas was a surprise, a series of contingent, rhythmic surprises: "There is no point in an act if you already know what it contains." In action painting, to paint is to experience something entirely different, entirely its own. "The new painting has broken down every distinction between art and life." (In this way, at least, Cezanne was a kind of ur-action painter. When Emile Bernard asked him, "Aren't nature and art different?," Cezanne proclaimed, "I want to make them the same.")

Is Dubrow a latter-day action painter? No, because in one crucial sense he works programmatically: he refers to the memory that exists outside him, that he falls into. He wants to create the conditions in paint in which he will feel again what he felt before. At least, part of him wants it that way. But John is indeed a kind of action painter because he knows that he cannot reproduce the old feeling perfectly. The painting will tell him what he feels. "I don't want another drink," James McMurtry sings, "I only want that last one again." John recognizes that he cannot have that last drink again. The slash of his palette knife cannot adequately conjure the whip of the wind on his face no matter how deftly he wields it, and half of him doesn't want it to do so. Half of him thinks in paint. So the act of creation is its own event, its own bizarre and unpredictable act. He sprints outward to the original memory and then inward toward something strange, some visceral painterliness, which transforms the memory into a new, other thing. Back and forth, back and forth. The canvas is stained with his sweat. The painting is the sweat. Accident, intention; creation, destruction; meditation, activity. All of it at once. Two hands, ten minds.

CM: *How much is serendipity part of your work?*
JD: *Everything is a surprise while working, every mark, and I'm hyperaware of the accidents that happen. Everything emerges from the paint while holding on to the memory, and the fixed ideas about the memory are very strong — and then the serendipitous stuff is when I'm reaching for a random thing which has nothing to do with it, I'll think okay I'll try THIS, and that's when really interesting things happen.*
CM: *But it still feels like the original thing when you're done with it?*
JD: *Yeah. Well, I think it does, but then... when I went back to the place where this memory took place it felt nothing like this. So the memory is transformed through the process of painting. These paintings in a way are all about transformation. They begin with a very concrete memory that then so completely transforms that they become like these living forms. This to me seems like something alive. And even though it's echoing the original memory, it becomes its own live thing. And it is its own life that has nothing to do with...*
CM: *But that's what you mean by painting?*
JD: *That's how I think of painting.*
CM: *What's interesting is that your "illegible" canvases are completely coherent. But you have to spend time with them —*
JD: *Yes, they are very slow. You have to really look, wait for them to open up, and not try to resolve the canvas into a comprehensible image but to understand it on its own terms, to recognize the internal coherence. What's interesting is that in the end they somehow seem inevitable. I know it's done when it feels like it's become what it wants to be and when it gets to that place... well, it shuts off, I mean it stops inviting me in and psychologically they shrink.*
CM: *Because there are no boundaries while you're painting it?*
JD: *Right. There are no boundaries for my brain. My brain is awakened by it and I can get into it and then when it reaches*

coherence it shuts me out and I have to stop.

CM: *So you know when it's done?*

JD: *There are a lot of false endings because it'll shut me out and I'll stop and then I'll look at it again and it's open again. But in the end, when the painting shrinks, and I turn around it, it's startling to see that suddenly the painting is completely contained —*

CM: *Does that feel like a relief? Or does it feel like being shut out?*

JD: *No, no. It feels like it's finally taken on its own life. I'm not part of it anymore. I feel like I've taken myself out of it. I am not in there anymore. I have a memory of doing all its stuff to it, but I don't know how that happened, and whatever force was moving through me, it doesn't need me anymore.*

LEON WIESELTIER

A Paschal Homily by Naomi Klein, with a Commentary

I

On the second night of Passover, in the year of our Lord 5784, a seder was held in the streets of Brooklyn, in Grand Army Plaza, a block away from the residence of Senator Chuck Schumer. The event was called the Seder in the Streets to Stop Arming Israel. It was addressed by a number of anti-Israeli, anti-Zionist, and/or anti-Semitic speakers — after the wild blurring of those distinctions in the past year, the burden of clarification falls on the demonstrators, many of whose intense hostility to the existence of the Jewish state, and promiscuous political rhetoric, crossed the line into the ancient foulness a long time ago. Hundreds of protesters attended and hundreds were arrested, thereby reversing the order of the holiday and going from freedom to bondage. Their bondage, of course, did not last long; he is a fortunate man whose bondage is purely gestural.

I have not been able to establish whether anything remotely resembling a seder took place at the Seder in the Streets. (It sounds like the name of an old Richard Widmark movie.) The political director of Jewish Voice for Peace explained at the gathering that "tonight's Seder in the Streets will be happening on the second night of Passover, a holiday we observe every year that is all about liberation and how our liberations are intertwined with one another." Well, not all our liberations: later in her statement she declared that "the Israeli government and the United States government are carrying out a genocide of Palestinians in Gaza, over 34,000 people killed in six months in the name of Jewish safety, in the false name of Jewish freedom." Here, for a start, was another instance of the popular misuse of the term "genocide," which has now become a regular feature of progressive discourse. For all of Israel's cruelties toward the Palestinians, it is a gross historical lie that the Jewish state ever set out to eliminate every last Palestinian and every last vestige of Palestinian culture, so that the people and the culture would disappear from the face of the earth.

Not even the Syrian war, before which the destruction in Gaza pales in grim comparison, was genocidal. Aren't war crimes, or crimes against humanity, in which the charnel house of Syria abounded, evil enough? "Genocide" has become the term with which to describe the atrocity of which one most disapproves. There certainly are genocides in the world now — the Uyghurs most notably — but the left never marches for them. It never marched for Syria, either. An encampment on campus for the Rohynga? Not a prayer. Scores of thousands dead Sudanese? It appears that you have to be fighting Israelis or Jews for progressives to bestir themselves on your behalf. Anyway, the definition of genocide is not quantitative: the Hamas savagery of October 7, even though it killed "only" twelve hundred people, was in fact genocidal, owing to the anti-Semitic and eliminationist motivations that are amply and explicitly articulated in Hamas's literature.

None of this exonerates the Israelis from the high number of non-combatant deaths in Gaza. No, "non-combatant" is too cold: innocent men, women, and children. The retaliation for the Hamas attack has been ruthless; and whereas I have no idea how to compute the proportionality that is demanded by the rules of war, I am quite certain that monstrously disproportionate actions have been taken place. We have been witnessing the hell of violations justifying violations justifying violations. The Israeli government — which, to the eternal disgrace of Zionism, includes a few ministers who do think genocidal thoughts — was dragged kicking and screaming to humanitarian assistance to Gaza; it was American pressure, that is to say, an expedient strategic consideration, that prodded the Israeli war cabinet to overcome its plain contempt for the population it was bombing. This was not the best it could have done. The Israeli notion that all Gazans are terrorists is as ludicrous as the Hamas notion that all Israelis are war criminals. The de-civilianization of others is a significant moment in their de-humanization.

Yet the tendentious application of the concept of genocide was not the most egregious bit of the peacenik's contribution to the seder in the street. If, as she says, all our liberations are intertwined with one another, why is the name of Jewish freedom false? What was Zionism if not the national liberation movement of the Jewish people? Perhaps someone would like to argue with a straight face that the Jews were not in need of national liberation, but it should not be controversial to suggest that such a person is an imbecile. "Have you ever tried playing the who-suffered-most game with Jews?" Dave Chapelle once remarked. "It's very hard." Unfortunately, versions of this malevolent imbecility now proliferate in the ubiquitous disqualification of Jews from the roster of oppressed peoples, as if the success of the Zionist endeavor to create a safe and strong and sovereign parcel for its hounded people should be held against it, and not as a sign of the moral seriousness with which a persecuted people went about rescuing itself.

The left's willed obliviousness to the epic history of Jewish victimization is doubly offensive because it is attended by a deep contempt for the equally epic efforts by Jews to put an end to their own victimization. Self-rescue in any group is wholly laudable. A people in pain may be forgiven for impatience, and admired for it if its impatience breeds practicality. Zionism is supremely an ideology of anti-wallowing. It represents an absolute refusal to tolerate the misery of one's own. In this respect, I have long wished, respectfully and as a steadfast friend of the idea of partition, that the Palestinians would Zionize themselves, that they would be done with historical excuses and come to admire the quickening mentality of state-building. Institutions are nobler than intifadas. The Jewish state existed before it was declared; its sovereignty came last. In a world of Jewish wretchedness, there was no other way. Diplomacy had its place, but agency was everything. Justice for the Jews was justice by the Jews, exactly as justice for the Palestinians will be justice by the Palestinians.

"At the core of the Passover story is that we cannot be free until all people are free," the JVP woman declaimed. She was right. The problem is that her own slogans vitiate the universalism of her teaching. Insofar as progressive anti-Zionists reject the legitimacy of a Jewish state, they advocate an Orwellian Passover, for which all people are free except one. There is *nothing* false about the name of Jewish freedom. This must be granted if the conversation is to proceed. In Grand Army Plaza, of course, the objective was not conversation. The gathering's immediate purpose was to protest an impending Senate vote on billions of dollars of military aid to Israel — hence its proximity to Schumer's home. Chuck was Pharaoh. "We're here to tell Senator Schumer that enough is enough," the JVP woman asserted, a few thousand rhetorical levels below Moses' original demands of Pharaoh. As in the original exodus, however, the Israelite bill passed.

II

Politically, the Seder in the Streets was a failure. Emotionally, it sounds like it was a success. It consisted in the sanctimonious intoning of an entire anthology of progressive platitudes about the Israeli-Palestinian conflict and its meanings. In its secular way, the seder was entirely liturgical. Its call-and-response of political chants by the assembly of bitter Herbs was supplemented by a sermon by Naomi Klein, whose presence in this context was surely more exciting for the participants than a visitation by Elijah the Prophet would have been. On April 24, the *Guardian* in London published the text of her homily. In its way it is a precious document. I reproduce it here, with its lines numbered to assist in a close reading, with a commentary.

1 I've been thinking about Moses, and his rage when he came down from the mount to find the Israelites worshipping a golden calf.

The ecofeminist in me was always uneasy about this story: what kind of God is jealous of animals? What kind of God wants to hoard all the sacredness of the Earth for himself?

But there is a less literal way of understanding this story. It is about false idols. About the human tendency to worship the profane and shiny, to look to the small and material rather than the large and transcendent.

What I want to say to you tonight at this revolutionary and historic Seder in the Streets is that too many of our people are worshipping a false idol once again. They are enraptured by it. Drunk on it. Profaned by it.

That false idol is called Zionism.

It is a false idol that takes our most profound biblical stories of justice and emancipation from slavery — the story of Passover itself — and turns them into brutalist weapons of colonial land theft, roadmaps for ethnic cleansing and genocide.

It is a false idol that has taken the transcendent idea of the promised land — a metaphor for human liberation that has traveled across multiple faiths to every corner of this globe — and dared to turn it into a deed of sale for a militaristic ethnostate.

Political Zionism's version of liberation is itself profane. From the start, it required the mass expulsion of Palestinians from their homes and ancestral lands in the Nakba.

From the start it has been at war with dreams of liberation. At a Seder it is worth remembering that this includes the dreams of liberation and self-determination of the Egyptian people. This false idol of Zionism equates Israeli safety with Egyptian dictatorship and client states.

From the start it has produced an ugly kind of freedom that saw Palestinian children not as human beings but as demographic threats — much as the pharaoh in the Book of Exodus feared the growing population of Israelites, and thus ordered the death of their sons.

Zionism has brought us to our present moment of cataclysm and it is time that we said clearly: it has always been leading us here.

It is a false idol that has led far too many of our own people down a deeply immoral path that now has them justifying the shredding of core commandments: thou shalt not kill. Thou shalt not steal. Thou shalt not covet.

It is a false idol that equates Jewish freedom with cluster bombs that kill and maim Palestinian children.

Zionism is a false idol that has betrayed every Jewish value, including the value we place on questioning – a practice embedded in the Seder with its four questions asked by the youngest child.

Including the love we have as a people for text and for education.

Today, this false idol justifies the bombing of every university in Gaza; the destruction of countless schools, of archives, of printing presses; the killing of hundreds of academics, of journalists, of poets — this is what Palestinians call scholasticide, the killing of the means of education.

Meanwhile, in this city, the universities call in the NYPD and barricade themselves against the grave threat posed by their own students daring to ask them basic questions, such as: how can you claim to believe in anything at all, least of all us, while you enable, invest in and collaborate with this genocide?

The false idol of Zionism has been allowed to grow unchecked for far too long.

So tonight we say: it ends here.

Our Judaism cannot be contained by an ethnostate, for our Judaism is internationalist by nature.

Our Judaism cannot be protected by the rampaging military of that state, for all that military does is sow sorrow and reap hatred — including against us as Jews.

Our Judaism is not threatened by people raising their voices in solidarity with Palestine across lines of race, ethnicity, physical ability, gender identity and generations.

Our Judaism is one of those voices and knows that in that chorus lies both our safety and our collective liberation.

Our Judaism is the Judaism of the Passover Seder: the gathering in ceremony to share food and wine with loved ones and strangers alike, the ritual that is inherently portable, light enough to carry on our backs, in need of nothing but each other: no walls, no temple, no rabbi, a role for everyone, even — especially — the smallest child. The Seder is a diaspora technology if ever there was one, made for collective grieving, contemplation, questioning, remembering and reviving the revolutionary spirit.

So look around. This, here, is our Judaism. As waters rise and forests burn and nothing is certain, we pray at the altar of solidarity and mutual aid, no matter the cost.

We don't need or want the false idol of Zionism. We want freedom from the project that commits genocide in our name. Freedom from an ideology that has no plan for peace other than deals with murderous theocratic petrostates next door, while selling the technologies of robo-assassinations to the world.

We seek to liberate Judaism from an ethnostate that wants Jews to be perennially afraid, that wants our children to be afraid, that wants us to believe the world is against us so that we go running to its fortress and beneath its iron dome, or at least keep the weapons and donations flowing.

That is the false idol.

And it's not just Netanyahu, it's the world he made and that made him — it's Zionism.

What are we? We, in these streets for months and months, are the exodus. The exodus from Zionism.

And to the Chuck Schumers of this world, we do not say: "Let our people go."

We say: "We have already gone. And your kids? They're with us now."

III

line 1: It is never a salutary impulse to identify with Moses on his way down the mountain. His rage was terrifying. He smashed God's own writing. He despised his own people, who had failed yet another test. He kept his compassion from them. As is often the case with holy wrath, corpses ensued. Three thousand people died, brothers killed by brothers. A bad day. Moses fixed things with God, but still a bad day.

line 4: Another unfortunate impulse. There are many ways to read Scripture, many methods of interpretation, but one's own politics is likely not the most rewarding of them. Why would one want to read this text as an ecofeminist even if one is an ecofeminist? (And what on earth does environmentalism and feminism have to do with the manufacture of an effigy of a calf out of the baubles of high net-worth individuals in the desert?) It is not the purpose of ancient writings to edify modern ideologies. Nor is it a shortcoming of the Torah if it is found to be lacking in ecofeminism. Why would one boast about a bias? The parochialism of the enlightened never fails to amuse. One of the goals of hermeneutics is to encourage the reader to get out more.

line 5: Before the interpreter moves on to arcane methods of interpretation, she should get the literal meaning straight. God's ferocity is in no plausible way an expression of jealousy. Nothing in the text, or in its larger theology, suggests otherwise. Yahweh has many troubling anthropomorphic quirks, but He is not an idiot. His indignation here is directed at falsehood: he had vouchsafed them a revelation of the truth. Having demonstrated the veracity of His existence to the Israelites with the evidence of their own senses, in miracle after miracle, He is shocked by their reversion to the idolatrous error, to the metaphysical illusions of materialist Egypt. This disappointment is premised on His confidence that the Israelites, who were the first people asked to live with the burdensome intellectual requirements of monotheism, and therefore with its retraction of the emotional gratifications of polytheism, could rise to the spiritual difficulty; and when they fail to meet the challenge, He is volcanically angry. He insists that these people understand the truth. Did he make a bad bet on the spiritual capabilities of the Israelites, of ordinary men and women? To be sure, an intolerance of the frailty of human beings is unbecoming in a Deity, as it is unbecoming in a political movement that speaks in their name; but the crisis at the foot of the mountain was not caused by the injured vanity of an abstract being who was envious of the blingy materiality of a cow.

Nor was it the result of God selfishly hoarding holiness. I do not mean to make God's apologies, but if this were a hoarder He would not have created the world to compete for His holiness. The medievals discussed this. They believed that creation was therefore the ultimate expression of divine love. Sanctity is not what God keeps but what God dispenses, and in certain schools of thought to the entirety of creation. There is nothing petty about the concept or its history. But Klein's contrarian questions do not deserve such serious answers. She was just trying to impress her congregation with her skepticism about religion. Her sermon really has nothing to do with theological reflection. She was just intellectually accessorizing.

line 9: False idols? There are no other kind.

line 10: Splendissima! Down with the material, up with the transcendent! But be careful about denouncing the small; trouble starts that way. The small is where we live. And what precisely is the progressive transcendent?

line 12: Rabbi, such an assessment of the event is for others to make.

line 14: Idolatry, in the Jewish tradition, is a very grave charge. The traditional understanding of idolatry is that it consists in the worship of the creation instead of the Creator. It is a misattribution of divinity. It comes in material and immaterial forms. Insofar as it consists in the overestimation of what one admires, it is a common malady.

line 16: Surprise! But the preacher is correct about one thing, which she and her congregation have abundantly illustrated over the years: one can have an idolatrous relationship to ideas, to ideologies.

line 20: The history of the acquisition of land by the founding Jewish settlers of the yishuv and by the relevant Zionist institutions is not remotely one of "colonial land theft." This is an empirical matter. It has been archivally documented. It is certainly the case that some territories were acquired in battle, but the battle was for survival and it was visited upon Israel by neighbors who refused to consider seriously either the historic right of the Jewish people to the land or the sublime compromise of partition. The armistice lines of 1949 left Jewish forces and Arab forces in places that the United Nations had not assigned to them. The presence of a Jewish state in the ancient land is not an occupation. (But its borders should have more to do with security and morality than with antiquity.) At no point in its history did Israel launch a war of conquest, even when its leaders harbored fantasies of territorial expansion. The preacher in Grand Army Plaza should make herself aware of inconvenient facts and do her best to deal honestly with them. Nothing about the conflict is simple. In this way it differs from many of its analysts.

But what about the occupied territories? The seizure of any or all of the territories that fell under Israeli dominion in the Six Day War was not an Israeli war aim, though a state that has successfully defended itself against many hostile armies cannot be blamed for wishing to end the hostilities in a strategically more advantageous position than when they began. In the aftermath of the Six Day War, the Jewish world was overwhelmed by a great triumphalism, which was only in part an expression of relief at not having been annihilated. There were ideological opportunists, too, who interpreted the unanticipated extension of Israeli rule over the new areas as a providential instrument for their own maximalist ambitions, secular and religious. But there were also some Israelis who, when the inebriation of victory wore off, recognized that sovereignty over the Palestinians in the newly acquired areas was a mortal trap for the Jewish state. I had an Israeli friend who wept with joy and then wept with dread. I remember arguing with my religious Zionist friends, still in high school, that if they really needed to find the hand of God in the new situation, they might consider that the Holy One had benevolently granted them, for the first time in Israel's embattled history, this: land that Israel could surrender without surrendering itself. Years later I learned that I was groping for the concept of a bargaining chip. The bargain, of course, would be peace.

And so, for fifty-seven years, with increasing intensity and increasing frustration, liberal Zionists in the Israeli Jewish community and the American Jewish community who believe that the survival of Israel depends upon reconciliation with the Palestinians, and that the Palestinians, unlike the Arab states that attacked Israel, have a moral and historical claim that Jews must respect, threw themselves into "peace work," politically and culturally — work from which today's progressive anti-Zionists would like us to desist. Our work spoils their paradigm, which is that liberalism and Zionism are incompatible. Historically and philosophically, this proposition is outrageously untrue. What is true is that we doves, or pragmatists, or moderates, or two-staters, are the big losers in present-day Israel. But progressives, of all people, should understand that historical reversal is not the same as philosophical refutation.

Stubbornness is sometimes an ingredient of integrity. We are not wrong in our hunger for Israeli-Palestinian reconciliation, we are merely unpopular — for now.

So why this rush to the exits? Why should liberal Zionists complacently accept defeat instead of persisting in their exertions? Why this progressive counsel of despair, except that it goes so nicely with other dogmas of the post-colonial faith, and that it makes certain people less likely to be despised by the left, which is their idea of perdition? And what is a more principled and more practicable solution to the conflict than the adjacent states of Israel and Palestine? I have not heard one. Justice that is purchased with injustice is injustice, and this goes for all sides. So I do not have the insolence to recommend to the Israelis that for their own good, or because of a wrinkle in critical theory, they should erase themselves. If Israel commits crimes or abuses that must be criticized, we have plentiful grounds, liberal grounds, Zionist grounds, Jewish grounds, universal grounds, on which to criticize it. We need no lessons in the practice of self-criticism from Naomi Klein or Judith Butler. If Israel cured cancer, they would defend cancer.

Zionism, before it is a historical worldview or a political program, is a conclusion drawn properly from the long history of Jewish weakness, an expression of Jewish self-respect, of Jewish honor. Do I mean to suggest that anti-Zionist Jews, or Jews who advocate for the dissolution of the Jewish state and a return to Jewish weakness, are dishonorable? I think I do.

One additional animadversion. Why do Klein and her camp followers assume that anybody who is a Zionist and who refuses to entertain the erasure of Israel also supports, and is even elated by, all the carnage in Gaza?

There was indeed a roadmap that led from Egypt, but

it led to Canaan, not to Israel. The command to exterminate the seven nations of Canaan was a ghastly thing — not only was it exceptionally cruel, but it prefigured the same hideous mistake that motivated the anti-Semitic murderers of medieval and modern Europe: that you can kill the belief by killing the believers. In the event, the archeologists tell us, the complete liquidation of the Canaanites never happened. And what about the Egyptians who pursued the Israelites in the desert and drowned in the Red Sea? The ancient rabbis propose that God himself was incensed about the Israelite celebrations of their destruction. "The works of my hands are drowning in the sea and you come before me with song?!" Most importantly, what does modern Zionism have to do with the Bible? Not nothing, certainly; the inspirations for the restoration of the Jewish commonwealth do not all date from Herzl's outrage at what they did to Dreyfus. But Klein is deploying the Bible exactly as the settlers in the West Bank deploy it: as some sort of blueprint, some sort of excuse, for modern politics. The Zionist exodus was different from the Biblical exodus. Nobody turned a river into blood or split a sea for the Zionists. There were no signs and wonders, except the wonder that people who staggered out of death camps could find the will to live again and cross the waters in the dark of night and participate in the construction of the secular means of their own salvation. There is a roadmap!

line 24: The promised land was not an idea, it was a place — it was, and is, soil. Before it became a metaphor — the Zion of the black churches in America, for example — it was soil. Before it was a metaphor, it was a place. This is a conflict about geography. For the Palestinians, too, the land is soil. They remember, and teach their children to remember, particular olive trees on particular slopes outside particular villages. (One of the conditions of peace is that they finally choose a state over the recovery of those olive trees.) To treat the promised land as a "transcendent idea" is to elide the earthly fury of this conflict. And also its perpetual danger: it is dangerous, after all, to sacralize soil. We have seen in many countries the catastrophic results of geographical mysticism. I confess that I have myself felt the pull of it. I love that land, whatever the political vicissitudes. I would love it even if an imperial power still ruled it. I love it for its beauty and its poetry. I love it because I am a Jew. And so I am here to bear witness that the love of the land, the vulnerability to the aura of its physical setting, does not make one a murderer. Instead it makes me wish more ardently to see peace in it. Note to progressive theorists: sometimes a concept can make you more heartless than a clump of dirt.

The de-materialization of the land has become a central idea of Jewish anti-Zionists. In *The Necessity of Exile*, a memoir of his spiritual instability disguised as a study of ideas, Shaul Magid lavishes praise upon Rabbi Shimon Gershon Rosenberg, a strange right-wing figure known as Rav Shagar, who died in 2007 at the age of fifty-eight. Until not long before his death, he lived in the West Bank and founded and directed a variety of yeshivot. I have been told that Shagar was an extraordinary teacher of Talmud. His contribution to contemporary Jewish thought was two-fold: a religious post-Zionism and a fusion of traditional Jewish concepts with post-modernism. (A religious zealot who propounded the indeterminacy of truth! Cool!) Shagar's anti-foundationalist program, which in my view marks the end of belief itself, included his endorsement of a great nineteenth-century Hasidic master's view that, in Magid's words, "*Eretz Yisrael* is not a place but a state of mind." Never mind that in his messianic thinking that *rebbe* spoke quite plainly about the land as a physical location. The excitement of a non-material land for the post-Zionist Magid is that it further enables his tedious swooning over exile, as if the romance of exile is not one of the oldest cliches of modern culture. The prolific Shagar once wrote an essay in which he taught, in Magid's enthusiastic paraphrase, that "we must fold exile into the state itself." By this he means more than a state of alienation (which Israel, like all states, long ago found ways to nurture). He is referring to a constitutive sense of ontological Jewish difference that not even the restoration of Jewish sovereignty can alter. We are getting into dark chauvinist waters here, in which any self-respecting progressive should be reluctant to swim. But not Magid; he will not be told that he came too late to be an exilic Jew. (Apparently there is not enough glamor in being only a diasporic Jew.) And so he concludes that "the establishment of the state is not a rejection of exile but rather a dialectical move, even a Hegelian one, that redirects exile into the state itself, and thereby elevates it to its next phase, the phase of the political, to a state of justice and compassion." Who's afraid of a dialectical move? Zionism has little to fear from such post-Zionism. But it peddles a distortion of Jewish ethics that must be rectified: the Jewish injunction to pursue justice makes no distinction between political dispensations, between physical locations, between exile and statehood, between homelessness and home. The Jew must seek justice wherever he is. The exilic condition is not ethically privileged, except perhaps in the sense that powerlessness makes many transgressions impractical. A state, by contrast, has the power to commit crimes. There has never been a state that has not committed crimes. And so a critical and even adversarial stance is therefore a prerequisite of responsible citizenship. Ethically speaking, territoriality is more exacting than extra-territoriality.

line 26: Having a military does not make you militarist. Militarism is the view that all problems should be solved by force. Sometimes I see evidence of that disastrous view — a despair of diplomacy — in certain Israeli politicians and governments, though not so much in the Israeli army. To defend yourself with a military is also not militarism. Neither is a people's army, if the security situation warrants it, or universal conscription, all those guns slung jarringly over the shoulders of young men and women who must disrupt their youth to guard their country against its enemies, who are not imaginary. Have Israeli soldiers committed abuses? Of course. But neither is that militarism. Owing to its geopolitical situation, Israel is a Western-style country that cannot suffice with Western-style consumerism as its way of life. (Though the Tel Aviv nights could fool you.) It must also organize itself for its security. Israel has provided an encouraging answer to the question of whether consumerist societies, materialist societies, lifestyle societies, can muster the inner resources that are required for their mobilization in their own defense, though I am not sure how generalizable to other Western societies, to us, its example is.

Israel is not an ethnostate, though its politics is now afflicted by a new ethnonationalism, like many other states. Israel is a nation-state modeled on the old European model of the nation-state, which I call the theory of the perfect fit. In this view, every nation should be incarnated in a state and every state should embody a nation. Ideally, the political borders and the cultural-religious-ethnic borders should coincide. The problem is that they never do, and so there appears what became known as the Problem of Minorities. As long as the minority on the "wrong" side of the border is small, such nation-states are workable. But when the minority grows larger, the majority would panic, and one of the manifestations of this panic was a xenophobic infatuation with itself; tolerance can metamorphose into intolerance in no time at all. (The Peel Commission of 1937, which proposed the idea of partition because it concluded that Arabs and Jews living together in a single state is a recipe for disaster, also recommended population transfers, voluntary or otherwise, in and out of the Jewish state and the Palestinian state.) Many European countries are now confronting this problem, or choosing not to confront it. So is the United States, where white panic has become a decisive force in our politics. And so is Israel.

There are only two possible solutions to the fiction of the perfect fit: the redefinition of the nation in the nation-state as multi-ethnic, or fascism. Such a redefinition, which has become even more urgent in our era of vast migrations, would render the "problem of minorities" moot. In a self-defined multi-ethnic society, there are no natives and no foreigners. The streets flow with legitimacy. Israel is a multi-ethnic nation. (The Jewish people is a multi-ethnic people.) This is the demographic fact. But its right-wing radicals fear this fact, and their fear has been promoted into hatred, and they themselves have been promoted to the upper echelons of Netanyahu's disgusting government. They have set out to overthrow the Enlightenment values that are enshrined in Israel's Declaration of Independence. But there is, again, a struggle. And progressives, when they describe Israel as an ethnostate, are pretending that the struggle is over and that the villains have won. *Genossen*, this is not helpful!

Pessimism is not only an analysis, it is also a choice. Why do Jewish anti-Zionists want to pull the plug on the struggle for liberal Zionism and the two-state solution? Because it appears to be losing? But a cause is not a fair-weather pursuit. When I read Naomi Klein's book on capitalism and the climate, I did not dismiss it as quixotic, even though the likelihood of her program's realization seems low. At present there is a strong basis in political and economic reality for pessimism about the renunciation of fossil fuels and the "extractivist" paradigm. Klein's cause seems doomed. So why doesn't she give up? For the same reason that I don't.

It is true that John Rawls would not have written the Israeli law of return. The law enshrines a prior ethnic preference. But who is so ignorant, or so callous, that they cannot comprehend why there must be a secure place on earth to which Jews may flee in the assurance that they will not be turned away? Fleeing, after all, has been a primary activity of Jews over the centuries. For the same reason, the Jews must always form a demographic majority in Israel, so that no blocking minority or other majority makes Jewish asylum impossible. I admit, as a proponent of equality in an open multi-ethnic nation-state, that this is morally embarrassing. In this respect, my liberal Zionism is not completely consistent, but neither was Camus' invocation of his mother in his discussion of justice in Algeria. If Jewish experience us teaches that we must be stringent and self-reliant about our survival, so be it. Survival, too, is a moral obligation. Anyway, a Palestinian right of return is a similar preference that one day will be extended by the state of Palestine. I would have thought that the extension of such a privilege as a response to their decades of displacement would be a significant Palestinian incentive for hastening the creation of a Palestinian state.

line 28: The Nakba was not the case "from the start." The expulsions that Klein regards as the essence of the Zionist enterprise did not occur until the war of 1948–1949, out of a mixture of strategy, battlefield improvisation, and chaos. I do not mean to excuse them, but such events are hardly unknown in the history of warfare, even in wars of liberation that have met with the approval of the left. The pre-Nakba years were also preceded by a protracted period of Arab violence against Jews, and by Arab alliances with the Third Reich. (In the 1920s and 1930s Arab attacks on Jewish towns and villages was accompanied by the cry *Itbah al-yahud*! or "slaughter the Jews!") Again, I do not mean to excuse the pain that Jews inflicted on Palestinians; not at all. How could an ethically and historically self-aware Jew excuse it? But it is not too much to ask that people who wish to make grandiose interventions in this debate know some history. The sloppiness is insulting.

line 34: I was not aware that Israel is responsible for the Sisi regime. As I recall, not long after a million Egyptians demonstrated against authoritarianism in Tahrir Square, a million Egyptians demonstrated for authoritarianism in Tahrir Square. To be sure, the election of Mohamed Morsi of the Muslim Brotherhood to the presidency of Egypt rattled the Americans, the Israelis, the other Sunni states, and many Egyptians, but we should all have kept our heads, at least if we are serious about democratization as an objective of foreign policy. (Of course progressives regard democratization as a sinister euphemism for American imperialism, but that is for another day.) Israel's lack of enthusiasm for democratization in the Arab world has roots in the old exilic preference for vertical alliances with rulers over horizontal alliances with populations, for reasons that are not hard to understand, though Yosef Hayim Yerushalmi showed that the vertical alliance, too, was a myth. The harsh disappointments of recent years notwithstanding, I am not prepared to give up once and for all on the hope for democracy in the Arab world. Sisi's regime is despicable, and it is an ISIS-making machine. But what does Zionism have to do with it, except insofar as Zionism is the cause of all evil?

line 36: An ugly kind of freedom for whom? I would not treat the achievement of Jewish freedom so lightly, especially at a seder. The plight of the Palestinians is not the entirety of what one needs to know about Israel.

line 39: The Jew as Pharaoh: there is always a cheap thrill in such an inversion. It unburdens the post-Zionist (and the anti-Semite, though I am not accusing Klein of anti-Semitism) of any special sensitivity to Jewish fate and its implications for politics. Yes, to regard human beings in the generalizations of social science — in this instance, as demographic threats — is inhumane, though policy and politics do so all the time. But the notion that Israelis have concluded from their insistence upon a Jewish majority in Israel that they must slaughter Palestinian children is grotesque. Moreover, if it has been a goal of the diabolical Israelis to diminish Palestinian fertility rates, they have failed miserably. Klein should pause to consider the distinction between criticism and slander. And she can take some comfort that Pharaoh spared the daughters. Maybe he was an ecofeminist, too.

line 42: No. What has brought us to our present moment of cataclysm is this: three thousand Hamas terrorists attacked Israel on October 7, 2023, and butchered and raped and incinerated men, women, and children. If they had not done so, all the Israelis and Palestinians who died violently since October 7 would still be alive. The absence of any mention of this depravity in Klein's paschal sermon is despicable. Another example of the left's universalism minus one.

line 51: Every Jewish value? Including holy war, which is also a Jewish value? Or anti-pagan violence? Or family purity? This woman who speaks so categorically about Judaism appears to know little or nothing about it. In American Jewry now, the surest sign of Jewish ignorance is to exalt "the value we place on questioning." But goyim ask questions, too! And the Zionist tradition is a parade of questions and challenges and quarrels. Oh yes, and answers. Questioning is the beginning, not the end, of intellectual responsibility. In the Talmudic tradition, the number of subjects about which we must suffice with the questions, because we will not have the answers until the prophet Elijah delivers them, is exceedingly small. We sometimes confer too much prestige on questions. (At the seder, as Klein points out, questioning is the child's task.) In any event, Klein is a creature of answers posing as a creature of questions. It is a neat trick, to traffic in certainties and portray yourself as a champion of doubts.

line 52: How on earth has Zionism betrayed the love we have as a people for text and for education? Pass the *maror*, please.

line 61: I had not encountered the term "scholasticide" before. I discovered that on April 18 a group of UN human rights experts in Geneva issued a press release in which they "expressed grave concern over the pattern of attacks on schools, universities, teachers, and students in the Gaza Strip, raising serious alarm over the systemic destruction of the Palestinian education system. 'With more than 80% of schools in Gaza damaged or destroyed, it may be reasonable to ask if there is an intentional effort to comprehensively destroy the Palestinian education system, an action known as 'scholasticide,' the experts said." The damage wrought upon education and culture in Gaza by the Israeli campaign must indeed be overwhelming. But there are collateral effects in war, in this war and every other. Not everything that is destroyed in war was targeted for destruction. That is one of the reasons that wars should be avoided: they are wanton. There is no such thing as "surgical" bombing. But there is something demagogic, an agit-prop quality, about the "-icide" construction. Is the destruction of a vineyard vinocide?

line 71: She flatters herself.

line 72: The phrase "our Judaism" contains much less authority than Klein thinks it does. Ben Gvir and Smotrich also have "their" Judaism. Their Judaism can indeed be contained by an ethnostate, so to hell with them. Such a Judaism, every customized Judaism, is nothing like the actually existing Judaism, historical Judaism, Judaism in its classical sources, Judaism in all its text-based variations, which is an irreducible alliance of universalism and particularism. The tangle, the incongruity, the simultaneity of all the imperatives, is the point. Every other version is cherry-picked. Klein's "internationalist" Judaism is similarly an arbitrary doctrine invented in the image of a political desire. Does she really not see the "nationalist" elements in the Bible and the rabbinical tradition? The gravity of her opinion about Judaism is not enhanced by her assumption that she can blithely wave them all away. Her rejection of particularism has no basis whatever in our religion. Even the prophets, the ones with the prooftexts beloved of lion-and-lamb progressives, were particularists; or more precisely, they taught the coincidence of the local with the global. The internationalist Klein should shop elsewhere for precursors.

line 76: Here is another post-Zionist shibboleth: that Israel is bad for the Jews. But Jewish nationalism never promised a world free of Judeophobia. It promised only a haven from it and a defense against it. And the world without the Jewish state was not exactly good for the Jews. O, the bliss of subalternity!

line 77: Neither is "my" Judaism. Solidarity with the downtrodden, including Palestinians, is perfectly compatible with it, and even required by it. Klein's air of moral superiority is insufferable.

line 79: Gender? See paragraph thirteen of the Declaration of Independence of the State of Israel, which includes a guarantee of "complete equality" with regard to sexual difference. In 1948! Klein might also take an interest in the shelter provided in Tel Aviv for Palestinian LGBTQ people who fear for their lives at home.

These debates discomfit me because they make truthful claims sound like apologetics. The rhetorical situation is rigged against elementary corrections, which come to seem like partisan pleadings. I do not deny my partisanship, obviously; but I insist that objectivity, or the search for it, is the obligatory accompaniment of partisanship. Not perfect objectivity, of course; but the impossibility of perfect objectivity must not provide cover for the whateverist epistemology that now governs our culture. The purpose of objectivity is not to ruin our commitments but to clarify them, to test them, to make them intellectually respectable. A wise philosopher has described our optimal mental situation as "positional objectivity." There is an easy way to check on positional objectivity: it comes with scars. Those scars are the traces of the positions that one wished to espouse but discovered that one could not, because their usefulness for one's side could not withstand the honest acknowledgement that that they are false. He who finds no fault in his own side, who lives without intellectual dissonance and moral friction, is a liar. (Honesty compels me to add that for this reason I have admired Klein's withering critique of the environmentalist elite and the "extractivist left.")

line 86: As it happens, the Passover seder is a peculiarly bad illustration of the portability of Judaism: it is a service — not a technology! — for a table set with symbolic objects and performed by housed people who are enjoined to imagine empathetically the unhoused existence in the desert and the unhoused generally. It is indeed portable — but so is all of Judaism since the fall of Jerusalem, when a far-seeing rabbi of the first century proclaimed the dissociation of the religion from its capital. The adjustment of Judaism to extra-territoriality was never a choice for extra-territoriality. And there are Passover duties beyond the Passover seder that require a synagogue or meeting place. Even when we wandered, we were not light on our feet.

(Oh, what's the use?)

line 91: Was the exodus a revolution? Modern revolutionaries have thought so, but they departed from the ancient model. The Egyptian tyranny was not deposed. The slaves did not replace the masters; the slaves left. (The Jews have never sought to overthrow their oppressors. They sought instead to get beyond their sway, to be left alone to be themselves.)

The freedom for which the slaves departed Egypt was not what we mean by political liberty. Instead they were given a new metaphysics of obedience. But there is one respect in which the saga of the Israelite liberation brings to mind our own perplexities about authoritarianism: the mentality of servitude survived the experience of servitude. The riddle of democratization is that you must already know what it is like to live democratically in order to live democratically. How, then, does democracy begin? Memory is a terrible saboteur.

line 99: The list of Zionist and Israeli peace plans is long, which is why it makes for melancholy reading. And the list of Zionists and Israelis who opposed those peace plans is also long, which is why it makes for even more melancholy reading. There has never been a Zionist consensus, except perhaps in the early 1940s, when the prospect of extermination concentrated the Jewish mind in favor of statehood. The old Zionist disputations have never been resolved. They will be on the ballot in the next Israeli election.

line 106: There is no more definitive sign of moral frivolity in the discussion of Israel than to mock Iron Dome.

line 112: You are the exodus? Then go away.

line 115: Oh, I see. You have already gone. Somehow we will have to manage without you.

As for our kids: you remind me of one of the most foolish comments of our time. "Young people are just smarter," Mark Zuckerberg instructed in 2007. It was a sentiment that updated the most ludicrous generational conceits of the 1960s, as does your little boast about stealing our children. Listen. You do not know our children. You know only the ones who follow you. But we have our little darlings, too, a prodigious number of them, and they live in a world, a world of young and old, beyond your grasp — a liberal world, a conservative world, a Jewish world, a Zionist world, a traditional world, a patriotic world, a peace- and decency-seeking world. Their loyalties are not blind and their sentiments are not inauthentic because they are not your loyalties and not your sentiments. You are making a mistake. Our kids are not with you now. Those are your kids. I wonder how many future venture capitalists and litigators are among them. Believe it or not, there are larger and deeper places than the quads, and places more consequential for the future of the world, and for its betterment, than Grand Army Plaza on the night when you choose to deliver a homily there. No cause will succeed that cannot see beyond itself. For heaven's sake, woman, look at life from both sides now.

In loving memory
of our friend and contributor
HELEN VENDLER
(1933–2024)
"No coward soul is mine."

We are proud to congratulate
our brave friend and contributor
VLADIMIR KARA-MURZA
on winning the 2024 Pulitzer Prize
for Commentary
(from a Russian prison cell).

336

Liberties

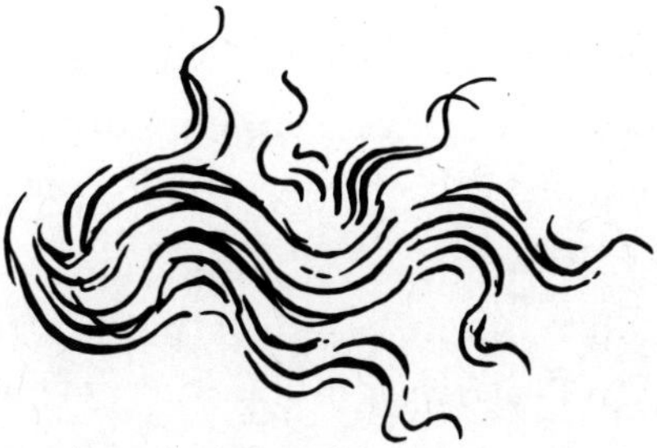

CONTRIBUTORS

PAUL BERMAN is the author of numerous books, including *Terror and Liberalism* and *The Flight of the Intellectuals*.

SERGEI LEBEDEV is a Russian novelist and the author of *Oblivion* and *Untraceable*. This essay was translated by Antonina W. Bouis.

ASSAF SHARON is a professor of philosophy at Tel Aviv University and a senior fellow at Molad: The Center for the Renewal of Israeli Democracy

ROSANNA WARREN is an American poet and the author most recently of *Max Jacob: A Life in Art and Letters*.

EKATERINA PRAVILOVA is a professor of history at Princeton, and the author of *A Public Empire: Property and the Quest for the Common Good in Imperial Russia*.

MOSAAB ABU TOHA is a Palestinian poet and the author of *Things You May Find Hidden in My Ear: Poems from Gaza*. His new book, *Forest of Noise: Poems*, will appear in the fall.

CARLOS FRAENKEL is the James McGill Professor of Philosophy and Religion at McGill University.

JUSTIN SMITH-RUIU is a professor of history and philosophy of science at the University of Paris, and the author among other books of *The Internet Is Not What You Think It Is: A History, A Philosophy, A Warning*.

KIT WILSON is a writer and musician based in London.

BENJAMIN BALINT is the author most recently of *Bruno Schulz: An Artist, A Murder, and The Hijacking of History*. The writing of this essay was supported by a grant from The Robert B. Silvers Foundation.

MITCHELL ABIDOR is a historian, writer, and translator. Among his translated works is an anthology of Victor Serge's anarchist writings, *Anarchists Never Surrender*.

MATTHEW ZIPF is a writer currently at work on a biography of Renata Adler.

ADRIAN NATHAN WEST is a writer and literary translator living in Spain. His first novel, *My Father's Diet*, was published in 2022.

DANIEL HALPERN is a poet, critic, and editor, and the founder of Ecco Press.

DAVID THOMSON is the author of many books on film and culture, most recently *Remotely: Travels in the Binge of TV*.

CELESTE MARCUS is the managing editor of *Liberties*.

LEON WIESELTIER is the editor of *Liberties*.

Liberties — A Journal of Culture and Politics is available by annual subscription and by individual purchase from bookstores and online booksellers.

Annual subscriptions provide a discount from the individual cover price and include complete digital access to current and previous issues along with the printed version. Subscriptions can be ordered from libertiesjournal.com. Professional discounts for active military; faculty, students, and education administrators; government employees; those working in the not-for-profit sector. Gift subscriptions are also available at libertiesjournal.com.

As a matter of principle, *Liberties Journal* does not accept advertising or other funding sources that might influence our independence.

We look to our readers and those individuals and institutions that believe in our mission for contributions — large and small — to support this not-for-profit publication.

If you are interested in making a donation to *Liberties*, please contact Bill Reichblum, publisher, by email at bill@libertiesjournal.com or by phone: 202-891-7159.

Liberties — A Journal of Culture and Politics is distributed to booksellers in the United States by Publishers Group West; in Canada by Publishers Group Canada; and internationally by Ingram Publisher Services International.

LIBERTIES, LIBERTIES: A JOURNAL OF CULTURE AND POLITICS, is published quarterly in Fall, Winter, Spring, and Summer by Liberties Journal Foundation.

ISBN ISBN 979-8-9854302-5-7
ISSN 2692-3904

Printed in Canada.

The insignia that appears throughout *Liberties* is derived from details in Botticelli's drawings for Dante's *Divine Comedy*, which were executed between 1480 and 1495.